Language & Globalization Series

Series Editors: **Sue Wright**, University of Portsmouth, UK and **Helen Kelly-Holmes**, University of Limerick, Ireland

In the context of current political and social developments, where the national group is not so clearly defined and delineated, the state language not so clearly dominant in every domain, and cross-border flow and transfers affect more than a small elite, new patterns of language use will develop. This series aims to provide a framework for reporting on and analysing the linguistic outcomes of globalization and localization.

Titles include:

David Block
MULTILINGUAL IDENTITIES IN A GLOBAL CITY

Jenny Carl and Patrick Stevenson (*editors*)
LANGUAGE, DISCOURSE AND IDENTITY IN CENTRAL EUROPE
The German Language in a Multilingual Space

Julian Edge (*editor*)
(RE-)LOCATING TESOL IN AN AGE OF EMPIRE

Alexandra Galasinska and Michał Krzyżanowski (*editors*)
DISCOURSES OF TRANSFORMATION IN CENTRAL AND EASTERN EUROPE

Roxy Harris
NEW ETHNICITIES AND LANGUAGE USE

Diarmait Mac Giolla Chríost
LANGUAGE AND THE CITY

Clare Mar-Molinero & Patrick Stevenson (*editors*)
LANGUAGE IDEOLOGIES, POLICIES AND PRACTICES
Language and the Future of Europe

Clare Mar-Molinero & Miranda Stewart (*editors*)
GLOBALIZATION AND LANGUAGE IN THE SPANISH SPEAKING WORLD
Macro and Micro Perspectives

Ulrike Hanna Meinhof & Dariusz Galasinski
THE LANGUAGE OF BELONGING

Richard C. M. Mole (*editor*)
DISCURSIVE CONSTRUCTIONS OF IDENTITY IN EUROPEAN POLITICS

Leigh Oakes and Jane Warren
LANGUAGE, CITIZENSHIP AND IDENTITY IN QUEBEC

Colin H. Williams
LINGUISTIC MINORITIES IN DEMOCRATIC CONTEXT

Forthcoming titles:

John Edwards
CHALLENGES IN THE SOCIAL LIFE OF LANGUAGE

Helen Kelly-Holmes and Gerlinde Mautner
LANGUAGE AND THE MARKET

Jane Jackson
INTERCULTURALITY IN STUDY AT HOME AND ABROAD

Mario Saraceni
THE RELOCATION OF ENGLISH

Christina Slade and Martina Mollering
FROM MIGRANT TO CITIZEN: TESTING LANGUAGE, TESTING CULTURE

Language and Globalization
Series Standing Order ISBN 978-1-4039-9731-9 Hardback
                               978-1-4039-9732-6 Paperback
(*outside North America only*)

You can receive future titles in this series as they are published by placing a standing order. Please contact your bookseller or, in case of difficulty, write to us at the address below with your name and address, the title of the series and the ISBN quoted above.

Customer Services Department, Macmillan Distribution Ltd, Houndmills, Basingstoke, Hampshire RG21 6XS, England

Language Ideologies, Policies and Practices

Language and the Future of Europe

Edited by

Clare Mar-Molinero

and

Patrick Stevenson
University of Southampton

First published in hardback 2006
This paperback edition published 2009 by
PALGRAVE MACMILLAN

Palgrave Macmillan in the UK is an imprint of Macmillan Publishers Limited,
registered in England, company number 785998, of Houndmills, Basingstoke,
Hampshire RG21 6XS.

Palgrave Macmillan in the US is a division of St Martin's Press LLC,
175 Fifth Avenue, New York, NY 10010.

Palgrave Macmillan is the global academic imprint of the above companies
and has companies and representatives throughout the world.

Palgrave® and Macmillan® are registered trademarks in the United States,
the United Kingdom, Europe and other countries.

ISBN-13: 978–1–4039–9899–6 hardback
ISBN-13: 978–0–230–58008–4 paperback

This book is printed on paper suitable for recycling and made from fully
managed and sustained forest sources. Logging, pulping and manufacturing
processes are expected to conform to the environmental regulations of the
country of origin.

A catalogue record for this book is available from the British Library.

Library of Congress Cataloging-in-Publication Data
Language ideologies, policies, and practices : language and the future of
   Europe / edited by Clare Mar-Molinero and Patrick Stevenson.
      p. cm. — (Language and globalization)
   Includes bibliographical references and index.
   ISBN 978–1–4039–9899–6 (cloth) 978–0–230–58008–4 (pbk)
   1. Language policy—Europe. 2. Language planning—Europe.
   3. Europe—Languages—Political aspects. I. Mar-Molinero, Clare,
   1948– II. Stevenson, Patrick, 1954– III. Series.
   P119.32.E85L284 2005
   306.44′ 94—dc22   2005050961

Printed and bound in Great Britain by
CPI Antony Rowe, Chippenham and Eastbourne

Contents

v

List of Tables and Figures

Tables

Figures

Acknowledgements

We would like to thank the many people who contributed to the preparation and production of this book and to acknowledge the support provided by our colleagues in Modern Languages at the University of Southampton. The book would never have taken shape without the highly successful and thought-provoking conference, by the same title, held at the Southampton Centre for Transnational Studies in July 2004 with financial support from the University Association for Contemporary European Studies. Versions of all the chapters of this book were first presented there, and the authors benefited greatly from the feedback and lively discussion that took place. We would especially like to acknowledge the tireless work and support that our research assistant Anna Efstathiadou-Adams provided throughout the organisation of this event. We also wish to thank our co-organisers Christopher Brumfit and Michael Kelly for their contribution to the planning, as well as our student helpers for their invaluable work: Michael Doleschal, Amanda Hilmarsson-Dunn, Michael Hornsby, Michèle Hynett Bonnin, Saman Jamshidi Fard, Tomasz Mazik and Rosalía Miró García. Particular thanks are due to Darren Paffey, who has contributed energetically throughout to the success of the conference and the subsequent production of the book. We are also grateful to our anonymous reviewers and the series editors, Sue Wright and Helen Kelly-Holmes, for insightful and helpful comments on drafts of the chapters, and to Jill Lake of Palgrave for her support and encouragement. Above all, we want to thank our co-contributors to this volume for their cooperation and their efficiency in meeting very tight deadlines!

Clare Mar-Molinero and
Patrick Stevenson

Shortly after the original publication of this volume in hardback we were greatly saddened to have to announce the death, in March 2006, of one of the contributors, Professor Christopher Brumfit. As well as being an internationally renowned scholar in applied linguistics and a tireless advocate of the need to raise the profile of language learning and linguistic rights in all walks of life, Christopher Brumfit was a much loved and highly valued colleague at the University of Southampton for over 20 years. He has been a lasting inspiration to countless colleagues, teachers and students, and his wisdom and wit are sorely missed. We are proud to include his chapter in this volume as one of his last contributions to our field of study.

Notes on Contributors

Lukas Bleichenbacher is a lecturer in linguistics at the University of Teacher Education Thurgau (PHTG) and the University of Zurich, Switzerland. His research interests include various aspects of language choice, language ideologies and multilingual policymaking. His most recent publication is the book *Multilingualism in the Movies: Hollywood Characters and Their Language Choices*.

Jan Blommaert is Professor of Linguistic Anthropology at Tilburg University, the Netherlands. He was formerly Professor of Language in Education at the Institute of Education, University of London and Professor of African Linguistics and Sociolinguistics at Ghent University, Belgium. His research interests include linguistic ideologies and inequality, discourse analysis and literary studies. His publications include *Discourse* and (with J. Verschueren) *Debating Diversity*, and the edited book *Language-ideological Debates*.

Gerrit Brand is the book editor of the daily newspaper *Die Burger* in Capetown, South Africa. He was formerly a Postdoctoral Fellow in the Department of Philosophy at Stellenbosch University, researching in philosophy and the politics of language. He is the author of a book on African Christian theology, *Speaking of a Fabulous Ghost*.

Christopher Brumfit was Professor of Applied Linguistics at the University of Southampton, UK until his death in March 2006. He was also Chair of the British Association of Applied Linguistics, Vice President of the Association Internationale de Linguistique Appliquée, and an Academician of the UK Academy of Social Sciences. He was the author of more than thirty books, including his most recent, *Individual Freedom in Language Teaching*.

Brigitta Busch is Senior Research Fellow at the Department of Applied Linguistics in the University of Vienna, Austria and was formerly Head of the Centre for Intercultural Studies at the University of Klagenfurt. During her work as an expert for the Council of Europe's Confidence-building Measures Programme she was involved in a number of intercultural projects in Eastern and South-Eastern Europe. Her books include *Sprachen im Disput,* and (edited with B. Hipfl and K. Robins) *Bewegte Identitäten,* and (edited with Helen Kelly-Holmes) *Language, Discourse and Borders.*

Anna Duszak is Head of the Institute of Applied Linguistics at Warsaw University, Poland where she is Professor of Linguistics, as well as Professor in the Warsaw School of Applied Psychology. Her research interests include discourse analysis, pragmatics, anthropological linguistics, crosscultural communication and critical discourse analysis. Her publications include *The Dynamics of Topics in English and Polish,* and *Tekst, Dyskurs, Komunikacja Międzykulturowa.* She edited the books *Culture and Styles of Academic Discourse,* and *Us and Others* and co-edited *Speaking from the Margin* and *Identity, Community, Discourse.*

Susan Gal is Mae and Sidney G. Metzl Distinguished Service Professor in Anthropology and Linguistics at the University of Chicago, USA. Her research areas include sociolinguistics and linguistic anthropology, with special interests in multilingualism, variation, language and gender, linguistic differentiation and linguistic ideology. She is currently working on a crosscultural, comparative project about the semiotic principles that constrain and orient linguistic and sociocultural differentiation, and another project exploring the nature and history of political rhetoric and practices of media censorship in Hungary. She is the author of *Language Shift* and (with Gail Kligman) *The Politics of Gender after Socialism.* She coedited (with K. Woolard) *Languages and Publics.*

Robert Gould is Adjunct Research Professor in the School of Linguistics and Applied Language Studies and in the Institute of European and Russian Studies of Carleton University, Ottawa, where he is also Associate Director of the Centre for European Studies. His recent publications have focused on the development of the public language of politics and nationalism in Germany and on the discourses of immigration and identity in European contexts. He is currently a consultant for the research project 'Sprache und Identitätspolitik in der Schweiz' at the University of Fribourg and for the project 'Shrinking Citizenship' conducted by the Centre for Public Policy PROVIDUS in Riga.

Clare Mar-Molinero holds a PhD from the University of Southampton, and is Professor of Spanish Sociolinguistics and Head of Modern Languages at the University of Southampton. She teaches and has published widely on language policies and on global Spanish. Her publications include: *The Politics of Language in the Spanish-Speaking World* (2000), *The Spanish-Speaking World: Introduction to Sociolinguistic Issues* (1997), co-edited with Angel Smith, *Nationalism and the Nation in the Iberian Peninsula* (1996), and, co-edited with Miranda Stewart, *Globalization and Language in the Spanish-Speaking World* (2006). She is chair of the *International Association for the Study of Spanish in Society (SiS)*.

Katrijn Maryns completed her PhD at Ghent University in 2004 on communicative practices in the Belgian asylum procedure. Her current research also investigates language in legal settings. She is teaching at the universities of Ghent and Lessius (KUL) and participating in a research project at the University of Antwerp on discursive strategies used in the Belgian Assize Court. Her publications include articles in *Multilingua, Pragmatics, Language & Communication* and *Speech, Language and the Law*, and the monograph *The Asylum Speaker: Language in the Belgian Asylum Procedure*.

Tommaso M. Milani is a postdoctoral research fellow on the AHRC-funded 'BBC Voices' project at the University of Leeds, UK, having recently completed his PhD at the Centre for Research on Bilingualism at Stockholm University on the ways in which language politics, language ideology and national identity are intertwined in debates over Swedish. His broader areas of research encompass language ideology and Critical Discourse Analysis. His publications include articles in *Language in Society, Linguistics and Education* and *Language Problems & Language Planning*, as well as several chapters in edited collections.

Thomas Ricento is Professor and Chair, English as an Additional Language, University of Calgary, Canada. He has published widely in the fields of language policy and language ideology. His recent publications include the edited books, *An Introduction to Language Policy*, and *Ideology, Politics and Language Policies*, and (with B. Burnaby) *Language and Politics in the United States and Canada*. He is also Editor, with Terrence Wiley, of the *Journal of Language, Identity and Education*.

Rémy Rouillard is a doctoral candidate in the Department of Anthropology at McGill University, Montreal, Canada. His current research is concerned with ways in which indigenous people and oil technoscientists relate to nature and to each other in the Russian North.

Massimiliano Spotti is a postdoctoral fellow at the Department of Language and Culture Studies as well as a member of Babylon, Centre for the Studies of the Multicultural Society, Tilburg University, the Netherlands. His research interests include multilingualism in education, identity construction, and language testing for citizenship. Recent publications have appeared in the *Journal of Linguistics and Education* and in the *Journal of Language, Identity and Education*, and he is co-editor (with Guus Extra and Piet van Avermaet) of *Language Testing, Migration and Citizenship: Cross-National Perspectives* (forthcoming).

Patrick Stevenson is Professor of German and Linguistic Studies at the University of Southampton. His current research interests include the politics of language, multilingualism, language and migration, and language biographies. He has published widely in the field of German sociolinguistics and his recent book publications include: *Language and German Disunity, Language Ideologies, Policies and Practices* (edited with Clare Mar-Molinero), *Testing Regimes: Critical Perspectives on Language, Migration and Citizenship in Europe* (edited with Gabrielle Hogan-Brun and Clare Mar-Molinero, in press), *Language, Discourse and Identity in Central Europe* (edited with Jenny Carl) and (with Jenny Carl) *Language Regimes in Central Europe* (forthcoming).

Christian Voss is Professor of South Slavic Linguistic and Cultural Studies at Humboldt-University, Berlin. He has published widely in journals and has edited volumes on the Slavic minorities in Greece and in Greek-speaking Macedonia and on Macedonian culture and identity. He co-edited (with D. Stern) *Marginal Linguistic Identities: Studies in Slavic Contact and Borderland Varieties*.

1
Language, the National and the Transnational in Contemporary Europe

Patrick Stevenson and Clare Mar-Molinero

This book takes its cue from the coincidence of two key moments in recent European history: 2004 saw both the 15th anniversary of the events of 1989 that launched the post-Cold War era and the accession to the European Union of ten new member states, which gave the process of social transformation within and across national boundaries throughout Europe a new impetus. At the same time, the accelerated process of unification has renewed and heightened the tension between national and supra-national interests. One of the most tangible manifestations of this tension – between the promotion of, and resistance to, social, economic and political unification – is in conflicting language ideologies, policies and practices. The contributions to this book offer the first attempt following the enlargement of the EU to describe, analyse and evaluate the nature and implications of these complex language issues and to construct an agenda for research on the politics of language in the new European context.

In the decade or so following the publication in 1991 of *A Language Policy for the European Community* (edited by Florian Coulmas), a substantial body of research emerged, addressing language policy questions primarily from a national perspective (for example, Barbour and Carmichael 2000, Extra and Gorter 2001, O'Reilly 2001 and Hogan-Brun and Wolff 2003). More recently, increasing attention has been paid to the effects of globalization and the transnational flow of goods and services but also the transnational traffic of people and therefore of language(s), both physical and virtual (see, for example, Maurais and Morris 2003, Gardt and Hüppauf 2004, Wright 2004). Yet a tension remains between these two preoccupations: between the static framework of the national, with its fixed parameters, and the fluid forms of the transnational. This book reflects this tension: some chapters, especially in Part

I, deal explicitly with transnational phenomena and processes, but even those that focus on case studies located within the political boundaries of nation-states explore issues that arise through social processes and individual practices which traverse and permeate these boundaries.

The book is organised in two parts. Part I scrutinizes the fundamental theoretical and conceptual issues that provide the thematic link between all the chapters and invites readers to take a critical stance towards language questions in the European context by confronting them with the contemporary legacy of European language policies in other parts of the world and by situating the ensuing debates in the context of globalization. These chapters ask questions such as: what kinds of linguistic phenomena are the proper object of study in this context? To what extent are language ideologies and policies today still influenced by the ideas that spawned linguistic nationalism in the 18th and 19th centuries? In what ways and to what effect have European ideas about language shaped notions of identity and belonging in former colonial settings? What are the implications of these non-European experiences for the newly emerging Europe? What is the relationship between transnational 'world' languages and their birthplace in Europe?

Part II then explores in detail some of the specific ways in which language ideologies underpin policies, and the relationships between policies and practices, in particular European settings. The chapters in this part of the book raise questions such as: in what ways and for what reasons is the concept of a 'national language' used to sustain the idea of homogeneous 'national cultures' in a supposedly 'post-national' Europe? What role does language play in discourses of citizenship? How do evaluations of particular linguistic practices (such as codeswitching) serve to marginalize and discriminate against migrants? How do individuals and organizations (such as internet users and broadcasters) respond to the increasingly complex demands and opportunities of a multilingual environment and of globalization?

The central topos on which the book is founded is the conflict between the stubborn persistence of the Herderian conception of the axiomatically monoglot nation on the one hand, and the constantly shifting multilingual constellations of European states on the other. The sober-sounding and well-intentioned rhetoric of language policies formulated by the Council of Europe and other supranational bodies is of course in tune with the grand design for the future of Europe envisaged in the proposed EU Constitution. However, it is not so clear how far the largely symbolic promotion of diversity at the supranational level is, or can be, consonant with the robustly centripetal pressures of standardization and homogenization at the national level. So by asking in what ways language policies emerge from and contribute to the contradictions between monolingual ideologies and multilingual practices the authors here collectively propose the need for a much more rigorous and critical examination of policy formulation than has previously been offered.

In her opening chapter, Susan Gal lays the groundwork for the following discussion by interrogating the key concepts of language, Europe and the future. Questioning the validity of 'languages' as discrete, bounded forms, she proposes instead that analysis should focus on linguistic practices and repertoires and on their deictic, or indexical, functions in relation to time and place. She argues that 'language' is a European invention and that its exportation to other parts of the world is a major aspect of the European legacy (a contention taken up by Gerrit Brand in his chapter). Crucial to Gal's thesis is the resilience of the Herderian ideology, the isomorphism of language, state and nation, shored up by policies that continue to invest 'national' standard language varieties with the authority and legitimation to undermine 'post-national' European credos of pluralism and diversity. In particular, she emphasizes the baleful effects of standardization, which both creates stigmatized (non-standard) speakers and, paradoxically, increases linguistic heterogeneity. And difference is of course not value-free, for minority populations may already satisfy the new European ideal of multilingual competence but their 'own' languages are not valued in the linguistic market, while multilingualism amongst majority populations remains an elite privilege.

Christopher Brumfit shares Gal's scepticism about the terms that none the less continue to form the common currency of debates on language policy. However, while suggesting that for linguists the term language 'may have outlived whatever usefulness it ever had', he concedes that it retains its potency as a political construct. Building on Gal's notion of language as a convenient if dangerous fiction, a fuzzy category in a world demanding sharp definition, he argues that languages should be conceived as 'liminal states', since their speakers are in constant transition, never firmly located in any one homogeneous linguistic space. This clearly has consequences for language policy: policy-makers need to recognize 'liminality and the development of a repertoire for the crossing of thresholds...as central concepts of theory'. What this might mean in practice remains to be explored, but Brumfit presents a challenge to policy-makers by emphasizing the importance of individual linguistic creativity on the one hand and the limits of what policy can achieve on the other.

Such (self-imposed) constraints were not a feature of the language policy-making process that contributed to the formation of American identities as analysed by Thomas Ricento. For here too European traditions of constructing homogenized conceptions of the state-as-nation around supposed common characteristics and properties, with language typically at the forefront, were always part of the American project, as he shows in his discussion of discourses of 'Americanism' articulated in a range of texts published over the last hundred years. While conservative commentators insisted (and continue to insist) on a highly specified prescription of what it means to be – or to become – American, requiring not only proficiency in English but the relinquishment of other languages, liberal and progressive discourses have constructed a more inclusive prospectus of Americanism. In this and other ways, European language ideologies have both fed and been fed by debates on Americanization, and there are clear parallels between the contestation of identities based on tensions between linguistic homogeneism and linguistic pluralism on both sides of the Atlantic.

Like Ricento, Gerrit Brand considers the European legacy in relation to language policy making in a specific historical and geo-political context, in his case South Africa. However, while 'Europe' is rarely invoked in contemporary discourses on language (or, some would say, on most other political issues) in the US, Brand shows that it continues to figure in public debates about language in South Africa. Not surprisingly, the image that emerges is ambivalent but one that cannot be ignored. Memories of the colonial past are, of course, imbued with a deep and abiding sense of injustice and discrimination, and this unequal distribution of power was both institutionalized and symbolized through the imposition of a linguistic regime privileging standard European languages at the expense of indigenous modes of expression. The benefits that accompanied the repression, such as the introduction of print technology and the promotion of linguistic scholarship, were a delayed good as far as their impact on the majority indigenous population is concerned and have to be seen in the longer term perspective of post-colonial renewal. Brand traces the ambiguous history of European influence as 'destroyer' and 'developer' of indigenous linguistic and cultural practices through to the present contribution of European ideas to the development of the South African constitution and to the reshaping of South African society, and argues that 'the demystification of linguistic identities – which is not the same as misrecognition of them – is probably one of the most important intellectual tasks facing the South African pro-multilingualism movement', a task to which European intellectuals can make an important contribution.

While Ricento's focus is on debates around the role of English as *the* American language, and Brand concentrates on the specific consequences of the European colonial legacy in southern Africa, Clare Mar-Molinero both widens the discussion by shifting the emphasis to the global plane and re-focuses it by invoking the challenge presented to the global supremacy of English by the continuing rise of Spanish across the world. She argues that an adequate account of contemporary processes of language spread should not rely exclusively on apparently undirected forces of globalization and the market but should rather acknowledge the agency of governmental organizations acting in support of vested national interests. By analyzing the standard language ideology promoted by the Spanish Royal Language Academy and above all by the Instituto Cervantes (the Spanish state-funded organization charged with the worldwide dissemination of Spanish language and culture), which constructs standard peninsular Castilian as the bedrock of *Hispanidad*, she shows how global cultural trends can be harnessed to serve the purposes of an international language policy in the interest of reinforcing Spain's status as a global player.

Anna Duszak returns the discussion to fundamentals in her consideration of key concepts, but she does so from the perspective of an active participant in a double process of transition: as a Polish citizen experiencing the radical social transformation of central and eastern Europe in daily life, and as a linguist witnessing the concomitant changing linguistic/communicative practices as well as changing academic preoccupations and models of analysis. How do these two conditions relate to and interact with each other? She argues that Poland's emergence from the former Soviet bloc and more recently its accession to the EU have resulted – albeit not for the first time in the country's complex history – in a recontextualization of its relationship with 'Europe' in terms of a renewed if problematic and contentious western orientation. Together with the heightened influence of English and the spread of other global cultural influences, this has led amongst other things to the development of new communicative genres and to the penetration of new linguistic practices into existing, traditional genres, combining to form 'an intertextual flow of discourses – a connected network of dependencies, ideologies and practices'. This more variegated blend of public discourses, and its impact on communicative conventions, is currently a highly controversial issue in Poland, as elsewhere in eastern Europe, and it has important implications for the development of the new European public space as a whole.

Duszak's chapter, focusing on the liminal condition of a society that finds itself both temporally and spatially on the threshold of this new

European space, is itself located at the interface between the two parts of the book. Its theoretical and conceptual discussion contributes to the evaluation of what we are calling the European legacy in Part I, and its exploration of linguistic and social change in a specific European context opens up the investigation in Part II of new sociolinguistic formations. Tommaso Milani begins this investigation with a critical study of language planning and national identity in Sweden. Starting from the position that national identity is a 'dynamic reality' which is in part an ongoing product of language (planning) debates and which emerges from specific historical, ideological and social conditions, Milani demonstrates how performativity theory (Butler 1990, 1993, 1997) can provide a framework for explaining how fundamental categories (such as language, nation and identity) are construed in multiple and ambiguous ways. He draws on a range of policy documents from the last 30–40 years, culminating in the publication in 2002 of *Mål i Mun*, the report of the Committee for Swedish Language, to show how the salience of language issues in political debates in Sweden has increased during this period and how through the complex interplay of different discursive processes they have contributed to a more explicit definition of Swedishness.

Language, as Christian Voss demonstrates in his chapter, has always been inextricably bound up in the highly intricate web of discourses surrounding questions of local, ethnic and national identity in the Balkans. Focusing on Macedonia, both before and after the establishment of the independent republic in 1991, he shows how the name itself gives rise to multiple ambiguities and provides an excellent example of the historical constructedness of 'national' 'standard' languages and of the coincidence of time and place in the formulation of language ideologies to which Gal refers in her chapter. His analysis charts a way through the negotiation of identities (Pavlenko and Blackledge 2004) in this region that straddles past and present national boundaries, exploring in particular the role of the standardization of Macedonian in this process and the problematic relationship between individual linguistic affiliation and the ethnification of Macedonian national identity.

Language loyalty and its political consequences are explored further in the chapters by Rémy Rouillard and Patrick Stevenson. Ethnic and national conflicts may have had less catastrophic outcomes in the Baltic states than in the Balkans, but as Rouillard shows the legacy of the Soviet empire has left deep traces in the public consciousness of the people in this region. The large Russian(-speaking) minority in Estonia, many of whom are effectively monolingual, now finds itself under pressure to commit itself to a conception of citizenship based on proficiency in Estonian as the sole national language or else to retain the status of outsider. Rouillard's interviews with Russian artists and writers living in Estonia reveal a wide variety of responses to this challenge and differing attitudes towards the relationship between attachments to particular languages and Russian, Estonian, European and hybrid patterns of identification. In particular, they show how individual biographies, as well as public discourses, condition the longer term outcome of social transformation processes.

Public discourses are the focus of Stevenson's chapter, in which he too analyzes political contexts in which proficiency in a 'national' language has assumed a salient position in relation to definitions of citizenship, but in this case the emphasis is on the ideological sources and effects of such discourses rather than individual responses to them. While the new arrangements in Estonia have their roots in specific historical circumstances resulting from Soviet imperialism, new policies on language and citizenship in Germany and Austria (as in other western European countries) are part of a broader institutional reaction by national governments to what they perceive as threats to national integrity posed by large-scale migration. Stevenson characterizes the debates on the (im)migration legislation recently introduced in these countries in terms of their orientation towards competing language ideologies: on the one hand, the post-national conception of the European citizen, with its emphasis on multilingual repertoires facilitating social mobility and inclusion, and on the other hand, the anachronistic conception of the citizen of the nation-state, with its insistence on commitment to a single legitimate 'national' language.

Migration is also an increasingly contentious issue in Swiss political discourse and there are many similarities between the current debates in the non-EU member state Switzerland and many of its EU neighbours. Robert Gould's discussion complements the two previous chapters by analyzing representative texts from mainstream public discourse on migration in terms of the ways in which they manifest signs of interdiscursivity: his analysis of migration discourses shows how they have been 'invaded' by discourses of (post-Cold War) security on the one hand and of globalization and business competition on the other. In the common European and North American security discourse, he argues, foreigners are positioned as potentially dangerous elements and population movements as threats to stability, while globalization discourses subsume the concept of competition between states-as-businesses, as articulated in common collocations such as 'la place industrielle et économique suisse' or 'Wirtschaftsstandort Schweiz' (Switzerland as business location). In this way Gould accounts for the apparent discursive paradox – by no means unique to Switzerland, as he points out – according to which foreigners are simultaneously desired and mistrusted.

The marginalization of foreigners through textual practices is further demonstrated by Katrijn Maryns and Jan Blommaert, whose close scrutiny of transcripts of interviews with asylum-seekers in Belgium reveals the pitfalls inherent in such institutional procedures where participants have unequal access to linguistic resources. Asylum-seekers' ability to give an 'adequate' account of their origins and the circumstances of their departure plays a critical role in their chances of satisfying the criteria for the granting of asylum, but this is frequently constrained by the limits on their ability to operate confidently in the authoritative language of the country in which they are seeking asylum or by their reliance on the mediation of an interpreter. Under these conditions, they are unable to retain control over the all-important stories they try to relate: their stories pass through 'a sequence of different entextualizations' as they are retold and reformulated, and they have no means of knowing how complete or how accurate the interpreters' representations of their stories are. For people quite literally on the threshold between languages and between places of danger and safety, therefore, multilingual repertoires and codeswitching skills are more than an accomplishment or a useful asset, they can have a major impact on people's life chances.

The same may apply even to those who do succeed in making the move from one country to another, as Massimiliano Spotti shows in his study of multilingual children in monolingual Flemish classrooms. In this case, too, the members of the non-indigenous group are evaluated according to their linguistic performance, but here it is less a question of the perceived credibility of what they say than of their teachers' assessment of their proficiency in the institutionally privileged standard language. Through detailed observations of classroom interactions, Spotti investigates the challenge posed to the knowledge of monolingual teachers by the presence of children with a home language other than Dutch. In particular, he argues that the categorization process through which monolingual teachers construct the social identities of children from minority groups relies on generalized and essentialist conceptions of ethnicity that are tied to degrees of proficiency in the majority language. Furthermore, such children are often doubly disadvantaged in the formal school context through their acquisition of socially dispreferred local varieties of Dutch.

To offset the many problems and challenges associated with multilingual encounters in many European situations, the final two chapters illustrate the opportunities for radical and often anti-hegemonic practices afforded by multilingual repertoires in conjunction with both established and new technologies. Brigitta Busch shows how the conventional medium of radio is increasingly being used to reach more diverse audiences and to develop hybrid or 'heteroglossic' linguistic practices. She detects a growing contrast between national broadcasters, who maintain the tradition of monolingual programming to an audience imagined as linguistically homogeneous, and transnational and translocal broadcasters, who have identified and seek to cater for audiences that are more fragmented and more eclectic in their practices and their patterns of consumption. Focusing on private radio stations in Berlin and Vienna, she demonstrates how flexible scheduling and creative multilingual performance in a range of genres from popular music programmes to sports commentaries have transformed the European 'media space'.

No medium has transformed the European – or indeed the global – media space more fundamentally than the internet, and Lukas Bleichenbacher's chapter concludes the book with evidence of its possibilities and its implications for the future of transnational communication. By analysing contributions to the official online guest-book of the city of Kosice in Slovakia, he identifies emerging patterns of language choice that point towards the development of the internet as an increasingly multilingual medium and the growing self-confidence of internet-users to express themselves in a range of languages. At the same time, he sounds a warning note in contrasting the practices of contributors from inside and from outside Slovakia: while codeswitching and metalinguistic comments are common features of the latter, the former are striking for their conformity to the monolingual norm of the official 'Slovak-only' ideology. Here in the very centre of Europe, therefore, tensions between ideologies, policies and practices persist.

This book does not attempt the impossible task of offering a comprehensive survey of language political issues in contemporary Europe. Its aim is rather to propose the possible scope of sociolinguistic explorations in this context and to stimulate further research. It therefore seeks to strike a balance between the theoretical, the descriptive and the analytical, and the various chapters represent a wide range of theoretical influences, draw on different types of data (from official policy papers through internet guestbooks to transcripts of spoken interaction) and relate both to general issues involving language in an era of globalization and to particular case-studies in all parts of Europe. In these ways the book aims to provide a coherent discussion of the diversity and complexity of language questions that characterize the current social and political development of Europe. At the same time, by situating these questions in a broader context that acknowledges the increasing interconnectedness of national economies and cultural practices both within and beyond Europe, it aims to make a contribution – in response to the challenge laid down by Jan Blommaert (2003) – to the project of developing a 'sociolinguistics of globalization'.

Part I

The European Legacy: Theoretical Issues

2
Migration, Minorities and Multilingualism: Language Ideologies in Europe

Susan Gal[1]

Introduction

For scholars of language-in-context, the terms 'language, Europe and future' participate in what many are calling language ideologies. That is, they label cultural ideas, presumptions and presuppositions with which different social groups name, frame and evaluate linguistic practices. My experience as a scholar made language ideologies impossible to ignore. For over thirty years I have thought I was writing about *language* in *Europe*. But in a certain sense I was not. The parts of the world I have written about most – Austria and Hungary – have only recently been admitted to the lofty regions that officially call themselves 'Europe'. From another perspective, however, belonging to Europe has a complex history in the east of the continent that long predates the current institutional arrangements of the European Union. If the definition of Europe changes with the perspective of the definer, it deserves analysis as an aspect of language ideology.

The term language is no less problematic. I have found that the linguistic practices of the populations I have studied – Hungarian speakers in Austria, German speakers in Hungary – were hardly considered 'language' by the speakers themselves, by their neighbours, and their governments. Until recently, even many linguists believed those practices did not merit the term language because they were supposedly mixed, chaotic, impure, hybrid forms. By contrast, my scholarly discipline of linguistic anthropology puts such communities and speakers at the centre of attention in order to study the whole range of speakers' linguistic practices in interaction.

The third term, future, is also a puzzle, inviting a consideration of time as a cultural construct. The ethnographic evidence I will examine includes studies from the 1970s to the early years of 2000, years that bracket the Cold War's end. During this time, power balances changed dramatically, and regions of the world economy have become more complexly interconnected. Both the institutional growth of the European Union and the accelerated global circulation of people and commodities have implications for linguistic practices, and for our understanding of them. Not only do linguistic practices occur *in* time, linguistic forms and geographical regions come to index cultural categories *of* time: some point to modernity or the future; others become indexes of tradition and the past. The signalling of culturally coded temporality emerges as a recurrent theme in my examples and analysis.

The aim in this chapter is twofold. First, I use the notion of language ideology to explore 'language' as a culturally specific concept, taken for granted in everyday understandings (often by scholars as well as ordinary speakers). The dominant ideology of language in Europe today is 'standard language'. It simultaneously shapes and hides many of the actual practices of speakers, especially minorities and migrants. To highlight the binds and paradoxes therefore faced by such speakers, I examine the interaction of linguistic practices and the metalinguistic assumptions (language ideologies) through which they are interpreted. The second aim is to examine 'Europe' as a similarly constructed cultural concept that is intertwined with standard language ideology. In conclusion, I turn to signs of change in this reigning ideology.

Language

It may seem odd to say so, but 'language' was invented in Europe. Speaking is a universal feature of our species, but 'language' as first used in Europe and now throughout the world is not equivalent to the capacity to speak, but presumes a very particular set of features. Languages in this limited sense are assumed to be nameable (English, Hungarian, Greek), countable property (one can 'have' several), bounded and differing from each other, but roughly inter-translatable, each with its charming idiosyncracies that are typical of the group that speaks it. The roots of this language ideology go back to the European Enlightenment and the Romantic reaction that followed. Philosophies of language that emerged at that time circulated subsequently as ideologies of language (Bauman and Briggs 2003). Although the name of Johann Gottfried Herder is often associated with this language ideology, historians have demonstrated that many of these notions existed well before his time (Kibbee 2002; Woolard 2002).

This profound invention has been elaborated in many ways: in function, language is assumed to be most basically a technology for naming the world, rather than accomplishing numerous other social tasks; monolingualism is taken to be the natural state of human life. As form, named languages are assumed to be internally homogeneous; boundaries between languages are thought to be obvious and based on lack of mutual intelligibility. Linguistic forms are accepted as languages only if they are written and have literatures and norms of correctness. Hence the spoken forms of colonial territories and the rural peripheries of European states have long been derogated as not-quite-language, whether or not they shared historical provenance with the national standard. Because they lacked some of the features I have listed, they were seen as undeveloped, not modern or civilized.

There are also political entailments of the definition. Languages are supposed to be the property of all citizens, hence no one's in particular. Yet, they are also and contrarily authorized as expressions of the distinct spirit of a particular group. Universality and authenticity, though apparently opposed, are nevertheless the two cultural values on which the authority of languages in Europe is based (Gal and Woolard 2001b). Furthermore, social groups, by virtue of their supposed linguistic homogeneity and distinctness are thought to deserve a state, a territory, some kind of political autonomy. If your language can be called a 'version' of mine, then I can claim your territory as a part of my state. In short, linguistic practices – by seeming to be independent of human will or intent – are effective in legitimating political arrangements within this Herderian discourse (Irvine and Gal 2000).[2]

Ironically, as scholars have repeatedly pointed out, such a perfect homology among nation, state, and language never existed in Europe, or anywhere else. As an ideal made of tightly interwoven strands, it is nevertheless a powerful, generative projection. Such a configuration of assumptions deserves to be called an *ideology* of language because it takes a perspective on the empirical world, erasing phenomena that do not fit its point of view; ideology too because it is linked to political positions. It is a set of cultural notions in the anthropological sense: a frame, not always conscious or within awareness, through which we understand linguistic practices (Woolard 1998).

One is tempted to discount all these familiar notions as mere clichés. Yet they continue to be the basis of sociological and political theories that have enormous influence (Anderson 1983; de Swaan 2001). And they continue to dominate conceptions of language all over the continent. Although ethnolinguistic nationalism is sometimes thought to be a special problem of eastern Europe, this set of default assumptions underpins the views expressed in the mainstream and liberal newspapers of western Europe as well as those of nationalist fringe groups (Blommaert and Verschueren 1998).

But are not the language policies associated with the European Union and its many institutional organs an exception? In their bureaucratic and not entirely democratic way, do they not work against the hegemony of linguistic nationalism? In the studies they fund, the policies they recommend, there is an ideal of diversity in language and culture. For example: the EC established and the EU supports the European Bureau for Lesser Used Languages. In a recent Action Plan for 2004–06, a communication from the Commission to the Council of Europe, the European Parliament, and the Committee of the Regions called for 'Promoting language learning and linguistic diversity'. A recent large tome commissioned by the Language Policy Unit of the Directorate for General Education and Culture, although mostly about 'regional languages', nevertheless, and to its credit, called for support of all 'minority languages in Europe' and the 'promotion and protection of linguistic diversity'. In 1992 the 'European Charter for Regional or Minority Languages' was issued, which encourages the support and maintenance of territorial as well as non-territorial languages, and even languages of immigration (Grin 2003). The Council of Europe is calling for more and better language teaching to realize a plan in which each European 'citizen [will] be able to communicate in a minimum of two languages in addition to his or her mother tongue'. These declarations are in line with the EU imagery of a 'Europe of Nations' and a 'Europe of Regions' (see Ahrens 2003; Wright 2000).

Yet, this emphasis on linguistic diversity is deceptive. Many analysts have pointed to the dearth of signatories on key agreements, or the lack of policy enforcement. From my perspective, however, the more fundamental issue is a matter of recognition. There is talk of national language, minority, regional language, foreign, migrant and third-country languages; mother tongues, sign languages, lesser used languages, ethnic minority, indigenous and non-territorial languages. Nevertheless, all the linguistic practices listed in such documents conform to Herderian assumptions. No other configurations of speaking are recognized.

In order to see the specificity of what, for convenience, I have called the Herderian definition, it is necessary to contrast it with some other perspective on language. Well suited to this task is a set of ideas that take linguistic form not as an object but rather as a social process and practice, one that always simultaneously produces a metacommentary on its own production. Such a perspective is shared by the approaches of Franz Boas and Mikhail Bakhtin, of Roman Jakobson and the Prague Circle, and has been developed further in the work of John Gumperz, Erving Goffman, Dell Hymes and younger generations. For these scholars, the (Herderian) category of 'language' is not a natural fact, it is a folk construct, a product of institutional and cultural processes of standardization.

The process of standardization is therefore itself an object of study. It roughly corresponds to Bakhtin's (1981) notion of a 'unitary language' created by centripetal forces of centralization and regimentation that are always opposed by centrifugal processes of increasing differentiation. Standardization is not primarily a matter of speaking but rather of exhibiting loyalty towards a denotational code whose high status and norms of correctness are created and supported by powerful institutions such as universal education, language academies, press capitalism, linguistic science, and linguistic markets that instill in speakers a respect for the norm. It is what Bourdieu (1981) has called the 'legitimate language' whose acceptance as correct even by those who do not know it produces symbolic domination. Standardization is only one kind of language regime. It contrasts with ideologies organized around sacred languages or unwritten languages. Within the general pattern of standardization – a 'culture of standard' – different values are attributed to different standard forms (Silverstein 1996). The French standard is understood to have properties that contrast with those of the Hungarian, for instance, and is maintained by somewhat different institutions. Indeed, standardization always happens in a world of standards which are then in a field of contrast with each other.

For those living in standardized linguistic regimes – as we all do – the institutional valorization of them makes all other forms seem inadequate or simply invisible. Rather than focusing on standards, then, this chapter attends to the whole range of forms in the functionally organized linguistic repertoires of speakers. Register, accent, voicing, variety, are all terms designating linguistic practices that come to index (point to, co-occur with) some set of social relations, social identities, situations, and values. Linguistic practices can often bring about, through social interaction, the very social relations that they then index. Linguistic practices are pragmatic phenomena, patterns of language use. They are always and necessarily interpreted by speakers and listeners through language ideologies that are about pragmatics, that is, *meta*pragmatic phenomena. When seen from the vantage point of this alternative approach, the ethnographic examples I discuss here show how the Herderian ideology produces ironies – contradictions – for the migrants, multilinguals and minorities who live in the world it creates but who rarely abide fully by its requirements. I focus on examples that illustrate five such ironies.

Ironies of minority travel

My earliest fieldwork, in the 1970s, was in an Austrian town, very near the Hungarian border: Oberwart/Felsőőr (Gal 1979). Until 1921 it had been part of Hungary; border changes following the Second World War turned the region's Hungarian speakers into a minority in German-speaking Austria. In the 1970s Austria was part of the capitalist world, Hungary part of the east bloc and relatively impoverished. The townspeople spoke linguistic forms historically identifiable as Hungarian, but those who were educated went to German-language schools. Oberwarters denigrated communism and considered themselves socially far above the Hungarians on the other side of the tense, barbed-wired border that divided Austria and Hungary. They nevertheless went to Hungary to get cheap shoes and dental care. I was surprised to find that the very people who at home were most fluent in local Hungarian never used Hungarian forms in Hungary. Despite the difficulties of communication this created, they spoke German and expected to be accommodated.

This was because, on the rare occasions when they used local Oberwart forms in Hungary, they were ridiculed by monolingual Hungarian-speakers, who heard the Oberwart pronunciation and non-standard lexicon as indexes of the past, in contrast to the newest Hungarian slang and school-taught standard. The rural forms made the Oberwart speakers sound 'old' to their Hungarian interlocutors. Or, even worse, if the Oberwarters were perceptibly young, they were indexed as stupid, backward, unsophisticated, the opposite of 'modern'. The results of spatial and political distance were heard as temporal distance.

Ironies of diasporic migration

Another village in which I have done long-term fieldwork is called Bóly, in southern Hungary (Gal 1993). Many of its inhabitants are descendants of German farmers, invited in the 18th century by the Habsburg Empress Maria Theresa to settle in southwestern Hungary after it was depopulated during the Turkish wars. Following the Second World War, a large part of the village's German-speaking population was deported to east or west Germany, amidst (sometimes false) accusations that they had been Nazis. As a result, virtually every family had relatives in

Germany when I first visited the village in the 1980s. By that time, and after decades of discrimination, it was once again politically permissible to claim a German–Hungarian identity in Hungary. But there was virtually no education in German, so the people of Bóly spoke their local, historically Germanic varieties, but were educated in standard Hungarian schools. Labour migration to western Germany was lucrative in those years, given east-west economic disparities.

The parallels and differences between Bóly and Oberwart are noteworthy: because of the relative positions of Hungary and west Germany in the continent-wide status system of the Cold War, Oberwarters could expect Hungarians to accommodate to their German, but people from Bóly could not use their knowledge of standard Hungarian in Stuttgart. So they used the German forms they knew. But when they did so, these highly educated workers were heard as foreign, backward, and unsophisticated. As in the case of Oberwart, indexicals of peripherality with respect to the centres of linguistic standardization were heard as a lag in time. Unlike the Oberwart case, however, the story of Bóly has a further complication. This late 20th century work migration was often bidirectional, diasporic. People and even whole families who had gone to Germany to work went back to Hungary to buy houses and fancy appliances with their valuable deutschmarks. On their return, when they used the linguistic forms and non-linguistic practices (for example, filtered coffee, lighter hair dyes) they had learned in Germany, they were envied, but also ostracized for putting on airs. They were perceived by their less well-travelled German–Hungarian neighbours as well as by monolingual Hungarians as condescending and vulgar.

The difficulties experienced by speakers of Oberwart and Bóly are only partly a function of named languages like Hungarian and German. Rather, aspects of speakers' repertoires (accents, registers, genres) indexed identities which were then recognized and judged from the perspective of variously placed others within the linguistic ideology of standard, but also in light of a pan-European scene in which Hungary and Germany were differently placed centres of linguistic and political-economic power. This phenomenon is by no means limited to eastern Europe; parallel phenomena occur among Portuguese migrants to France (Koven 2004). Perhaps not surprisingly, given the interpersonal stakes, all such speakers became painfully self-conscious of their speech.

Boundary dilemmas

Of particular, obsessive attention were any practices that – from the viewpoint of the two standard languages involved – could be heard as foreign. And here we see that boundaries are dynamic, part of the puristic process of making separate standard languages in the first place. Linguistic boundaries are created and maintained through forms of policing accomplished by schools, academies and dictionaries. Boundaries are also matters of time: people from Bóly and Oberwart had most trouble distinguishing between old borrowings that had been integrated as standard forms, and new or nonce borrowings that they accessed through bilingualism. Linguistically these two kinds of borrowings can seem identical, but the first is heard by standard speakers as 'ours' while the second is heard as 'foreign'. Depending on the cultural value of the donor language, the foreign can gain indexical meanings of time or status. The impression of differentiation between languages is not created by isolation and separation between linguistic forms, but rather by a consciousness of mixture and interpenetration. The mixing of languages that is anathema for Herderian ideology is part of the Herderian imperative of keeping them apart.

Translation and school instruction are also boundary devices that often work in paradoxical ways. In the formal teaching of Corsican to young Corsicans, there is explicit juxtaposition of Corsican forms with the more prestigious French they already know. This creates a situation in which any difference between the two is seen as a lack or problem in Corsican, thereby demoting it in the eyes of the students, the very people who would like to learn it better. Similarly, translation can be a double bind for minority languages: to translate literary works implies there are not enough such works in Corsican; but to fail to translate implies that Corsican cannot be used for the high art of other languages (Jaffe 1999).

Ironies of standardization

For most of the period following the Second World War, it was taboo in Hungary to discuss the linguistic practices of the large numbers of Hungarian speakers outside the borders of Hungary, in Slovakia, Romania, Serbia, Croatia and Austria. Separated from the Hungarian state's territory by the border changes of the Versailles Treaty that closed the First World War, these populations have since constituted the largest minorities in Europe. In the late 1980s, I was there at the very first meeting – in Budapest – of Hungarian-speaking language-teachers and cultural specialists from each of these countries. All of them were bilingual in Hungarian and in one other standard language. They were shocked to discover that Budapest intellectuals – eager to extend a metropolitan Hungarian standard – did not understand the problems of the bilingual minorities as well as the leaders of those minorities understood each other, despite the great linguistic differences dividing them. Some have raised the question of whether there should be a single Budapest-based standard of Hungarian in the Carpathian basin, or several 'centres' (Lanstyák 1995). In the attempt to gain recognition, minority speakers within the European regime of national, standard languages have often tried the strategy of making their regional and minority forms into standards. What are now called the minority languages of Europe have all undergone these regimenting steps.

In these situations a characteristic contradiction of values always arises: once some forms are chosen (through language planning) as the standard ones, speakers/users of alternative forms are doubly stigmatized. From the perspective of the state they are 'second language speakers' of the national language, and now their minority linguistic practices are seen as impure, inauthentic or inadequate with reference to the standards set up for the minority language by language planners. By the nature of the standardization process, every creation of a standard orientation also creates stigmatized forms, supposed 'non-languages', among the very speakers whose linguistic practices it was supposed to valorize. Contrary to the commonsense view, standardization creates not uniformity but more (and hierarchical) heterogeneity.

As many observers have pointed out, this situation creates a social contradiction too. While the doubly stigmatized speakers may well want to abandon the minority language, the jobs of minority-language standardizers depend on 'maintaining' the use of the language. The language attitudes of language specialists, intellectuals, media workers come to be at odds with the preferences of other minority speakers. Sometimes minority or immigrant elites on different sides of the standardization issue struggle with each other. Stark oppositions in language attitudes and interests develop within what was imagined by state agencies and minority speakers to be a unified ethnolinguistic group.

Standardization also brings contradictions concerning linguistic form, ones that I believe are aptly characterized as killing the language in order to save it (Whiteley 2003). Romani provides a European example. Spread across the continent, Romani speakers share many linguistic forms identified by linguists as historically Indic. Other linguistic characteristics are the result of large-scale borrowing from a great many historical traditions. All Romani speakers also use at least one and often several national languages. At the level of linguistic pragmatics and linguistic genre, European Roms practise oral, improvisational poetic forms that have no parallels in other contemporary European communities (Stewart 1989, Friedman 2001). If Romani is to be 'reduced' to writing and standardization, its uses regimented to match the range of uses of other standard languages, these often hybrid genres will be destroyed, eliminating the pragmatic features that constitute for speakers the character of Romani linguistic practices.

Ironies of neither/nor

The history of war, deportation and border changes in eastern Europe provides fertile ground for negotiating the difference between standard languages. The speakers of Opole Silesia, another border population, were wooed both by the German state during the Nazi period but also by the Polish state during the Communist period, and remained suspicious of both. Today, the people of this highly industrialized district sometimes present themselves as Poles, sometimes as Germans. This, I think, is true of all such border minorities. But the Opole Silesians are different in that they also have a self-consciousness of being neither Polish nor German, but 'Silesian,' even though they eschew the use of this term because of its war-time connotations. Their Silesian linguistic forms are not standardized, and the most vivid proof of their sense of separate consciousness is their linguistic ideology. In the face of the purist, Herderian ideologies around them, Opole Silesians revel in mixing forms, in practices of cross-lingual punning, and question-answer sequences that violate the supposed boundaries of the standard languages. Silesians see their linguistic system as inextricably a combination of German and Polish, and prize exactly that quality. They elaborate multilingualism itself as the sign of a distinctive cultural identity (Vann 2000).

My aim in discussing these five 'ironies' was to make visible the continuing power of standardizing, national regimes that are reinforced – sometimes at regional scales – despite or exactly because of European supranational agencies. Adopting a processual perspective on language, I illustrated the ways in which the linguistic practices of speakers systematically violate – and yet are interpreted through – the deceptively neat Herderian picture offered by a centuries-old ideology.

Europe

A second goal of this chapter is to consider 'Europe' itself from the perspective of language ideology. Language planning, language censuses and the literature on language teaching in Europe today certainly contribute to creating the idea of 'Europe'. But here I take a different tack, focusing instead on ethnographic and anthropological approaches to describe how the borders of Europe are linguistically constructed, and conversely, how language ideological debates are shaped by shifting institutional borders.

Institutional borders

When the term 'Europe' is understood to be a set of institutional structures, the spatial and territorial extension of those institutions has effects on how language ideologies are deployed. Accession to the EU has had consequences for debates about language within the new member states because there are forums for political pressure and claims to be made. This is an important change, even though the claims are all authorized through standardizing, Herderian ideology. In Estonia, for instance, the Russian-speaking population, once the privileged speakers, now consider themselves to be in a marginalized position due to post-Soviet language laws requiring knowledge of Estonian for many everyday and official uses (see Rouillard, this volume). Estonian leaders justify their policies to voters inside Estonia by invoking the equation of language with nation and state. In Europe-wide forums, by contrast, while Russian minority leaders use Herderian arguments to plead for their minority rights, Estonian leaders claim to be considerate of minorities, thereby attempting to show themselves to be proper Europeans (Yarian 2004).

In addition to providing the venue for such arguments, the new institutions also change the implications of debate. As one EU bureaucrat noted: before accession, the claims of Russian speakers in the Baltics were mixed up with Cold War defences against Moscow; now they are internal EU questions of 'language rights'. Time is a less obvious component of these debates. Are Estonian speakers oppressed because their language was not official for many decades? Or are the Russian speakers oppressed because Estonian is now required for state jobs? Who counts as victim and object of discrimination depends on when you start the narrative. The principle can be applied to all the language minorities throughout the former Soviet sphere.

Cultural constructions

Europe as institutional structure and Europe as geographical unit both rely on the cultural category of Europe that was historically the replacement for 'Christendom'. In the current politics of European integration, many different definitions of Europe are implied or explicitly invoked. Some focus on religious as opposed to cultural traditions, or on economic relations as opposed to political forms (Balibar 2001). Choice of the critical features with which to define 'Europe' signals the writer's political stance on key issues such as the exclusion or inclusion of potential EU members, the viability of a united Europe as a political entity, or the preferred treatment of migrants and Islamic populations. These are vital matters, but I put them aside in order to make a more general point about Europe as a cultural concept.

As a mode of self-understanding for European intellectuals, 'Europe' is what Bakhtin (1981) called a 'chronotope', a virtual space-time unit seen by its creators as the seat of modernity, development, and progress. In this guise, Europe is as much an ideology as is the notion of standard language. The two are closely related because standardization of linguistic forms has been one of the key features that has historically provided the cultural justification for aspiring polities to be recognized as properly European nation-states or as regional–ethnic minorities.

Europe is a cultural concept in another sense as well. It is a sign that gains its meaning in contrast to a set of 'others'. These others are virtualized world regions with their own temporal connotations. The borders of Europe shift not only with the expansion of the EU, but with the position from which one views the non-institutional, virtual space-time that is also 'Europe'. In this sense, 'Europe' is a Jakobsonian 'shifter', whose scope and reference changes, depending on the contrast set that is invoked in the specific context of use. Some years ago I analyzed the Hungarian version of this phenomenon. In Hungarian public discourse, Europe is routinely contrasted with the east and Asia, from which Hungarian ancestors are supposed to have come. Depending on the perspective taken in any segment of discourse, Hungarians could see themselves as Europeans contrasted with Asia, or alternatively as Asians contrasted with Europe. When speaking as Europeans, Hungarians dismissed Asia as backward and corrupt, the opposite of Europe. This stance also worked as a criticism of communism, when the Soviet Union was a stand-in for Asia. But Hungarians could also call themselves Asians, as a form of self-criticism, deriding the lack of modern values of restraint and development in the whole country, when compared to the west, or in the country's eastern half in comparison to its western half. As this example suggests, such mental maps or virtual borders were never stable. Within any zone labelled as Europe, Hungarians could subdivide (for the moment) to call a part of it 'not really, or not even' Europe because not developed or up-to-date enough in comparison to other imagined space-time zones (Gal 1991).

This fractal geography, the discourse of an infinitely splittable Europe, endlessly able to project stereotypical inclusion and exclusion according to perspective taken in interactional context, exists in all the central and eastern countries of the continent. It has been well documented for the Balkans (with Macedonia often tagged the Balkan of the Balkans), Russia and the German lands, as well as Scandinavia, in addition to Hungary. A surprising Scandinavian graffito exclaims: 'Asia begins in Malmö.' In the European south, a similar fractal contrast with Africa is often invoked, producing tags such as 'Sicily, the Africa of Europe'. In this sense, Europe is a moving entity, a perspectival cultural object whose borders can change in interactional time. The fractal splitting of space-time can also be triggered for some people by migrant populations and their linguistic practices, so that European cities are divided by certain speakers into streets and neighbourhoods that are less European or 'not-European' at all.

Across borders

For many speakers resident in Europe, the discourse of Europe is not the only organizing principle of their sociolinguistic lives. Rather, the standardized linguistic correctness to which they orient is located on other continents. It is useful here to invoke the classic distinction between speech communities and language communities. Migrant and diasporic populations are part of a European *speech* community, interacting with speakers of many other languages and linguistic varieties, noticing the significance of indexical signals that designate origin, age, gender and other categories of personhood even across languages. But their sense of linguistic correctness, their orientation to a denotational code and its literary norms, links them to other regions where there are speakers of the named languages they use. They are members of *language* communities of Hindi, Urdu, Indonesian, Turkish or Yoruba speakers that have their highly valued, standardizing centres outside of Europe.

In a different kind of linkage, Moslem populations in Bosnia are being connected to Moslem migrants from north Africa or Turkey who live in Paris or Berlin, as well as to practising Moslems elsewhere in the world through Koranic schools and their associated Arabic linguistic practices. And in yet another kind of connection that cross cuts the discourse of Europe, groups such as the Saami are being mobilized as 'indigenous peoples' with connections to international NGOs defending indigenous rights. Within such political networks, the Saami are seen as the 'Indians of Europe'. They face some of the same dilemmas as indigenous groups on other continents, required to prove their linguistic or customary 'authenticity' in order to make territorial or institutional claims.

Conclusion

The standardizing language ideology whose analysis has occupied much of this chapter remains powerful, if sometimes at regional scales, in addition to the older linkage to nation-states. This ideology does not succeed in regimenting all practices, yet the 'ironies' I have examined show how it quite effectively creates stresses and strains for speakers. By contrast, in this conclusion I consider the way that the tight Herderian weave of culture, language and state in Europe is itself being stretched and frayed in subtle ways.

Although cultural diversity and standardized linguistic diversity are part of the official ideology of the EU, territorially organized linguistic difference is an obstacle to another fundamental EU value, economic success through ease of movement for labour and commodities (Shore 2000). This has led to some shifts in the way the relations between language and culture are discussed, that is in language ideology. We find ethnolinguistic diversity understood not only as a value in itself, but also as economic advantage. Whether in attempts to legitimate support for minority languages, or to justify support for French as lingua franca, multi-standardism is touted as indispensable for high competitiveness in the global marketplace, in the great knowledge industry and economy of the future (Nelde 1996; Oakes 2002). While some languages such as German and English have lucrative markets in education, others such as Saami, Gaelic and Basque are imagined to have monetary value as exotic markers of place that regional developers hope to sell as touristic destinations.

The ideological linkage between speaker's identity and first language remains strong, but the connections to territory and state do not. For a new European elite with extensive education, fluency in one national language is augmented by knowledge of one or more (other) languages of wide distribution – English, German and/or French. What indexes such elite speakers is not any one shared code linked to a territory, but rather the isomorphic breadth of their linguistic repertoires and perhaps the situational switching among these standards. One may speculate that for such speakers, ethnolinguistic identity is only an occasional issue, the situations for signalling it arise on a limited basis. In a different pattern that is differently deterritorialized, speakers of some regional, minority languages are not learning the state language. Although they remain citizens of Macedonia, Albanian-speakers there acquire English and not Macedonian as a second language (Ismajli 1988). The earlier example of migrants in Europe orienting to non-European centres of standardization provides another case of such deterritorialization of linguistic practices.

And finally, there are intriguing shifts in the temporal indexing that was so evident in the European chronotope and in the ironies of standardization. Minority languages and rural accents whose use has historically signalled authentic group identity gained their value by indexing the past and tradition, in contrast to urban, state-centred modernity. Some of these minority linguistic forms are being reframed through new technologies such as the internet, and through their use in genres such as world music and other forms of popular, youth culture (see, for example, Urla 2001). Linguistically there is often a concomitant and self-conscious *anti*-standardizing move: combinations of forms from several standard languages are intentionally used together; single lexical items come to stand for the entire language; interlingual puns and other bivalent forms are positively valued and encouraged in such genres. These tactics do not necessarily increase the number of speakers of a minority language or lead to the acceptance of migrant languages by state agencies (Eisenlohr 2004). But they do sometimes result in ideological transformation, so that minority languages, rural accents, and immigrant forms are aligned less with the past and backward looking traditions, and more with forms of cultural production that have come to signal global youth culture and forward looking, urban sophistication. It remains to be seen how these linguistic forms and practices fare as they circulate in the future of Europe.

Notes

1. This chapter was written while I was the recipient of a John Simon Guggenheim Foundation Fellowship and an ACLS–SSRC International Program Fellowship. I would like to express my thanks to both, as well as to an anonymous reviewer who offered helpful bibliographic advice, and to Patrick Stevenson and Clare Mar-Molinero for the kind invitation to participate in this volume.
2. Indeed, the results of comparative and genetic linguistics have often been recruited to buttress political claims made in the name of linguistic 'similarity'.

3
A European Perspective on Language as Liminality

Christopher Brumfit

Limen, liminis, *the threshold.* I. A. Lit. intrare limen, Cic. B. Meton.
1 = *house, dwelling;* 2. *entrance;* 3, a. *the starting point of a chariot-race
in the circus;* b. *border, boundary; a beginning.* II. Fig. *a beginning.*
Cassell's *Latin Dictionary* (literary citations omitted)

> The self suspended between languages is a liminal self, living
> unsteadily in two languages and therefore living fully in neither...the
> second-language learner, positioned on the blurred border-line
> between first and second languages, unable either to turn back and
> regain the old self or to move forward, unencumbered, into a new one.
> Granger, C. A. (2004) *Silence in Second Language Learning*
> (Clevedon: Multilingual Matters), 62

> ...the data...illustrate the degree to which members of the group
> studied engaged in crossing from one language to another and,
> most significantly, as part of day-to-day exchanges which are
> characterised by what is termed *liminality.* In Rampton's data,
> liminal exchanges take place in contexts which are socially fluid.
> They are fluid because normally ordered social life is loosened...
> Carter, R. (2004) *Language and Creativity*
> (London: Routledge), 172

> Watch carefully, and you will note that in the area covered by the
> great official languages, most people are bilingual. They can speak the
> official language, but they also speak among themselves a dialect of
> their own, usually a dialect more or less cousin to the official language.
> Hilaire Belloc (1925) *The Cruise of the Nona*
> (London: Constable), 14

> The language in which we are speaking is his before it is mine. How different are the words *home, Christ, ale, master*, on his lips and on mine! I cannot speak or write these words without unrest of spirit. His language, so familiar and so foreign, will always be for me an acquired speech. I have not made or accepted its words. My voice holds them at bay. My soul frets in the shadow of his language.
>
> James Joyce (1916) *Portrait of the Artist as a Young Man*
> (London: Collins) 1983 ed., 172

Language

The quotations above illustrate the argument of the first part of my chapter. The chapter as a whole is going to take a now widely accepted position, to modify it by referring to the diversity within languages as well as across languages, and, in the second part, to consider its implications for language policies in Europe. However, we should not progress without noting the extensions of the concept 'liminal' implied by the Latin definitions. Not only may we be crossing the threshold to someone's dwelling and home, but we may also be making a new beginning. Crossing thresholds can take us into private and protected space, and it can involve us in repudiation as well as entry, starting again as well as continuing. It is small wonder that the 'year abroad' for language undergraduates is seen both as a threatening and a liberating experience (Coleman, 1996; Johnston *et al.* 2004).

The position can be broadly articulated as follows. Human beings are born with a capacity to acquire the languages to which they are exposed. There is no genetic predisposition to particular languages, but there is a predisposition, manifesting itself from birth if not before, to acquire those languages that are provided by interlocutors. Unless there is brain damage, they may acquire language visually, through touch, or through hearing – though humans without impairment normally acquire it initially through hearing. But acquisition in normal circumstances is interactional: hearing and the creation of sounds operate simultaneously. Even when there is some impairment of the senses, for example when sight and/or hearing are damaged, the process of language acquisition becomes interactional once opportunities are provided.

'Language acquisition' is a misleading term, however, for we do not acquire something which is pre-existent and fixed 'out there', and we do not possess it once we acquire it; more accurately, we perform with it in order to make it. And we create with it not just unique sentences to express our own unique messages, but unique displays of our decorative, analytical, mimetic, melodic, symbolic and allusive capacities. These capacities enable us to exploit not just the formal properties of the code, but the properties of the referents and of the associations of the referents. Consider some examples that came immediately to hand:

February brought home the serious issue of unregulated gangmasters.
Labour Today, Summer 2004: 5

Working together with the newly launched Southampton's Real Nappy Network, the council is keen to help encourage the use of reusable nappies. The group organises regular two monthly 'Nappucino' events...
Southampton City View: 25, June/July 2004: 2

If you stand with your feet just inches above the water of the River Itchen as it roars through the races of the mill, you will experience one of Winchester's best kept secrets: the thrill of the mill!
National Trust Thames & Solent News, Summer 2004: 1

Smacking Bans: Children are Unbeatable.
Guardian editorial headline, 5 July 2004: 17

These quotations are taken respectively from the Labour Party magazine for party members, from a free local government newsletter for Southampton residents, from a Newsletter of a charity devoted to preserving old buildings and rural landscape, and from a national newspaper. All were delivered to my house within a few weeks, and such examples could be replicated in any household in the country. Some of our creativity with language uses widely accepted metaphors which will be more or less tired to the user, depending on their maturity and experience with language ('brought home the serious issue...'), while some may be conventional in style but probably genuinely new to the writer ('as it roars through the races of the mill'). But, as also in these examples, we play with alliteration, rhythm, metaphor, idiom and cross-linguistic quotation as naturally as we use the grammar of our language. So too we tell stories, and not just for amusement. Consider the following, from a discipline that is not conventionally thought of as addicted to fictional narrative:

> If you went to a police station to report that you had seen a car being vandalized and were accused of having been the vandal yourself, you might well say 'If I had done it, I would hardly be drawing attention to myself in this way.' You would be temporarily entertaining the (untrue) hypothesis that you were the vandal, in order to show how ridiculous it was.
>
> Gowers, T. (2002) *Mathematics: A Very Short Introduction*
> (Oxford: Oxford University Press)

Thus the language we acquire is modified and created by our use of it, and the world to which it may refer is described and modified, but also imagined and created. By the age of forty each of us has encountered many words that did not exist at our birth, and serious readers will encounter many more that have rarely been spoken in their lifetime but which were once spoken, and others that are common in writing but have always been rare in speech. Native-speakers live happily either half-understanding or ignoring the precise meanings of much that we encounter in reading, as the following examples will indicate, unless you are a seventeenth century literary scholar:

> *Flamineo*: I will now give you some politic instructions.
> John Webster (1612) *The White Devil*, Act V, Scene 1
>
> Wherein Christians, who deck their Coffins with Bays, have found a more elegant Embleme. For that he seeming dead, will restore itself from the root, and its dry and exuccous leaves resume their verdure again.
> Thomas Browne (1658) *Hydriotaphia: Urn Burial*
> (London: Dent) 1906, 125

Now if, as an educated person, you have never read *The White Devil* or *Urn Burial* it is probably because you have chosen not to; although *Southampton City View* may have missed the attention of non-residents in the city, classics are available in libraries and heard in theatres, radio or television and the relative numbers of those who choose to be exposed to them are dependent on fashion, willingness and taste.

We are perhaps constrained by fashion, willingness and taste, but we are not coerced by them, as I have just demonstrated. The *Zeitgeist* may assist in making some options more available than others, but, especially with wider education, larger numbers of people speaking particular languages, and Internet access, *some* members of any large speech community are likely to choose minority options.

We also adopt and abandon styles of language. 'Taking in a scope' (improbable as it may seem) was a phrase widely used in my undergraduate days for 'going to a film'. Associated with that were a range of in-phrases that I have mercifully now forgotten but which would no doubt resonate for some people at a reunion of former students. Recordings of the royal family demonstrate subtle changes in individual phonology even in that protected environment, while there are records of politicians and others quite deliberately discarding (or more rarely adopting) the less-educated-sounding accents and lexicon of their youth. Both by conscious choice and by unconscious change we move out of (and occasionally in to) speech communities that continue their lives independent of the floating speakers on the margins.

But speech communities are not completely independent. As Brutt-Griffler (2002a) so cogently argues, thinking about speech communities rather than individuals as the possessors of language enables us not to be threatened by the facts of language variation within any speech community, and removes a number of problems about 'ownership' of the language. Learners share in the ownership of the language by participation in the speech community, and are not placed by definition in a deficit relationship with native speakers. In Rampton's (1990) terms, 'expertise' rather than 'affiliation' can become the normative reference points if evaluation is called upon at all.

There are major and complex concerns to be raised about the term 'speech community' of course (see Patrick 2001), but for the purposes of the argument here they are not relevant. The key issues are (1) that members of groups whose language is for all major purposes mutually intelligible will still show wide variation as individuals; (2) that the cultural and linguistic experiences of individuals will be reflected in the meanings and formal features of language they operate with; (3) that time as well as space is reflected by these: 'the past is another country' but those who have visited it participate linguistically in its life – indeed just as Auden remarked that for the poet 'a poem is never finished', so too past linguistic forms and meanings have the potential to be resurrected by writers like Joyce or Nabokov, and no language is ever completely dead while there is writing or memory. The symbolic values both of the meanings and of the formal features will certainly be used by some (and may be used by all) as part of power-based negotiation within political relations; stereotyping (England as a nation of shopkeepers), anecdote (Alfred and the cakes) etc form a bank of intertextual references for almost any discourse.

Identity

> The most natural state is one nation, an extended family with one national character.
>
> J. G. Herder cited in Gilbert, P. (2000) *Peoples, Cultures and Nations in Political Philosophy* (Edinburgh: Edinburgh University Press), 154

This is not the place to enter into a major analysis of identity and language (see Joseph, 2004 for a full discussion), but a few points need to be made against the notion of essentialism, and particularly essentialism based on language. Let me open the topic by referring to Balkan history, for that illustrates very clearly the dilemma faced by any analyst of European, and perhaps any other history (see Voss, this volume).

> The kingdom of Greece is not Greece; it is only a part, the smallest and poorest, of Greece. The Greek is not only he who inhabits the kingdom, but also he who lives in Janina, or Thessaloniki, or Seres, or Adrianople, or Constantinople, or Trebizonde, or Crete, or Samos, or any other country of the Greek history or race.
>
> Greek Prime Minister Ioannis Kolettis, 1844, quoted in Jelavich, B. 1983, *History of the Balkans*, Vol.1 (Cambridge: Cambridge University Press), 262
>
> As far as the religious hierarchies and the Ottoman state were concerned, religion always took precedence over culture, language and race in defining one's identity.
>
> ... throughout the region ... national identity or identities do not remain stable. They change over a few generations; they mutate during the course of a war; they are reinvented following the break-up of a large empire or state; and they emerge anew during the construction of new states.
>
> Glenny, M. (1999) *The Balkans 1804–1999* (London: Granta), 71 and 158.

Now of course it is possible to discuss language identities and associated issues such as language rights without necessarily accepting an essentialist view of language (see May, 2003 for example). But it is important that we recognize not just the role of language in the symbolism of the nation state, but the wider cultural phenomena that were closely associated also. Herder's 'family' image sounds attractive without close thought, and images of fatherlands, motherlands and children of the revolution abound in national discourses. But, as subsequent events have shown all too clearly, the relationship between identity and nationalism has implications for religion, for other cultural practices that constitute lifestyles, as well as for such class-related phenomena as educational expectations, income, and social aspirations, let alone common ancestry. Wars have been frequently fought over religion, of course, but the rhetoric of pre-democratic South Africa is not alone in defending a 'nation' through class interwoven with other cultural constructs to maintain a standard of living (see Simons and Simons, 1969 for a historical analysis, and Brand, this volume, for a discussion of changes in the contemporary context).

Not only are 'national' identities predicated on a selection of symbolic practices which may vary from time to time, as political exigencies demand, but identity may also be completely separated from nationalism. For example, it is commonplace to see identity, an individual's conception of 'self', as closely related to linguistic practices and to power.

The following assumptions – deriving from schools like poststructuralism, postcolonialism, social constructionism, and feminism – are now widely shared in the field of applied linguistics:

- That the self is shaped considerably by language and discourses;
- That the self is composed of multiple subjectivities, deriving from the heterogeneous codes, registers, and discourses that are found in society;
- That these subjectivities enjoy unequal status and power, deriving from differential positioning in socio-economic terms;
- That, because of these inequalities, there is conflict within and between subjects;
- That, in order to find coherence and empowerment, the subject has to negotiate these competing identities and subject positions in relation to the changing discursive and material contexts.

Canagarajah, S. (2004) 'Multilingual writers and the struggle for voice in academic discourse', in Pavlenko, A. and Blackledge, A. (eds) (2004) *Negotiation of Identities in Multilingual Contexts* (Clevedon: Multilingual Matters), 267

But we should note that the 'schools' from which these assumptions are drawn do not refer only to cross-linguistic communication, but communication within what have been conventionally regarded as homogeneous cultures. The multiple subjectivities expressed and reflected in heterogeneous codes may be as much within languages as across them. As Rampton (1995) shows, language crossing and style-shift follows patterns within single states that are indistinguishable in principle from those found in cross-state casual contact. An outside observer following discussion of, for example, access to higher education in the British context could interpret discussion of identity within London without any awareness of any mismatch with theoretical categories listed by Canagarajah.

It may be sensible, then, to propose a test for almost any observation made about language crossing and perceptions of language use by users, whether about 'learners' or about non-native speakers. If the substitution of 'native-speaker' for 'non-native-speaker' in the argument could still lead to a well-formed and interesting discussion, then the key issue may be human communication, rather than so-called separate languages. Indeed, it is possible to sympathize with Makoni and Meinhof (2004) in their frustration about the construct 'language' when contemplating the seamless robe of 'multilingualism' in Africa. The term 'language' may have outlived whatever usefulness it ever had (see also Gal, this volume).

But, as linguistic purism and language riots indicate, the term clearly fulfils a need for many people, and where there is a gap between apparent need and theoretical discussion, politics becomes necessary. The 2004 European elections, in which language was a live issue for commentary and lobbying in (at least) Spain, Poland, and Ireland are a recent witness to this, if any is needed.

Language power

But the extent to which the literature on the politics of language use, particularly the language rights discussions, has concentrated on cross-languages behaviour risks rendering invisible the same issues within languages. Thresholds are found not only between languages, but also within them, and liminality is characteristic of contemporary language use. But the perceptions of the self and the other, of insider-ness and outsiderness, of membership and non-membership have been surprisingly little discussed in relation to 'languages', although there is a thriving industry on the topic within English in relation to the role of standard English (Leith, 1983; Crowley, 1991 to name but two).

> All researchers agree that a distinction between American English and British English provenance is impossible to make with regard to loanwords in European languages in any consistent way.
>
> Görlach, M. (2002) *English in Europe* (Oxford: Oxford University Press), 3

It seems reasonable to believe, though, that like identities languages are constructs that come and go according to political need and individual or group choice. Naming a language (or dialect, or style) is a social act, since it involves defining a particular social group as some kind of sharing community. The more potentially powerful members of that group may be seen in relation to those being excluded, the more overtly political the act of naming and defining.

If our purpose is to understand how social agents operate with language, we can make one definite prediction: the current status of English is temporary. But on the timescale within which we have to operate, it is likely to be significant, though in due course it is likely to be replaced by another language (or possibly other languages) to which the term global may have to apply.

What we have to accept is that inherent in this is a condition of permanent liminality. I have occasionally been frightened by the awareness that (unlike human beings throughout most of history) I sit in an airport or on a metro train surrounded by hundreds of people whom I have never ever seen before and whom I shall never ever see again. Some of them I may speak to, but a condition of outsiderness is common for most professionals for much of their time. And an increasing proportion of the world's population literally crosses new thresholds many times a year, while many more aspire to this condition, and observe it vicariously through their screens. It is now a commonplace to attribute this contact without communication to jet travel, mobile phones, the Internet, and satellite TV, but few foresaw the extent and speed of the penetration of these technologies into what we used to call the third world. Mains electricity is no longer a condition of access for many. Thresholds advance on everyone, fast.

Language policy

So where does this leave policy-making in Europe?

First, we have to recognize that policy-making is normally aspirational and symbolic. A policy rarely guarantees funding, and it may be more significant for what it excludes than for what it includes. Nonetheless it does attempt to draw lines, and to define goals that policy-makers feel are, in principle at least, desirable.

But built into this is a risk of policy remaining far away from the practices of individuals and groups. On language policy people vote with their tongues. Much of the debate about language, rights and identity (see, for example, Brutt-Griffler 2002b, and particularly contributors to the Forum discussing these issues in the *Journal of Language, Identity, and Education* 3, 2, 2004) centres on conflicts between individual rights and communal rights (see also significant philosophical discussions by Habermas and Taylor in Taylor and Gutman, 1994, and my attempt to tease out some language issues in Brumfit, 2001). Because language is impossible to constrain, individuals, families and broader groups will do what they will do, perhaps regardless of and perhaps responsive to, persuasion or policy. We can accept, as we should, that rational choice theory is not enough to account for linguistic behaviour without ignoring the power of economic and other aspirations on language use.

But thinking consistently in terms of 'his or her mother tongue', 'their own language', while deeply embedded in European thinking, belies what is happening on the ground. As I tried to show at the beginning of this chapter, our individual repertoires are full of creativity, and play. So-called language contact research indicates the constant permeability of so-called language boundaries. Yet we remain the prisoner of a simplification which is becoming harmful by our retention of terms like 'English', 'German', 'French', 'Hungarian' as if they are more than metaphors for affiliation and aspirational identity.

The effect of this is to lead us towards a model of European language use which is dysfunctional because it does not reflect linguistic practices. Speakers are held to acquire their 'own' language from birth, to augment it with a language of national or regional communication, and eventually to add a language of wider, international communication. Speakers of the 'successful' international languages are thus held to obtain unfair advantage, with all three levels of activity being performed by the same language (see model on p. 38).

This 'tectonic' model inevitably leads to friction between the levels. Level I grates with Level II which grates with Level III, and inherent in thinking with a common-sense model such as this is a view that there will inevitably be friction. But, is this model a reflection of what people actually do with their own linguistic repertoires? If we want to retain a geological metaphor, is what people in fact do closer to a volcanic than

I	Language of wider communication	*'French'? 'English'? 'German?' 'Spanish'?* 'Esperanto'?
II	'Other' Language	*'French', 'German', 'Spanish', 'English'*, etc.
III	'Own' Language	'French'....
		'Breton'....
		'German'...
		'English'....
		'Welsh'....
		'Russian'....
		'Italian'...
		'Polish'....
		'Norwegian'
		'Spanish'., etc.

Italics = a language which some users would believe to be unfairly imposed because it advantages some speakers over others.

a tectonic plate model? Or is it more a model of gradual change through erosion and climatic shift than one of violent explosions at all? From the individual Level III with childhood language acquisition, people increase their repertoire by rising through and assimilating relevant parts of the levels above with more or less force according to need and motivation.

I would not wish to press this second analogy very hard, but the image may make us think more about the nature of our linguistic repertoires, for they are fluid and merge with the landscape, creating new shapes and sometimes gradually and sometimes violently modifying, reshaping and displacing previous formations. And they happen irrespective of planning, because individuals develop their own repertoires from their store of linguistic capacity, crossing language and dialect boundaries as they do so.

People who wish to communicate more widely, whether beyond the home, beyond the village or town, beyond the region, the state or across the world, have more opportunities now than at any earlier time to develop their own multilingual linguistic repertoires. Each of these (idealized) terms, 'home', village', etc represents a base from which a threshold is crossed to another. The question is whether seeing these as bases for discrete languages, or discrete varieties, is compatible with what we have learnt from many decades of sociolinguistic research.

The 'tectonic' model above may reflect perceptions of power relations, and thus may have its value as a way of looking at the impact of international politics on languages. But it cannot reflect what language practices look like, in non-political discourse, from below. Individuals choosing to communicate with other individuals, whether to do business, to achieve access to higher education, to travel efficiently, or for any other purpose, are extending their repertoire in relation to norms of behaviour that are subtly transmitted by the practices of their peers and of those in groups that they aspire to join. For some, this process may be perceived in political terms, but for many it will be a process of voting with their tongues that has been familiar to members of multilingual communities throughout the world probably ever since language emerged.

I am not trying to argue that there are no issues of power or economic weight to address, but I am asking us to recognize that from individuals' perspectives, multilingualism/multidialectalism is and always has been the norm for the majority of human beings. To interpret the current multilingual situation in Europe as a deviation from (largely nineteenth century) expectations of national monolingualism is false to the history of every country in Europe and false to the nature of language. In a sense, just as – and because – there are no homogeneous speech communities, there are no native-speakers to idealize. As Belloc observed in 1925 before the quotation I used at the beginning of this paper, 'human speech is naturally not a set of a few official languages, but a mass of innumerable dialects, all melting one into the other' (Belloc 1925: 14). In a world like this language becomes liminality by definition, as every speech act is an engagement with a subtly different dialect, and the further we roam the more thresholds we cross.

Policy thus becomes a way of minimising negative effects of the practices of communication and identity-formation that take place through language. On the one hand, the fact that most countries in the world had, by the end of the 1990s, adopted English as the first foreign language, created a unique situation where (with the partial exception of Latin America) one single language was the default language for international communication. On the other, the rise in minority language support has made people in the major monolingual-thinking nations more aware of local multilingualism. Both from above and below, all (except English native-speakers) are being reminded far more than they were of multilingualism and liminality. For the English native-speakers, despite decades of exhortation from language professionals, the reminder comes from below, as Spanish most forcefully in the United States, and Urdu, Panjabi, Cantonese, Welsh, Irish, and other languages in the UK assert their various claims – and similar statements could be made for Australia, Ireland and other primarily-English-speaking states.

This situation will necessarily generate friction as well as good relations, if only because some people will act as if the tectonic model applies, and others will resent language opportunities apparently open to some and not to others. Language can easily become a surrogate for economic, political, educational and personal disadvantage.

Predicting future areas of friction is a responsibility of language policy-makers, and we can be sure that some of the risks associated with majority and minority access to languages will continue to need addressing. Concerns of the impact of English on other languages have been well articulated (see, for example, Phillipson 2003). But there are also risks, less frequently discussed, for speakers of the 'successful' languages. These are not only found in the friction deriving from attempts to maintain the 'integrity' or intelligibility of international languages against the inevitable tendencies towards fragmentation (see, for example, Kachru 1990; Quirk 1990), or the attempts to maintain a perceived national language against multilingual pressure (Crawford 1992; Stevenson, this volume). Even more they are likely to be in the retreat from multilingualism that is already showing itself. The realization that the other's English will, for most people, be far more efficient than one's own foreign language proficiency, is arguably already having major effects on the motivation to learn foreign languages in traditionally English-speaking countries (Edwards 2001). Not only may English speakers become the only educated monolinguals in the world, but some of them will become very defensive about this state and more and more aggressively mono-cultural in attitude. Relatively trivially, a trade war, based on the perceived 'ownership' of English, is not an impossible to conceive scenario, as more and more students throughout the world make teaching through the medium of English a requirement for engagement in the lucrative higher education industry. Every other country having a substantial number of highly competent English users will be perceived as threatening by some. Less trivially, English speakers need to be helped to see foreign languages as sources for the extension of their repertoire, not as all-or-nothing adoption of others' cultures. Language policy is more likely to reduce the negative effects of people hiding behind 'a language' if it acknowledges the permeability of languages, in all directions.

It would be absurd to suggest that a reformulation of theory or a new metaphor would completely resolve such conflicts. Because language is an epiphenomenon in power relations, and because it can so easily be seized upon as a defining marker of group and individual identities, conflict using language as an overt symbol for loyalty will remain for many years. But a recognition of the permeability of language would nonetheless make it harder for public discussion to hide behind the smokescreen provided by reifying idealized languages as fixed and easily defined entities. If we recognize that no two individuals speak the same language exactly, that they differ in range of their lexicon, in the relations between active use and recognition of lexical items, in the distribution and frequency of syntactic features, in the cultural codes that they combine with their language use – let alone in accent and personal tone of voice; if we recognize this, we begin to acknowledge the insufficiency of the term 'language' as unit of analysis. Thinking in this way will enable us to see that the naming of a language is a political, not a linguistic act. We see this overtly in the ways in which language rights are promoted over individual rights in advancing the claims of particular languages within the polity or within education (see, for example, discussion of Welsh in Mitchell and Brumfit 1993).

It is not my purpose here to suggest that language should never be associated with political movements, nor that cultural groupings should be forbidden to have their causes advanced through democratically arrived at policy decisions. But we should be clear that such decisions are indeed political, to be accompanied by all the checks and balances that should accompany the use of power in public space.

Nonetheless, as an account of how language typically operates in human communities, the notion of a single language, whether it adopts us at birth ('this is your mother tongue'), or whether it is learnt as a foreign language ('this is your first, second, third foreign language') is simply wrong, at best a device to assist education, a pedagogic tool, at worst an instrument for the identification and exploitation of outsiders. It is not just that the lexicon borrows from contact, so that a sentence like 'Somewhere in the zeitgeist is the notion of the apparachnik as a bete noire' while inelegant is not obviously unusable by an English speaker, but that individuals, like speech communities, have repertoires, not languages. These repertoires cross languages/language varieties in many different ways, no doubt in as many ways as there are individuals. Some will use a range of codes relatively discretely; others, especially in speech, will combine and mix, either seriously or in play (Rampton 1995, 1999). Some will combine literacy and oracy; others will be limited to one or the other for parts of their repertoire; some will aspire to convergence with other cultures; others will maintain a more rigid 'outsider' identity while still using or understanding other varieties fluently. Some will operate entirely with contemporary language; others will be addicted to reading and will operate primarily in the language of the past for their understanding. However we conceptualize liminality, once we acknowledge the phenomenon of 'crossing', and once we recognize that comprehension constitutes language competence as much as production, the firm boundaries around what we have been taught to regard as 'languages' collapse.

For a European Union that rides on a tradition of nineteenth century nationalism deriving from such philosophers as Herder, quoted earlier in this chapter (and discussed at greater length by Susan Gal in her chapter), the argument presented here poses a major challenge. Yet it is a commonplace to recognize that the Masaryk-Wilson principles of nationality that tacitly accepted much of this tradition for the Versailles treaty was based on a complete falsification of the realities of European (or, we might add, any other) language behaviour. Monolingual regions do not exist (even in principle they could only exist occasionally, and temporarily, as a result of genocide). Like 'nations', they are theoretical constructs, and they risk becoming as dangerous constructs as those that falsely claimed groups were 'united by a common language, a common territory, a common history, a common culture, and a common fate' (Popper 1994: 186). This is because 'the theories on which they are constructed are wholly inadequate' to quote Popper again.

Because of these inadequate theories, many of the thresholds that languages cross are ignored, rejected or rendered invisible. The repertoires of many European residents exploit features of Arabic, Turkish, Cantonese, Urdu, Kiswahili, Russian, to name only a few, more than the recognized majority and minority languages of the Union. Because there are acknowledged languages, there have to be unacknowledged ones; a repertoire, on the other hand, can be open-ended and unrepressive in effect. To persuade people to accept a more open-ended view of our language capacities is a large educational project – but it accords with our lived linguistic experience, so it should be possible. Certainly we have to learn to see the constructs 'French', 'English', 'German', 'Italian', 'Spanish' etc as ideological constructs that have to be treated with great care. They will not go away as terms, for they perform useful functions in everyday discourse. But used inappropriately they can be dangerous. They need to come with a health warning.

Conclusion

Perhaps the most potent and memorable images we have of contemporary thresholds are from the television screens: the kick through the door and the rushing in of armed soldiers. But in fact we walk through our own – and many other – thresholds every day and scarcely notice them. And our behaviour changes with each shift of location. Recognising liminality as a feature of violent confrontations makes for good journalistic copy, and reflects real issues of conflict. But liminality is a feature of peaceful co-existence too. Liminality in language is not just a condition of use; it is a condition of structure and acquisition, of comprehension and of production. The concept erodes the integrity of grammars and dictionaries of particular languages (though they retain their usefulness as pedagogic tools to assist the development of a greater variety of competences). For education, we can usefully simplify, even (if experience shows it to be helpful) usefully falsify slightly. But for policy we have to start with the clearest account of the practices of those who live in Europe. If European policy-making is not to be out of touch with the linguistic practices of its citizens, emphasis on 'languages' must go to the political arena where it belongs. For language policy, liminality and the development of a repertoire for the crossing of thresholds must be seen as central concepts for theory.

4

Americanization, Language Ideologies and the Construction of European Identities

Thomas Ricento

Introduction

Few of us today would question the centrality of ideology in matters concerning language status and use. In fact it has become increasingly clear to many of us who work in language policy and planning (LPP) that it is impossible to look at social structures and processes apart from ideologies, which van Dijk (1998: 8), defines as the 'shared framework(s) of social beliefs that organize and coordinate the social interpretations and practices of groups and their members.' In this chapter, I discuss the inherent ideological nature of all language discussions, including those in social science. I then provide a summary of the findings from an empirical study I conducted on the role of ideologies of language in the construction of American national identity. Finally, I consider aspects of the US historical and discursive process that constituted language ideologies which are relevant to language policies and policy approaches in Europe today, and the implications for the future of European identity.

It is important to be specific about what I mean by 'ideology' and how ideologies can be identified in some principled way. Before discussing ways of identifying ideologies, I want to make a few general comments about the nature of ideologies. First, ideologies apply not just to situations 'out there' in the 'real world,' but also to intellectual constructs and conceptual frameworks which may be invoked in applied research on language status and use. Second, these constructs and categories may be applied uncritically and inappropriately in arguments in favor of, for example, the promotion of linguistic diversity and more equal access to the political economy of states or supra-national entities, such as the European Union. Finally, ideologies are not properties of some discourses or some speech communities and not others; rather, as Silverstein (1992: 315–16) notes, '...every system or modality of social signs is infused with indexicality, [and] therefore such indexicality is caught up in a dialectic process mediated by ideological formations, and...therefore there is no possible *absolutely* pre-ideological, i.e. *zero-order*, social semiotic – neither a purely 'sense'-driven denotational system for the referential-and-predicational expressions of any language, nor a totalizing system of purely "symbolic" values for any culture.'

To illustrate the ways in which ideologies are imbricated in the selection and interpretation of linguistic data, I now turn to three popular theoretical constructs in the literatures of language policy, sociolinguistics, and the sociology of language: diglossia, language-as-resource, and language ecology. The construct of diglossia has been widely accepted as a neutral description of 'reality' in mainstream sociolinguistic theory. Yet, a case can be made that this construct *prescribes* as much as it *describes* societal arrangements with regard to language(s). Woolard & Schieffelin (1994: 69), for example, criticize diglossia as 'an ideological naturalization of sociolinguistic arrangements,' perpetuating linguistic (and, relatedly, societal) inequalities. By naturalizing binaries such as High and Low status languages or varieties, which tend to correlate with instrumental (H) and identity (L) functions of language, the construct of diglossia tends to naturalize the legitimacy and dominance of the 'big' languages in Europe and elsewhere which already have established High instrumental functions and domains, while also providing identity functions for their speakers. As long as some languages in Europe, for example., English, French, German, and Spanish are identified as having greater instrumental utility than, say, Portuguese or Polish, then this supposedly natural arrangement will help perpetuate asymmetries in access to cultural and political power, despite the support for specific language policies designed to promote foreign language teaching/learning and even with the existence of widespread translation services.

Another example of an academic construct which may help promote values that are counter to linguistic diversity and social equity is the metaphor 'language as resource' (Ruiz 1984). While potentially useful as an antidote to a 'language as problem' orientation, 'language as resource' has been invoked in support, for example, of highly selective foreign language education programmes to serve state national security needs and international trade at the expense of the needs and aspirations of ethnolinguistic communities, as is occurring in the US today (see Ricento in press). When researchers and policy-makers use main-stream economic models in dealing with language, with the implicit ideologies that are associated with constructs like supply/demand and need/capacity (as in, for example., Brecht and Rivers 2002), they need to be cognizant of the myriad ways that languages are highly *atypical* compared to most commodities or services analyzed by economists. As François Grin (in press) has argued, approaches that commodify language do not take into account market failure in the case of 'super-public' or 'hypercollective' goods (De Swaan 2001), such as language. For example, in classical economic models, the value of a commodity correlates inversely with its supply, that is, minority languages should be *more* valuable than majority languages. Yet, in the case of language, as Grin notes, the more people use a language, the *more* valuable it becomes as a tool for communication to people who already use it. There are many other ways in which mainstream economic models are counterproductive when applied to LPP research and theorizing (see Grin in press, for example).

Another example of how conceptual frameworks borrowed from another discipline may be inappropriately applied to LPP theorizing and research is seen in the application of environmental metaphors to the study of language 'ecologies.' While linguistic diversity is a fact (there are 6,000 to 8,000 oral languages worldwide), analogies between biological ecosystems and linguistic 'ecosystems' break down very quickly upon close inspection. For example, language contact, shift and loss have been features of human societies throughout history and do not entail species extinction, among many other differences. Dubious analogies like these weaken the credibility of linguistic ecology as a serious alternative model to the *laissez-faire* approach which benefits large languages, like English, at the expense of smaller ones.

The point of this brief discussion is to remind us that epistemologies in the social sciences are not exempt from the ideological formations extant in any system of social signs. Ideologies are part and parcel of academic theories and constructs just as much as they are attributes of the 'objects' which academics (including critical scholars) routinely scrutinize in their research. Critical scholars who seek to identify and oppose ideologies which perpetuate socioeconomic and political asym-metries related to language status and function must be careful in how they conceptualize alternative approaches in their academic theorizing and research, lest they help perpetuate the very ideologies (and policies) they wish to defeat. This is especially true in interdisciplinary work in which ideologies from different fields are uncritically accepted by scholars who are trying to fortify their positions with the importation of models and terminology from other 'hard' sciences. It is for these reasons that critical research concerned with uncovering and analyzing ideologies must employ methods of data gathering, analysis, and interpretation that are carefully scrutinized for the 'hidden' promotion of ideologies or other shortcomings. In the section that follows, I report on research that I conducted on the role of ideologies in the construction of national (in this case, United States) identity. I argue that the theoretical/methodological framework I employed – Critical Discourse Analysis (CDA) – takes cognizance of the complexity and embedded nature of ideologies in discourse and social processes.

The construction of American identity

I have been fascinated for many years with the question of American identity: Who or what is an American? There are certainly many ways to approach this question. The method most aligned with my training in linguistics and applied linguistics is Critical Discourse Analysis (CDA). CDA can provide a fine-grained empirical analysis on the topic of national identity and the ideologies which inform such identities. This is because, as van Dijk (1993: 253) points out, 'it [CDA] requires true multidisciplinarity, and an account of intricate relationships between text, talk, social cognition, power, society and culture.'

My focus in this research was to understand how dominant (even prototypical) attributes of 'American' as a cultural type evolved in discourses produced by Americans from the colonial period to the present day. I was especially interested in looking at the ways in which language, ethnicity, gender, religion, and expectations regarding appropriate behavior and beliefs were highlighted, backgrounded, or ignored. The goal was to see how particular constructions of Americanism and American identity came to be seen as commonsense and mundane through the use of a variety of linguistic and rhetorical strategies in a variety of discourses, texts, and contexts. An additional goal was to speculate on whether this methodology could be applied to other contexts, such as Europe.

Historical context

Before presenting this study's major findings, I will briefly provide the historical context. Most nations and states (and they usually are not isomorphic (Edwards 2003)) have national myths and narratives characterizing the people who founded or occupy the land, which often predate the establishment of the state. This was normally the case in Europe. However, in the case of the United States of America, there was not much time between the War of Independence and the establishment of the republic to develop the tropes and discourses of national identity. The facts on the ground also created a major challenge, since at the time of the 1790 census, only about 49 per cent of the national population was of English origin (Pitt 1976), and nearly 19 per cent was of African origin, 14 per cent was of Spanish origin, 15 per cent was of Scottish, Scottish Irish, or Irish origin; millions of Native Americans were ignored. To gain dominance from the earliest years of the new Republic, the numerical minority (Americans of British background) developed discourses to convince the numerical majority that the numerical majority's interests and the national interest as conceived largely by the numerical minority were one and the same. To achieve this goal it was important to establish that both the dominant group and all other groups shared a common American identity, despite the obvious differences in languages, cultures, ethnicity/race, socioeconomic status, etc. among the various groups. Thus, as early as 1788, John Jay in *The Federalist*, No. 2, characterized the nation as '... one united people – a people descended from the same ancestors, speaking the same language, professing the same religion ... very similar in their manners and customs ...'. At the same time, Americans sought to distance themselves from British and European ways of thinking, in part, by developing a 'new' American language. There certainly was a great deal of discussion and debate in the 18th century about how best to 'ascertain' and 'fix' the language, and the importance of language (especially written language and metaphor) in making the case for independence has been discussed extensively (see, for example, Howe 2004).

The difficult challenge was how to define or characterize America as a unique cultural collective, when its roots had been most closely associated with the Anglo-Saxon culture of England. As historian Richard Hofstadter (1989) famously said about the United States: 'It has been our fate as a nation not to have ideologies, but to be one.'

Given this historical background, it was not surprising that what I found in the texts[1] and their discourses was a complicated picture of the nature and goals of Americanism, both in terms of multiple discourses and in terms of contradictions within these identified discourses. For example, although there is ample historical documentation on the demographics of colonial and 19th century America (discussed above), this history in many of what I call conservative discourses is erased and replaced with a totally constructed – and often false – account of American history. Other, what I call, liberal discourses acknowledged the ways in which America had not yet lived up to its lofty ideals expressed in iconic texts, for example, by having the institution of slavery, religious intolerance, etc. while still arguing for a core set of American values that could be aspired to, even if they had not yet been fully achieved. A third discourse, which I call progressive, explicitly criticized the discourses of Americanization which positioned some groups (Caucasian/European), religions (Christianity), and language (English) as being more authentically 'American' than others. This discourse argued that democracy benefits by cultural diversity and held that Americanism was not tethered to any particular ethnicity, culture, religion, or language.

What I also came to understand was that the interpretation as well as the production of this history reflected different ideological orienta-tions on matters of language, race, religion, democracy, and civil society. Further, these ideologies – even when fairly coherent – were not applied consistently to particular issues. For example, while promoting the American value of freedom of expression in speeches and pamphlets, many Americanizers also supported restrictions on the use of languages other than English in schools, church services, in telephone conversa-tions, and newspapers. Another example concerns the meaning(s) of citizenship. There was support (along with opposition, which eventually won out) in the US Congress to require immigrants to take their 'first papers' towards gaining citizenship within five years of arriving in the US. Critics argued that becoming an American citizen should be volun-tary and freely chosen. While it was claimed by some Americanization leaders that immigrants would freely choose to become Americans, given the chance, other Americanizers (in speeches and pamphlets published by Americanization organizations) argued that for those who did not 'see the light' voluntarily, other more compulsory methods would be used to ensure they 'got the message.' While critics of this brand of Americanization would denounce such inconsistencies as examples of hypocrisy, or worse, supporters (apparently oblivious to contradictions in their discourses) believed that becoming an American required certain outcomes, and that freedom required 'right thinking' to protect its proper operation.

The tension between the 'is' of a diverse nation (or 'super' nation, in the case of Europe), comprised of a great number of ethnic/cultural groups and languages, and the 'ought' of an often imagined 'American' nation is evident in many of the discourses and texts examined in this study. I have rather briefly summarized here some of the key findings in my investigation of the construction of American identity(ies) (see Ricento 2003 for detailed discussion). Whether or not these identities are deeply felt, and whether or not they influence, specifically, language attitudes, their basic features are transmitted and reinforced through education and the media and are constantly revisited and reinforced through mainstream political discourse. This does not mean, of course, that individuals do not have views about American values and beliefs different from those presented in this study (they clearly do); rather, most people understand what they are *expected* to know and believe to be true about American ideals, American history, American values, the 'nation', human nature and so on. Many of these beliefs and values are informed by ideologies of and about language and thought, language and culture, language and human understanding, and language and patriotism. These ideologies are shared frameworks that organize and coordinate the social interpretations and practices of groups. When these ideologies are shared, or at least not opposed, by substantial majorities within a nation, they cease to be recognized as *ideologies*, but instead are understood as commonsense *knowledge*. When this occurs, attempts to change public opinion on matters, for example, relating to language learning, use, status, varieties, etc. often are viewed as political attempts to overturn politically neutral, commonsense knowledge, and are not supported. In other words, ideologies end up having very real effects on language policies and practices because they are socially shared. While ideologies have contradictory elements and are often not applied consistently in diverse contexts, those that political institutions, the media and education constitute and reproduce tend to persist. Understanding how ideas and beliefs become ideologies, and how ideologies provide frameworks to coordinate the social interpretations and practices of dominant groups allows us to predict with some confidence how particular language policies and practices might be interpreted – and supported or opposed – by dominant or majoritarian social groups. Such understanding can also help advocates for particular policies or policy orientations develop strategies to counter such dominant ideologies in specific domains (for example, schools, the media) while, at the same time, realizing that all ideologies (including those we may support) have inconsistencies and contradictions, and so are at once vulnerable and resistant to change in the short term. Such a view is realistic and therefore more useful in developing practical and practicable strategies for advancing policy goal agendas.

nation is evident in many of the discourses and texts examined in this study. I have rather briefly summarized here some of the key findings in my investigation of the construction of American identity(ies) (see Ricento 2003 for detailed discussion). Whether or not these identities are deeply felt, and whether or not they influence, specifically, language attitudes, their basic features are transmitted and reinforced through education and the media and are constantly revisited and reinforced through mainstream political discourse. This does not mean, of course, that individuals do not have views about American values and beliefs different from those presented in this study (they clearly do); rather, most people understand what they are *expected* to know and believe to be true about American ideals, American history, American values, the 'nation', human nature and so on. Many of these beliefs and values are informed by ideologies of and about language and thought, language and culture, language and human understanding, and language and patriotism. These ideologies are shared frameworks that organize and coordinate the social interpretations and practices of groups. When these ideologies are shared, or at least not opposed, by substantial majorities within a nation, they cease to be recognized as *ideologies*, but instead are understood as commonsense *knowledge*. When this occurs, attempts to change public opinion on matters, for example, relating to language learning, use, status, varieties, etc. often are viewed as political attempts to overturn politically neutral, commonsense knowledge, and are not supported. In other words, ideologies end up having very real effects on language policies and practices because they are socially shared. While ideologies have contradictory elements and are often not applied consistently in diverse contexts, those that political institutions, the media and education constitute and reproduce tend to persist. Understanding how ideas and beliefs become ideologies, and how ideologies provide frameworks to coordinate the social inter-pretations and practices of dominant groups allows us to predict with some confidence how particular language policies and practices might be interpreted – and supported or opposed – by dominant or majoritarian social groups. Such understanding can also help advocates for particular policies or policy orientations develop strategies to counter such domi-nant ideologies in specific domains (for example, schools, the media) while, at the same time, realizing that all ideologies (including those we may support) have inconsistencies and contradictions, and so are at once vulnerable and resistant to change in the short term. Such a view is realistic and therefore more useful in developing practical and practicable strategies for advancing policy goal agendas.

The relevance of the findings for European identities

My purpose here is not to present a detailed comparison between the histories of the US and Europe; rather, I suggest that the methods that were used to investigate the roles of ideologies in the construction of the American 'nation' may be fruitfully applied to the European context. I also suggest that Europe is tied to the US in ways that may not always be apparent to Europeans – or Americans – and that European intellectuals have engaged in the same sort of historical constructionism that has typified the American experience.

Let me first briefly summarize the Americanization process, at least as I understand it, based on the research described above. Over the course of about 150 years, the constitutional Republic of the United States became a nation (America) largely through a discursive process. This involved a complex interweaving of discourses from science, philosophy, and religion with societal discourses informed by the lived experience of diverse groups. Ideologies imported from Europe and extrapolated from the work of Darwin, Spencer, Herder, John Locke and many others were influential in both scholarly and popular literatures, but they were not always accepted nor applied to social policies in consistent ways. Confronted by 'social reality,' American science devised theories to justify extermination of Native Americans and the enslavement of Africans, including radical interpretations of human evolution. Later, beginning in the mid-1800s, with the influx of German immigrants and the increasing regional tensions caused by the practice of slavery in the South, discourses about the superiority of Anglo-Saxon culture (including language), influenced no doubt, and ironically, by German Romantic theorizing on nation and national identity, developed. This ideology was used in justifying passage of highly restrictive and racially-based immigration policies and laws beginning around the 1880s and continuing into the 1920s, and to proscribe the teaching of foreign languages in schools in the early decades of the 20th century.

Although the US was founded on the Enlightenment ideals of universal equality, fraternity, and liberty, there continued to be tensions between these ideals and the claims of dominant political and economic interests that America had a cultural (national) identity and in order for *that* America to survive, that cultural identity, which privileged English-speaking, Christian, Anglo-Saxonism, had to be maintained and protected. This led, among other things, to the institutionalization of Americanization in all aspects of American public education. The tension between the idea of America and the reality of the lived experiences of Americans can be seen in the variety of discourses which I have briefly described in this chapter. To the extent some in Europe call for the development, or construction, of a European identity, the lessons from the US experience are cautionary.

An example of the persistence of conservative discourses on Americanism alluded to earlier in this paper is found in a recent article by Harvard professor Samuel P. Huntington in the journal *Foreign Policy* (2004a) entitled 'The Hispanic Challenge' (see also a book-length treatment of these ideas in Huntington 2004b). Huntington argues that the infusion of immigrants from Latin America, and especially Mexico, is changing American identity by creating an unassimilated, culturally and linguistically distinct population that is indifferent, or even hostile, to the American creed, key elements of which include the English language, Christianity, religious commitment, values of individualism, and the work ethic. He claims that 'There is only the American dream created by an Anglo-Protestant society. Mexican Americans will share in that dream and in that society only if they dream in English.'

It may be useful to consider how European philosophers and social critics have characterized the historical and philosophical relations between European and American identities. Martin Heidegger, at least in some of his formulations, found Americanism to be something European. According to Heidegger, 'It [Americanism] represents a working out of modern European thought... it is the culmination of the entire Western metaphysical tradition' (Ceaser 1997: 196). Heidegger calls the modern language of information and technical communication 'American'; this is the foreign language used for communication for purposes of business and science. However, in another (metaphorical) sense, 'American' is the name Heidegger gives to the deformation of all the advanced languages. Heidegger wrote, 'Our language is "German", but we actually talk "American"' (cited in Ceaser 1997: 197); for Heidegger, of course, this was nothing short of disaster. America was a moment in history that was the spatial manifestation of the temporal fact of the 'darkening of the world' and the 'forgetting of Being' that is characteristic of our age. America represented, for Heidegger, the ahistorical; America is the homogenization of culture, the loss of authenticity.

In his book *America* (1988), the French postmodernist Jean Baudrillard also says Americans have no sense of history: America 'cultivates no origin or mythical authenticity; it has no past and no founding truth. Having known no primitive accumulation of time, it lives in a perpetual present' (p. 76). According to Baudrillard, the problem with Europeans is that they have been paralyzed in the wake of the French Revolution which created an ideal of the transcendent pictured in history; they are self-conscious of quality and therefore helpless. In contrast, the American Revolution promoted the idea of building a reality in this world. Since America skipped over nineteenth-century thought, according to Baudrillard at least, Americans can create unself-consciously in this world without experiencing the difficulty that comes from searching for the 'authentic.' It is this primitive American mind-set, according to Baudrillard, which has allowed America to become powerful and confident (there is, he notes, not even an American equivalent for Angst!). Thus, although European thinkers came up with the idea of modernity, America is the fulfillment of Europe, the end point of the Old World's development because, for Baudrillard, Europe's past is an obstacle to action, while America has no such past to impede it.

The notion that the US is not an 'authentic' nation reflects, of course, deep-seated ideologies on the nature of authenticity itself. A number of studies on European identity have revealed gaps between the 'is' and 'ought' of characterizations of Europe by Europeans in various genres of text and through analysis of social policies towards immigrant groups (for example, Blommaert and Verschueren 1998; Wodak, *et al.* 1999). Depicting the US as either the prodigal offspring or genetic mutant of Europe does little to advance European thinking on how it might understand itself as a collectivity comprised of great linguistic and cultural diversity.

An important question to ask is: Does Europe *need* to see itself as a unified entity as a prerequisite to attaining political and economic power necessary to compete with the US (assuming this is an important reason for promoting a European identity/identities)? Is the assertion of a European identity desirable, let alone attainable? These are the issues which are fundamental to discussions on European identity. Perhaps the crucial question is whether the cultivation of a European identity is compatible with the goals of sociopolitical and socioeconomic equity among the nations of Europe.

The assumption by Baudrillard that the US was able to become 'powerful and competent', in part, because of its un-selfconscious and primitive 'identity' misses the point that identities are connected to the lived experiences of peoples (for example, Americans or Europeans); they cannot be 'cooked up' or made to order, regretted or obliterated. In this regard, scholars interested in fashioning language policies to promote equity and integration in Europe, generally, and the European Union, specifically, need to first examine the ideologies and presuppositions represented in the writings of influential European thinkers, such as Heidegger, Baudrillard, and others. As constructions themselves, such systems of thought are, of course, highly ideological and, therefore, reductive of more complex histories and discourses in Europe, where the processes of identity formation, contestation, and revision have gone on for much longer periods of time compared to the US, and certainly pre-date the French Revolution.

The existence of regional languages and multinational states means that matters of identity are more important, different, and more complicated in Europe compared to the US. For example, although only about 7 per cent of the US population labels itself primarily as American on census forms (*New York Times* 2002), most Americans imagine themselves as part of a bounded nation. English is unrivaled as the national language. There is no parallel for this in Europe (although the argument for a Europeanized English as the best candidate for a Lingua Franca is evidence of the 'blow back' of Americanism on Europe described by Heidegger). Given the truism that language and power cannot be separated, I do not see how any conventions, agreements, or language policies could *in and of themselves* change the current sociolinguistic reality of Europe. Thus, policies which, for example, seek to level the playing field with regard to languages by, for example, advocating Esperanto as a Lingua Franca for the EU, are unrealistic because they skirt the ideological formations which render such a proposal a dead letter in the context of current (and historical) power relations within which languages (and cultures) have evolved and knowledge about them has become common sense.

Even the proponent of such an apparently idealistic solution of promoting Esperanto as a lingua franca in Europe, Robert Phillipson, confirms the political embeddedness of language practices in his book *English-Only Europe? Challenging Language Policy* (2003: 191–2):

Whether the EU in its present form – with intensive interaction between Eurocrats, representatives of member states, and lobbies – is equipped to play an influential role in language policy is an open question, but it is extremely unlikely. The fact that the EU's achievements are confined to producing every few years a resolution on multilingualism that merely has advisory status, and funding for various schemes for international liaison and student mobility, shows that language policy has a low priority, and has been accorded only modest funding. It has evidently been too politically sensitive for more serious engagement at the supranational level. EU funding for research in the area, and the occasional report, has been minimal, and mostly concerned with regional minority languages. The few relevant activities fit into the pattern of nation-states competing for power and influence within the EU, burdened by the dead weight of linguistic nationalism and the different conceptual universes that have evolved over centuries.

It is difficult to imagine exactly what would constitute a common European identity, given these 'different conceptual universes', different languages, different national histories, and so on. In the end, it may not matter that much. The continued importance of the state in international politics – despite countervailing pressures caused by globalization in the economic and cultural spheres – means that language policies that require the lowering of boundaries – political and linguistic – are not likely to have much success. All of the apparatus associated with the construct of 'modernity' – states, national standardized languages, print capitalism, sovereignty, borders and national identities often developed, and contested, over centuries – mitigates against processes which require the devolution, at least to a significant degree, of the state system.

My research on the development of American identity, and its effects on attitudes towards linguistic and cultural diversity, suggests that the forging of nationalist (or supra-nationalist in the case of Europe) identities comes at a high price and is generally detrimental to the status of minority languages. Scholars in language policy and planning argue that intervention by the state on behalf of language minority groups is both warranted and necessary (see, for example, Grin in press). Robert Phillipson (2003), for example, lists 45 detailed language policy recommendations to enhance the sociopolitical access of users of minority languages and, thereby, enhance European integration. These suggestions represent aspects of an idealized blueprint for motivating changes in language behaviour. However, European states, analogous to the US, have their own ideologies of language and national identities and will not easily forfeit them for the 'greater good' of a 'unified' Europe. Meanwhile, the market for 'big' languages, notably English, appears to be robust and may continue to assert itself in Europe in ways that are unfavourable to the long-term viability of minority languages, if favourable to economic development and supra-national integration.

The relevance of the US experience for Europe is this: suppression of linguistic and cultural difference *can* be compatible with the development of national (and supra-national) identity and economic development. The price, however, of such suppression is substantial and often difficult to measure. The US has a chronic shortage of qualified speakers of 'strategically important' languages such as Arabic, Farsi, Urdu, and Pashto. The marginalization and stigmatization of the cultures and languages of most immigrant groups in the US lowers the status of other languages and cultures, with negative effects on enrolments in foreign language classrooms and heightened social tensions, especially in urban areas. The abhorrent historical treatment of Native, African, and Mexican Americans (among other groups) continues to have negative effects on both the groups in question and on relations between these groups and the dominant (White, Christian, English-speaking) group. Language continues to be a divisive issue in civic life. In recent years, California, Arizona, and Massachusetts have essentially outlawed bilingual education programs for language minority children. Successful (and unsuccessful) attempts to declare English the official language at the federal and state level continue to divide Americans along ethnic and linguistic lines. This is only a partial accounting of the negative effects related to the construction and assertion of a particular (and exclusionary) version of Americanism (see Ricento in press).

The lesson for Europe may be to consider in the most broad and deep ways the consequences of European integration. If language policies which aim to 'level the playing field' among the diverse ethnolinguistic communities in Europe promote a greater degree of sociopolitical and economic access and equity *within* states, while enhancing inter-state communications, they may be worth pursuing. However, to the extent such policies reaffirm the status quo with regard to the status of national languages *vis-à-vis* minority languages within states and regions, they may be less supportive of the goal of promoting linguistic and cultural diversity in Europe, generally. Therefore, academics should carefully consider how their recommendations and plans for intervening in language practices within states and regions (as, for example., with the Basques in Spain and France) can contribute to more equitable outcomes for minority groups *vis-à-vis* majority groups, while enhancing inter-state communication and cooperation. This is a tall order, given the likely resistance to such an approach by majority groups; however, the US experience suggests that language plans and policies which focus primarily on unity/unification for the purpose of economic development and centralization of political power will almost certainly favour dominant elites and have deleterious effects on the aspirations – linguistic and cultural – of those who, historically, have the least power, including members of language minority communities.

Notes

1. The texts analyzed for this study came from a large corpus of period texts. Five hundred and fourteen pages of text totaling about 266,000 words were analyzed for this study out of a total corpus of approximately 1,500 pages of text and more than a half million words. Although the texts are all written, a number of text types, or genres, are included in the current study:

   1. speeches and addresses (spoken and written) on Americanization
   2. a handbook on Americanization, its goals, processes, requirements
   3. bulletins produced by the Department of Interior and the Bureau of Education
   4. bulletins produced by State Americanization committees
   5. pamphlets produced by the National Security League
   6. Memoranda on Americanization by prominent Americanizers
   7. A monograph, *Theories of Americanization: A Critical Study*

   The texts in this data set are all products of the Americanization movement, written by employees of state or federal governments, academics, civic leaders, or others with expertise and opinions relevant to Americanization. They cover a variety of topics that deal with the general theme of Americanism, its nature, characteristics, methods of promoting it, and so forth. From this larger corpus, a subset of texts was selected that deal predominately with the theme of American identity.

5
The Role of 'Europe' in the South African Language Debate, with Special Reference to Political Traditions

Gerrit Brand

Introduction

Why talk about Africa in a discussion on language and Europe? The best place to begin with an answer is perhaps an African proverb:[1] 'Motho ke motho ka batho' ('A human being is a human being through/with human beings'). This could be taken to mean, first, that identity is not only claimed by the self, but also given by others; second, that one's self-identity is linked to how one perceives others; and third, that identity is therefore thoroughly relational. From this we may infer that what Europe will be in the future will depend partly on how Europe is perceived by non-Europe, how Europe in turn perceives non-Europe, and the nature of relations between Europe and non-Europe. To talk about Africa – and especially about traces of Europe in Africa – is, then, also to talk about Europe.

Surveying public discussions about language in South Africa, one finds that 'Europe' is invoked or referred to quite often. The figure of 'Europe', as it appears in these discussions, is a very ambivalent one. On the one hand, Europe is associated with colonialism and therefore with linguistic imperialism. The emphasis then falls on Europe as the destroyer of indigenous languages and cultures, which were replaced by European languages, institutions and practices. On the other hand, Europe is associated with the coming of print technology and linguistic scholarship to the continent. Europeans are often praised for their role in helping to turn African languages into print languages, publishing dictionaries and other literature in these languages, and generally contributing to the standardization and modernization of indigenous languages. Thanks, partly, to missionaries and other Western agents, Africans came to think of their diverse forms of speech as 'languages', and for the first time had the opportunity to read and write in their languages and use it for certain high status functions in the newly emerging modern setting. 'Europe' was, then, not only the 'destroyer', but also the 'developer' of indigenous language and culture. Both of these roles are, in turn, interpreted in positive as well as negative ways. Europe as the colonizer can be blamed for her linguistic imperialism, yet, as we shall see, the fact that languages like English, French and Portuguese are of colonial origin can also count in their favour – their foreign status lends them an apparent neutrality between different language groups in the continent. Moreover, imperialist languages are, for that very reason, also world languages – as such, they provide access to power and prestige, and broaden horizons beyond local worlds towards a global cosmopolitanism. All this makes them attractive among elites as languages for public use within African states.

Likewise, Europe's role as 'developer' of languages is judged both positively and negatively. The positive interpretation has been mentioned already. However, it is also sometimes argued that Europeans took wrongful possession of African languages in studying and codifying them, that they unjustifiably favoured certain dialects over others as 'standard' varieties, and that they distorted the true nature of indigenous languages. Moreover, their work is seen as having contributed to 'tribalism' by making people aware of their distinctive languages and ethnicities. Focus on indigenous languages, and efforts to modernize and develop them, can also be interpreted as a type of divide-and-rule policy. To this could be added the ambiguity and controversy about the 'value' of literacy for non-literate languages, and the extent to which this transforms the (African) languages into a Eurocentric model.[2]

European political traditions in South Africa

The same ambivalence applies to another way in which Europe has exerted influence on the South African debate, through the impact of certain Western political traditions like republicanism, nationalism, liberalism and socialism.[3] These political traditions, and the reactions of African intellectuals to them, provided frameworks within which debates about language continue to be conducted. Given the themes of this book, it is this more ideological element of the European heritage in South Africa that will be the main focus of this chapter.

The figure of 'Europe' as both colonizer and 'language developer' will appear in all its ambivalence throughout.

A more clearly 'African' political tradition, like (Pan) Africanism, can only be properly understood with reference to the impact of 'Western' traditions, firstly, because it appropriated and developed many elements from those traditions, and secondly, because, at least in its modern forms, it emerged as a conscious (and often critical) reaction to those traditions.

Liberalism

In South Africa, liberalism is strongly, though not exclusively, associated with the English speaking community. It shaped, to a large extent, the discourses and ideological strategies with which this community – and those who identified with it – have tried to make sense of their place and mission in the territory. Certain elements in the liberal tradition, as inherited from Europe, lent themselves very well to a legitimizing function in a colonial context,[4] and these soon became prominent in South African liberal discourse, also with regard to the politics of language.[5] Liberal ideas could, for instance, be used to justify the policies of active (and sometimes coercive) Anglicization. This use of liberalism depended on the assumption that the English language is both expressive and constitutive of the British 'spirit' and 'British civilization'. The latter was associated, in this discourse, with liberal (Enlightenment) notions of 'free trade', 'liberty', 'justice', 'progress', and the like. According to this logic, efforts to anglicize the South African population could be seen as part of Britain's 'civilizing mission' in South Africa: in place of the 'backwardness' of Afrikaners and Africans,[6] agents of the benevolent British empire would establish a humane and liberal order from which all would benefit in the long term.

Once colonization had been carried through to its ultimate conclusion – that is,. once the entire territory had come under white control and whites had become permanently part of the South African population – relations between white and black came to be regulated according to the principle of segregation. Segregation differed from the later apartheid policy in that it was not tied to a notion of African self-determination or parallel development. Rather, the basic development model was assimilationist. In a paradoxical manner, the very purported aim of culturally assimilating the local population into the larger British empire came to function as a rationale for racial segregation: Blacks could only enjoy the privileges of British subjects and achieve the status of 'exempted natives' in the Union of South Africa (as in the former British colonies of the Cape and Natal before unification in 1910) once they had become 'civilized' – that is, once they met certain requirements in terms of, among other things, amount of property, level of Western education, style of dress and proficiency in English. In this way, liberalism came to function as a legitimizing ideology with which to justify colonial conquest and, later, racial segregation.

Naturally, there was resistance from some speakers of other languages against the dominance of English. Again, liberalism provided discourses that were useful in deflecting and deligitimizing demands for the recognition of other languages. Predominant among these was the liberal principle of freedom of choice. Once English had become thoroughly hegemonic, it was easy for those who sought to maintain the status quo to criticize (proposed) attempts to strengthen the position of other languages by characterizing them as attempts to 'impose' those languages. The logic here is clearly analogous to that of free marketeerism, where state intervention in the economy is regarded as against the spirit of free enterprise. The underlying assumption – whether it concerns the economy or the linguistic situation – is, of course, that the market is free to begin with.[7] This particular argument against attempts to resist the hegemony of English is still quite common in the South African language debate (see on this Painter 2002a, b; Painter 2003; Painter and Baldwin 2004).

Initially, there was strong resistance, especially from African populations, against the 'liberal' agenda in linguistic as in other respects. The various independent black polities each resisted as soon as their traditional way of life, including their linguistic habits, came under pressure from colonial encroachment. It took a long time for a united black resistance to emerge, with the result that different groups resisted at different times and in different ways. However, these scattered liberation struggles and uprisings were, in a certain sense, much more radical than the later united black struggle in the sense that the colonial presence was not yet accepted as a normal feature of the local landscape – much less was the hegemony of Western institutions, practices and discourses regarded as natural. Resistance to the British colonial agenda could take this form only as long as Africans were still ruled by strong and independent traditional leaders and relatively secure in their rural subsistence.

All this changed radically once urbanization set in – partly due to the discovery of gold and the consequent industrialization, partly because Africans had been robbed of most of their land – and especially after the establishment of the Union of South Africa in 1910, when Africans started to realize that they now faced a common threat in the form of systematic racial discrimination in a unified state. Leadership of the political and ideological resistance now shifted from the traditional leaders to the emerging urban elite among the black population. Instead of resisting liberal ideology, these leaders, including students, ministers, teachers, and lawyers who had received a Western education, appropriated the liberal discourse for their own purposes. Africans now demanded recognition as British subjects with an equal claim to the advantages of citizenship in a liberal order.[8]

The need for a united black front against racism also strengthened the position of English among black South Africans, since it could be seen, precisely because of its colonial origin, as a neutral and unifying language that would help Africans overcome tribal divisions. In this way, English, together with central liberal ideas, came to be associated with the struggle against racial discrimination and, as such, with progressiveness. 'Imprisonment' in African languages or Afrikaans was contrasted with proud membership of the British empire, with black unity, and with an internationalist perspective.

Thus, while liberalism initially served to legitimize white domination in South Africa, it was later employed in the struggle against white domination. In both guises, however, it tended to favour English as the main or only language of the public domain. It should be observed, at this point, that 'left liberal' perspectives were, for the most part, never very prominent in South Africa. The type of liberal ideas that came to be influential were those that suited the colonial project, that is to say, those versions of liberalism that are closely allied with capitalism and on the whole quite comfortable with huge social inequalities. Only very occasionally did liberal politicians, white or black, take seriously the socio-economic dimensions of the language question in South Africa.

It should be pointed out, however, that liberal arguments are occasionally also invoked against English hegemony (see e.g. Heugh 2000). The freedom of choice argument is sometimes used to demand that the state create options and choices by institutionalizing the use of other languages besides English. Behind this type of liberal argument lies a more substantive conception of freedom than the purely formal one that often leads to acceptance of the status quo. From a liberal perspective, the principles of state neutrality and non-discrimination can also be invoked to argue for equitable treatment of all languages by the state. Moreover, the utilitarian strand in the liberal tradition can be employed, not only to argue for the purported 'impracticability' of multilingualism, but also to defend the contrary, namely, the benefits for individuals and society at large – for instance in the educational domain – of respecting linguistic diversity.

Republicanism/nationalism

Whereas liberalism in South Africa is typically associated with the English speaking community and those that identify with it, republican and nationalist tendencies were initially very much the currency of the Afrikaner community. In linguistic terms, it is therefore closely associated with the Afrikaans language.[9]

While the term 'nationalism' can only really be accurately applied to Afrikaner politics in the 20th century, when the 19th century romantic ideas of Herder and others first came to influence many among the Afrikaner elite, the republican tradition goes much further back. Its roots lie already in the resistance to their employers of the so-called 'free burghers' After the British takeover, the republican spirit grew stronger among this increasingly self-conscious group. It only came to full expression with the establishment of independent 'Boer republics' in the north during the second half of the 19th century.

The South African republican tradition had roots in early Dutch republicanism and, to a lesser extent, the French Revolution. After the destruction of the Boer republics in the Anglo-Boer War (1899–1902), a more clearly ethnic (rather than territorial) identity came to the fore as the defeated Afrikaners sought, through an aggressive nationalism inspired by European examples,[10] to uplift themselves and regain control of their destiny.

A central motif in the Afrikaner republican-nationalist tradition is what one may term 'localism'. This involved a rejection of the under-standing of South Africa as, in the first place, a part of the British Empire. The task of the Union government, according to this view, was to look after the interests of (white) South Africans rather than imperial interests, and patriotism meant putting one's loyalty to South Africa above loyalty to the empire or commonwealth. It is a view that enjoyed growing support among Afrikaners, but scandalized many English speaking South Africans and the emerging black elite who sought recognition as British subjects. Attachment to Dutch and, later, Afrikaans[11] became strongly symbolic of the anti-imperialist, localist perspective in South Africa.

Another central idea in this tradition is that of self-determination or independence. Against the more individualistic liberal notion of freedom, which could be used to justify the hegemony of English, the republican-nationalist tradition had access to a more collectivist notion of freedom, which could be used very effectively to characterize the dominance of English as oppression of one 'people' by another.

Finally, the republican-nationalist tradition places much emphasis on the political significance of language and culture. Especially during the 20th century, Afrikaners tended to employ the discourse of cultural freedom for communities rather than that of individual rights, and Afrikaans was seen as the most important marker of Afrikaner culture and identity.

The way in which Afrikaner nationalists sought to maintain white supremacy differed from the segregation-strategy of English liberals. Rather than assimilation, the policy was now to promote so-called 'separate freedoms' (apartheid) for the different ethnic groups in South Africa. This had several implications at the linguistic level. Apartheid ideologues and strategists sought to develop, not only Afrikaans, but also the African languages. Rather than trying to overcome tribal divisions, the apartheid government wanted to ensure that ethnic consciousness and ethnic identities remained strong. Blacks became citizens of ethnic 'homelands' even if they had never set foot there. Those who lived in 'white South Africa' had to carry passes as if they were resident aliens. As under segregation, they were still forced to live in separate residential areas, but now these black townships were further divided into ethnic blocks. Each black ethnic group had its own schools where education was provided through the mother tongue. Under the policy of Bantu Education, the syllabi for black schools were no longer the same as those in white schools. The argument was that their education had to be 'culturally suitable'. Language boards were established to develop grammars and dictionaries, and state sponsored anthropological research into the traditional cultures of the different black 'peoples' was initiated. Radio (and, later, television) stations for the different African languages were established.

These policies were not always pursued with the purest of intentions. Bantu Education was experienced by blacks, not as 'culturally suitable', but as inferior – a way to retard the progress of Africans. Ethnic 'homelands', separate schools and mother tongue education were perceived as elements in a policy of divide and rule. This impression was confirmed by the apartheid government's efforts to strengthen traditional African leadership and rural cultures, while failing to recognize the leadership of the emerging urban elite. Moreover, in the 'white area', blacks had to learn – and, after the primary phase, be educated through the medium of – both English and Afrikaans.

The idea that communities sharing a common geographical space (even if this was, in theory, regarded as a temporary state of affairs) can retain different life-worlds and remain separate, in the sense of not mixing, by providing separate schools, radio stations etc. was probably influenced by the now defunct policy of 'verzuiling' ('pillarization') in the Netherlands, according to which Reformed, Catholic, humanist, etc. Dutch citizens retained their different identities in precisely this way. While, under Afrikaner nationalism, there were thus real efforts to protect and promote linguistic diversity as opposed to English hegemony, this diversity was understood in terms of separate, unilingual institutions for the different ethnic groups rather than integrated multilingual ones, and language rights were seen as group rights rather than individual rights.

After the first democratic election in 1994 – a date that can be used as a rough marker of the collapse of apartheid and of Afrikaner nationalism – many Afrikaner intellectuals sought, on the one hand, to return to earlier, pre-nationalistic and pre-apartheid republican models and, on the other, to link up with international (including European) discussions about minority rights, multiculturalism, communitarianism etc. The three central motifs of localism, self-determination and emphasis on language and culture are, thus, still prominent, but these now have to be thought through from the perspective of a minority who no longer have the power to dictate the national agenda (see Rossouw 2003).

Socialism

The socialist tradition, which emerged in South Africa in the 20th century in tandem with industrialization, is characterized by its emphases on worker solidarity, non-racialism, non-tribalism, and social equality.[12] As such, it has always been suspicious of both Afrikaner nationalism and English liberalism. Both these traditions are viewed as capitalist ideologies – Afrikaner nationalism due to its emphasis on ethnic consciousness, which weakens worker solidarity (see Alexander 1985a, b),[13] and liberalism due to its bourgeois individualism, which tends to mask social inequalities.

Socialists of varying shades played a leading role in the struggle against apartheid, which they believed constituted a necessary first phase of struggle against capitalism: once apartheid was defeated and popular democracy introduced, the second phase – the establishment of a socialist state – would follow. Socialists in South Africa have therefore always been uncomfortable with identity politics, ethnic consciousness and tendencies towards separatism. As can be expected, this translated into opposition against the apartheid ideal of separate 'homelands' and institutions for different language groups.

Although socialists in South Africa therefore often tended to lean towards English as South African lingua franca, this was not always the case. Within the broader anti-apartheid movement, it was often from the socialist wing that criticism of English dominance emerged.[14] Here, English dominance is equated with capitalist hegemony. Some socialists understand English in South Africa as the lingua franca of the elite, and a marker of class identity and socio-economic status. Linked to such perspectives is the belief that English dominance, and the associated misrecognition of linguistic diversity, creates rather than neutralizes ethnic hostilities. Consequently, the only way to strengthen trans-ethnic solidarity is to give full recognition to all languages spoken in the country.

Among those South African socialists who favour the latter strand in the Marxist tradition, a view of multilingualism emerges that is very different from that proposed by Afrikaner nationalists under apartheid. According to this view, multilingualism means many languages sharing the same space. This type of multilingualism requires equitable treatment of all languages by the state and – importantly – multilingual citizens.

Africanism

The Africanist tradition is not a European tradition. Nevertheless, it cannot be adequately understood without reference to the colonial impact to which it is a response. Africanists incorporated many elements from liberalism, nationalism and socialism into their thinking, and combined these with indigenous concepts that were now self-consciously understood as 'black' or 'African' as opposed to 'white' or 'European'.

Two modern Africanist movements of the 20th century can be distinguished in South Africa. The first, which emerged during the 1950s and 60s, drew inspiration from, and contributed to, the continent-wide Pan Africanist movement associated with figures like Leopold Senghor of Senegal, Kwame Nkrumah of Ghana, Julius Nyerere of Tanzania and Kenneth Kaunda of Zambia. Characteristic of this post-independence African movement were concepts like 'negritude', African socialism, African humanism, cultural authenticity, and a Pan African, rather than predominantly tribal or national, consciousness. Its political slogan was 'Africa for the Africans!'. Whereas the liberal, and to some extent socialist, traditions in the anti-apartheid struggle were borne by the African National Congress (ANC), the Pan Africanist tradition found political expression in a breakaway movement, the Pan Africanist Congress (PAC) (see the 'Pan Africanist Congress Publications Collection, 1958–1995'). The PAC have tended to favour the development of indigenous languages, including Afrikaans, and, at times, have even pleaded for English to be discarded as an official language of South Africa. In practice, however, they have followed the example of the ANC by using English as a means of overcoming tribalism among the leaders of the movement, although African languages are certainly used at popular gatherings.

A very similar set of sentiments and ideas came to fruition in the 1970s under the leadership of people like Steve Biko. This movement soon came to be known as the Black Consciousness Movement.[15] Unlike the Pan Africanist movement, it was predominantly urban based. Its battle-cry was 'Black man, you are on your own!'. There was a strong emphasis on inner liberation or 'liberation of the mind' in the movement. This involved a proud embrace of the 'black experience' and of 'black culture'. 'Self-reliance' was another characteristic emphasis. Black Consciousness thinkers rejected 'whiteness' and 'Europe' as universal reference points or standards, and emphasized the importance of self-chosen values and goals for black people.

The Black Consciousness Movement was a conscious attempt to establish a new 'black' identity in the place of traditional ethnic solidarities. This translated into strong opposition against the apartheid government's attempts to entrench separate ethnic identities among different black groups. At the same time, the movement's emphasis on black pride and self-reliance led to a rejection of liberalism, which was experienced as paternalistic and ultimately in the interests of whites only. This created a tension within the Black Consciousness Movement. On the one hand, English was thought to be useful as a unifying language among especially urban blacks. On the other, reliance on English could be seen as acceptance of the superiority of 'white' culture. This tension was never really resolved in the struggle years, but in post-apartheid South Africa, Black Consciousness leaders have been among the most vocal critics of English hegemony.[16]

When the use of 'black languages' is propagated from a Black Consciousness perspective, it is done in terms of an identity discourse, but quite consciously a 'black' or 'African' rather than an ethnic (e.g. isiZulu or Sesotho) one. Multilingualism, rather than any particular African language, becomes the marker of this identity. It is argued that the ability to use different languages and acceptance of linguistic diversity are characteristic of African culture and the black experience as opposed to what is perceived as a 'white', European monolingual model.

Language in the South African constitution

From the above, it will be clear that none of the four traditions discussed can be said to be essentially hostile or sympathetic towards linguistic diversity. While some traditions have tended, historically, to favour monolingualism, all contain elements and motifs that can be, and have, been invoked in favour of multilingual policies. All four are therefore, like the European impact in general, thoroughly ambivalent. In all likelihood, future developments in Europe – including developments at the ideological level – will continue to influence the ways in which South Africans debate the language issue.

Interestingly, the constitution of the post-apartheid state contains elements from all four political traditions discussed above (see Constitution of the Republic of South Africa 1996[17]). This is the case for the constitution as a whole, but also more specifically for those parts of the constitution that deal with language. In this sense, the South African constitution cannot be comprehended without taking into account the impact of European ideas and discourses on the South African mind. One implication of this is that the European mind can only understand itself, its own identity, by viewing the South African constitution, including its language clauses, as somehow part of European history: the future of language in South Africa, in the light of the constitution, is, in a very real sense, also part of the future of Europe.

The South African constitution is often described as 'liberal democratic'. While this is probably a one-sided characterization, it is true that central motifs from the liberal tradition are very prominent in it. As far as language is concerned, the most striking of these is the fact that language rights are understood, in the constitution, as individual rights. This is not to say that the group rights dimension is completely absent, but most of the formulations tend in the direction of individual rights. The constitution states that 'Everyone has the right to use the language and to participate in the cultural life of their choice' (Section 30) and 'the right to receive education in the official language or languages of their choice in public educational institutions' (Section 29(2)), and that 'Every accused person has a right...to be tried in a language that the accused person understands or, if that is not practicable, to have the proceedings interpreted in that language' (Section 35(3)(k)). The notion of free choice is thus also very central. The South African constitution further mentions 'language' together with 'race, gender, sex, pregnancy, marital status, ethnic or social origin, colour, sexual orientation, age, disability, religion, conscience, belief, culture, ... and birth' as an illegitimate basis for discrimination (Section 9(3)) – that is to say, discrimination on grounds of language, like, say, racial or gender discrimination, is defined as, by definition, 'unfair'. The liberal principle of non-discrimination is thus also clearly underlined in connection with language. In other words, in the language domain, the constitution draws on precisely those liberal arguments for multilingualism that have historically been relatively marginal to the liberal tradition in South Africa, thereby contributing to the development of this tradition. In a more general sense, the whole rights discourse, in terms of which the language clauses are formulated, can also be seen as a fruit of the liberal tradition.

The republican-nationalist tradition also left its imprint on the South African constitution, first, in the wide sense that the strong concentration on linguistic and cultural rights is itself largely the result of the input, in the transitional negotiations, by representatives of this tradition, and second, in the constitutional formulations that presuppose some notion of collective or group rights. 'Persons belonging to a cultural, religious or linguistic community' are, for instance, given the right, 'with other members of that community', 'to enjoy their culture, practise their religion and use their language' and 'to form, join and maintain cultural, religious and linguistic associations' (Section 31(1)(a–b)). The constitution further makes provision for the establishment of a 'Commission for the Promotion and Protection of the Rights of Cultural, Religious and Linguistic Communities', which has as its tasks 'to promote respect for the rights of cultural, religious and linguistic communities', 'to promote and develop peace, friendship, humanity, tolerance and national unity among cultural, religious and linguistic communities', and 'to recommend the establishment or recognition, in accordance with national legislation, of a cultural or other council or councils for a community or communities in South Africa' (Section 185(1)). Most strikingly, Section 235 declares that 'The right of the South African people as a whole to self-determination, as manifested in this Constitution, does not preclude, within the framework of this right, recognition of the notion of the right of self-determination of any community sharing a common cultural and language heritage, within a territorial entity in the Republic or in any other way, determined by national legislation'. All these rights are, however, quite strongly qualified, and made subject to considerations of 'equity', 'practicability' and 'the need to redress the results of past racially discriminatory laws and practices' (Section 29(2); see also Sections 30 and 31(2)).

The latter formulation points to the influence of the more leftist, socialist tradition with its emphasis on socio-economic rights and equality. The constitution requires, not only 'parity of esteem' (a more republican-nationalist concept) but also 'equitable treatment' for all 11 official languages recognized by the constitution (Section 6(4)). The equal recognition of 11 official languages (Section 6(1)) and the demand that the state always communicate with the public in 'at least two official languages' (Section 6(3)(a)) fits very well the kind of vision of multilingualism that has historically been characteristic of those in the socialist tradition who were critical of English dominance. It is a multilingualism that tries to avoid ethnocentrism and separatism. 'Recognizing the historically diminished use and status of the indigenous languages of our people', the constitution further obligates the state to 'take practical and positive measures to elevate the status and advance the use of these languages' (Section 6(2)), a section that can be interpreted as being part of a more general tendency in the constitution to make room for interventionist affirmative action policies, and to guarantee socio-economic rights like rights to housing, healthcare, a safe environment, etc. This also sits better with leftist sentiments than with South African versions of the liberal and republican-nationalist traditions.

However, the demand that the state strengthen the position of indigenous African languages that were marginalized in the past can also be understood as aiming at the valorization of African culture as a way of rectifying the Eurocentric tendencies of previous regimes. In this respect, the constitution's language articles can be interpreted as taking up and developing further the Africanist tradition: the state has an obligation to ensure that the dignity of black Africans and their cultures and languages are restored through legislative and other measures. The section in question can thus be understood as a critique of the assumption that 'white' or European languages and cultures are superior to those of Africa.

A new vision for both continents?

Not only in legal documents like the constitution, but also in civil society, the pro-multilingual strands in the different political traditions have started to converge in a number of ways, albeit not without tensions and continuing disagreements. Perhaps the most striking example of this is the formation, towards the end of 2002, of the Multilingualism Action Group (i-MAG).[18] I-MAG is a coalition of about twenty different organizations and a number of individuals involved in language-related work. Their mission is to promote multilingualism and the use of all South Africa's official languages in all spheres of life. They do this through projects, advocacy, policy proposals, and negotiation with government departments and other institutions. I-MAG's membership is drawn from different language communities and racial groups and, of particular interest for our topic, from all four political traditions discussed in this paper: Afrikaner nationalists, English and black liberals, socialists of varying complexions, and people inspired by Pan Africanist and Black Consciousness ideals. Time will tell whether civil society initiatives such as these can succeed in launching new influential discourses drawing on a variety of sources that were traditionally viewed as mutually exclusive, and whether linguistic diversity will, in this way, become a unifying rallying point rather than a cause of social division and instability.

In an address at the first annual general meeting of i-MAG in Cape Town, one member, well known linguist and veteran anti-apartheid activist Neville Alexander, said that it was the aim of i-MAG to initiate 'a language movement, which is not an ethnic movement, but a movement for multilingualism' (quoted in I-MAG 2003[19]). He emphasized that i-MAG viewed the struggle for multilingualism as part of the transformation of South African society from a 'colonial, apartheid society' to a 'non-racial, post-colonial society'. He defined multilingualism in terms of greater visibility of previously marginalized languages, and the growth of personal multilingualism among all South Africans, with the ideal that every South African should know at least three official languages. This formulation is fairly representative of the kinds of views that have been emerging from the organization ever since, and to which speakers of different languages, with roots in different political traditions and communities, are equally committed.

Clearly, recent developments in the political history of South Africa have given rise to renewed reflection on language as a social issue. In political negotiations, the drafting of new legislation and the forging of new civil alliances, creative use had to be made of ideas and motifs drawn from a variety of sources. As a result, an understanding of multilingualism is starting to emerge – even if the struggle for its actual implementation has just begun – which may also be of value to other societies struggling with the challenges of linguistic diversity, including the European Union. What is distinctive about this conception is that multilingualism is now increasingly understood in terms of a model where more than one language can share the same political and institutional space, and where it is not assumed that individuals are typically, or should ideally be, monolingual.

For Europe, as for (South) Africa itself, it will be very important to see whether this vision of a multilingual society can be realized in practice. In a more critical vein, it is necessary to point to certain weaknesses and potential sources of difficulties in the new discourses on language that are developing out of the different political traditions. Prominent among these is the assumption, common to all four political traditions as they developed during the 20th century, that the notion of 'a language' is unproblematic. It has been said that Europe invented language,[20] a statement by which is meant, not that speech is uniquely European or that European languages are somehow more developed or superior in some other way, but rather that the concept of 'a language' as a unified and bounded system of signs and meanings had its origin in European modernity. This conception of language has been criticized by contemporary linguists and philosophers (see for example, Van Brakel 1998). However, it is still assumed as quite natural by nearly all participants in the South African debate, as well as by most European policy makers.

The assumption that languages are (or should be) discreet bounded units finds expression in a number of ways in the South African context. One clear example is the debate about the harmonization of cognate African languages. Among the 11 languages recognized as 'official' by the constitution, four (some would argue five, including Xitsonga) are said to belong to the Nguni group: isiZulu, isiXhosa, SiNdebele and SiSwati, and three (some would argue four including Tshivenda) to the Sotho group: Sepedi, Sesotho and Setswana. Some participants in the debate have proposed that these different languages should be harmonized into two written standards in order to simplify the implementation of multilingualism.

Most speakers of the languages in question resist this proposal quite strongly. In fact, a virtually opposite tendency has also emerged, a 'proliferation of languages'. A debate is still continuing as to whether 'Sepedi' and 'Sesotho sa Leboa' (Northern Sotho) are different names for the same language, or whether Sepedi is only one language or dialect within a larger Northern Sotho group. Some communities who used to be regarded as Sepedi speakers claim that they speak Lovedu, which is closer to Tshivenda than to Sepedi. Other examples abound.

What the whole debate illustrates is the extent to which it is simply assumed, either that the identity of 'a language' is something that is objectively given, or that a unified standard – a single language – is the only way in which language forms within the same family can be treated as a unit for certain purposes.

This 'received view' runs into problems in the educational domain. In initiatives to promote 'mother tongue education', it is often discovered that, say, 'isiXhosa speakers' have difficulty understanding 'standard isiXhosa'. Clearly, there is a need for practices of standardization that are pursued in full consciousness of the fact that standardization is, at least partly, a political business, and that it can be done in ways that either empower or disempower certain sections of the population.

Just as Europeans have much to learn from the way in which 'their' political traditions have been critiqued, appropriated and combined in creative ways by South Africans in developing a novel vision of multi-lingualism, a broader awareness among South Africans of recent developments in European linguistics and philosophy of language might bring new perspectives to their debate, such as the insight that where one language ends and another begins is often more of a political than a purely linguistic judgement. This might help participants in the debate – and practitioners in the field – to give more explicit expression to the political considerations that lie behind their respective positions, and to find compromises and solutions rather than remain stuck in fruitless debates about the boundaries or 'true nature' of a language. In practice, many of the strategies used to accommodate linguistic diversity in South Africa are already more in tune with newer developments in European linguistics and philosophy, even though they are rarely explained in such terms, and were probably motivated by practical considerations rather than theoretical reflections. On television and radio, for instance, programmes that are officially designated, say, Sesotho, often use Setswana and Sepedi as well. However, as soon as it is proposed that this be officially recognized, objections are raised, as this would seem to imply that Sesotho, Sepedi and Setswana are not separate languages.

The recently promulgated National Language Policy Framework (2003) uses a rotational principle for regulating the translation of government documents into the official languages. Those documents that need not be translated into all 11 official languages, are to be translated, nevertheless, into at least six official languages: Afrikaans, English, a Nguni language, a Sotho language, Tshivenda, and Xitsonga. In deciding which Nguni or Sotho language is to be used for a translation, a rotational policy should be followed so that each of the varieties gets a share equal to the others in the same group. While this policy has been widely welcomed among language activists because of its furtherance of multilingualism, it has also been criticized, precisely on the six language principle, mostly on the grounds that the policy appears to deny the differences between languages in the same linguistic family.

The challenge is, then, to develop policies that will respect and valorise linguistic diversity, but without creating new dominant standards and elites or misrecognizing certain groups in society on the basis of their supposedly 'deviant' language forms. A more nuanced understanding of the nature of 'languages' might go a long way towards solving problems that arise in this area. If boundaries between languages are constructions rather than natural facts, it seems perfectly rational to draw those boundaries at different points depending on the context.

Likewise, recognition – and fruitful exploitation – of mutual comprehensibility between different language forms need not necessarily lead to strict, unified standard varieties to which everyone should conform. Different though related language forms can be mixed or used interchangeably for certain purposes, and where standards are developed, these could be made flexible, inclusive, and responsive to the needs of the affected communities.

The demystification of linguistic identities – which is not the same as misrecognition of them – is probably one of the most important intellectual tasks facing the South African pro-multilingualism movement, and one to which European intellectuals can make a very helpful contribution.

Indications are, then, that the futures of Europe and Africa will remain entangled in both helpful and problematic ways for some time to come.

Notes

1. The proverb, quoted here in its Sesotho form, exists in many African languages, including the 9 African languages that share official status with English and Afrikaans in South Africa.
2. See for example, J. van Brakel (1998).
3. For a general historical survey, see Marks and Trapido (1987). A brief characterization of the political traditions treated here is given in Brand 2004a, b.
4. See, for example,. John Stuart Mill, who worked for the East India Company and, in his *On liberty* (ch.III), wrote of the Chinese that 'they have become stationary – have remained so for thousands of years; and if they are ever to be farther improved, it must be by foreigners' (Mill 1996:1074).
5. For more detailed treatments of the themes touched on here, see for example, Butler *et al.* (1987); Dubow (1987); Giliomee (2003), especially. pp.193–9, 447–9; Hoernlé (1939); Sturgis (1982).

6. Although Afrikaners and Africans were placed differently in the status hierarchy of British colonialism, both groups were regarded as inferior to the British. Whereas Africans were seen as 'uncivilized savages' simpliciter, the Afrikaners (of Dutch descent) were seen as having 'regressed' to virtually the same level due to their isolation from the 'civilized' European influence. This liberal attitude has survived into 20th century academic writing on the Afrikaners.

7. For a thorough survey and critique of the ideology of free marketeerism in South African history, see Terreblanche (2002).

8. On the appropriation of liberalism by black liberation leaders, see e.g. Bradford (1984); Marks (1975).

9. See Giliomee (2003). The most prominent contemporary exponent of the republican tradition is Danie Goosen (see for example, Goosen 2000).

10. Anderson (1983) argues that modern European nationalism was inspired by independence movements among people of European descent in colonial territories like South America and South Africa, rather than vice versa. My formulation here refers to a later stage when a fully developed European nationalism started to influence Afrikaner thinkers.

11. Afrikaans shares about 95% of its vocabulary with Dutch, but the spelling, grammar and pronunciation differ quite significantly. Whether the two are different languages or simply two variants of the same language is a moot point. The main reason why Afrikaner elites eventually opted for Afrikaans as a vehicle for the new nationalism, is simply that, by the early 20th century, very few Afrikaners were proficient in Dutch. Afrikaans became a medium of instruction in former Dutch schools in 1910. In 1925, the Union senate decided to interpret the constitution's reference to 'Dutch' as one of the two official languages (next to English) as including Afrikaans. This made Afrikaans the de facto second official language, a situation that was formalized only in 1961, when South Africa was declared a republic.

12. For a historical perspective on socialism in South Africa, see Drew (2002). For recent exponents of the socialist tradition see. Alexander (2002); Bond (2004); and. Slovo (2004).

13. It is interesting to note that Afrikaner nationalist thinkers were, at one stage, very concerned about the 'proletarianization' of Afrikaner workers, which was thought to lead to their 'denationalization' and even assimilation with blacks, i.e. loss of ethnic identity, and sought to remedy this trend by solving the 'poor white problem' through job reservation, preferential wage scales and the like, see Scholtz (1954), esp. Ch.XII,.

14. Alexander (1989) discusses some historical examples.

15. See Biko (2004); Ramphele (1995).

16. See, e.g. Mangena (2001); Seepe (2000a, b).

17. http://www.polity.org.za/html/govdocs/constitution/saconst.html

18. I-MAG's website is at www.imag.org.za.

19. I-MAG, 'Berig oor die eerste algemene jaarvergadering van die Meertaligheidsaksiegroep op 5 Junie 2003' (Report on the first annual general meeting of the Multilingualism Action Group on 5 June 2003) http://www.litnet.co.za/taaldebat/ajmag.asp

20. See Susan Gal, this volume.

6
The European Linguistic Legacy in a Global Era: Linguistic Imperialism, Spanish and the *Instituto Cervantes*

Clare Mar-Molinero

Introduction

In this chapter I will be arguing that when examining language and the future of Europe it is important to remind ourselves that in the present postcolonial era a European/Western legacy continues to dominate language spread beyond solely continental Europe although its nature may have changed since the familiar military, political imperialism of earlier eras. I will refer to concepts of linguistic imperialism and the recent criticism of these theories which has resulted in a trend away from their theoretical focus. Today language spread is more commonly discussed in the framework of globalization (for example, Crystal 1997; Gardt and Hüppauf 2004; Maurais and Morris 2003; Wright 2004). However, it can be argued that globalization is in itself a form of imperialism. As Hamel (2003) has pointed out an over-emphasis on 'globalization' in analysing language spread and language survival can lead to an obscuring of who the agents or actors in power relationships really are. By revisiting theories of imperialism we may be able to pinpoint more accurately who these actors might be. In the case of language spread we can thus identify the significance of European and Western colonial and postcolonial influence in shaping language behaviour and producing language hierarchies which categorize a few so-called world languages or global languages at the top of the pile, and ever-fewer smaller languages underneath. Whilst acknowledging, as, for example, Brutt-Griffler (2002a) claims, that in societies where these world languages are used, there is also impact and influence 'bottom-up' from grassroots local language behaviour and attitudes, I believe that ultimately the dominance and power of globalization and linguistic imperialism determine language choice, use and survival.

In particular in this chapter I will focus on the role of standard language ideologies and the delivery of foreign language teaching in the expansion of knowledge of world languages. In the case of most world languages it is the original European (or, certainly, Western) form that remains the acknowledged and codified 'standard' prestige form, despite the language's wide use beyond the continent of Europe. To illustrate this argument I will concentrate on the case of Spanish. The literature on global languages and on language and globalization has to date largely concentrated on English (Brutt Griffler 2002a; Crystal 1997; Graddol 1997; Pennycook 1994, 1998) with only a very few contributions on other world languages (but see Maurais and Morris 2003), such as French (Calvet 1994), German (Gardt and Hüppauf 2004) and Spanish (Tamarón 1995; Mar-Molinero 2004; and the regular *Anuarios* of the Instituto Cervantes). As English is without doubt *the* global language this is hardly surprising, but both its impact on and its role model for other competing world languages is also of interest. In this chapter I will be limiting my investigation to exploring the role of Spain's Instituto Cervantes as one important actor on the stage of contemporary – imperialistic – Eurocentric language spread. Before moving to the discussion of Spanish and the Instituto Cervantes, I will make some general observations about the issues implied by the terms 'globalization' and 'linguistic imperialism'.

Theoretical issues

Globalization

Globalization is the most common concept used today to frame our understanding of world systems and our social, political and cultural inter-connections. I understand globalization to mean 'an increasing inter-connectivity on all levels' (Hamel 2003: 6). It is especially associated with the economic impact 'whereby financial capital is taking the lead over productive capital' (ibid.). Modern electronic technology has enhanced dramatically the communications that underpin these relationships. However, Blommaert (2003: 612) stresses that the fact that we are envisaging interactions on such a wide geographical level should not lead us to believe there is total uniformity about globalization processes. As these processes cross boundaries and connect at transna- tional levels, there are tensions between both the national and the transnational reactions to global trends. Blommaert argues that 'the system is marked by both the existence of separate spaces (e.g. states) and deep inter-connectiveness of the different spaces, often, precisely, through the existence of worldwide elites' (ibid.). Blommaert goes on to state that 'Globalisation implies that developments at the 'top' or the core of the world system have a wide variety of effects at the 'bottom' or the periphery of that system' (ibid.).

Such an identification of a hierarchy leads me to argue that we should still understand much of the inter-connectiveness in terms of power dominance and therefore 'empires' and imperialism. Moreover, by using an imperialist theoretical framework we can explore more readily who it is that controls and acts in these processes, whereas with the concept of globalization we have tended to move away from pinpointing such actors or agents. I will limit my discussion here of these general ideas about globalization to the specific situation of language, whilst emphasizing that this is of course very closely bound up with wider social, political and economic processes.

Contemporary global processes inevitably do affect language use and spread, and provide us with interesting situations to analyze. Coupland (2003: 467) suggests that there are four key processes to take into account when analyzing language in a global era. These are: *interdependence, the compression of time and space, disembedding*, and *commodification*. All of these are closely related too to issues of dominance and imposition. These will be traced below in the specific case of Spanish.

Linguistic imperialism

In his pioneering (and much criticized) book on this concept Phillipson argues that Linguistic Imperialism is a 'subset of linguicism' which in turn he defines as 'ideologies, structures and practices which are used to legitimate, effectuate and reproduce an unequal division of power and resources (both material and immaterial) between groups which are defined on the basis of language' (Phillipson 1992: 47) Whilst Phillipson is criticized for explaining the spread and creation of 'world' English as being *solely* the product of linguistic imperialism and linguicism (for example, Brutt-Griffler 2002a) his contribution to a theory of language spread and language hierarchies is useful and frequently applicable. The link between language spread, imposition and dominance and the political and economic dominance imposed by colonial and neo-colonial powers also highlights how this has been, above all, a European and Western led process.

A key factor in linguistic imperialism is the provision of (foreign and/ or second) language teaching and learning of the world language in question. This in turn raises questions about what form of the language – the Standard Language question – and also what cultural values are reflected in the language curriculum. To discuss these issues in a contemporary situation I will turn to the case of Spanish and its historical and current spread around the world.

Spanish language spread

Castilianization and the Empire

That the spread of Spanish can be accounted for historically in terms of colonization and imperialism cannot be denied. The language of Spain was exported and imposed across the Spanish Empire in the Americas from the sixteenth century onwards. In all of the colonies it was the language of the Church, the Administration, education and the elites in general. However, it was not until after the wars of independence and, ironically, when the newly established republics of Latin America were no longer part of the empire that the use of Spanish became widespread, a trend that has continued to this day. Nonetheless it is the legacy of a European imperial power that has established itself totally as the national and most widely-spoken language of the twenty former Spanish colonies of Latin America. This situation came about as the result of explicit language policies, both under the Spanish Crown and later in the newly-formed republics, which privileged and promoted Spanish over and above any indigenous language (Mar-Molinero 2000; Siguan 1992).

Linguistic imperialism in a post-colonial era

Having originated in Spain, Spanish has subsequently established itself, first, as the majority language in twenty Latin American countries and, later, as the mother tongue of a sizeable community in the US. Moreover, it has also become an important second or foreign language for speakers across the world. Whilst still not on the scale of English world-wide, it is nonetheless experiencing a growing and popular demand (Instituto Cervantes 2000). As a result, it is estimated that there are now over 400 million speakers of Spanish worldwide (SIL 2002).[1] Spanish, therefore, sees itself as a world language and needs to be analyzed in the context of language and globalization discussed above.

Taking Coupland's (2003) four characteristics of language in relation to globalization, we can see that this spread of Spanish means that the global *interdependence* of these communities to one another and to other parts of the world system has a significant impact on the language itself. The Spanish-speaking world shares media and cultural production, in particular those available through fast technological forms of communication such as television, film, recorded music and the internet. Collectively this language community responds to new linguistic needs and creates or borrows new words and terms. The second marker identified by Coupland, the *compression across time and space*, experienced by this large population of Spanish speakers is part of the same phenomenon with electronic communication making the geographical distances insignificant.

There is no doubt, too, that the Spanish language is increasingly seen as a *'commodity'* as will be seen in the Instituto Cervantes' packaging of it on behalf of the Spanish government. Hüppauf (2004: 17) argues in a discussion about the success of English and the perceived decline in popularity of German that 'the global language [i.e. English] is highly attractive and successful in seducing people the world over.... It is the idiom of hopes and promises... of consumption and unrestricted movement'. This kind of popularity and 'seduction' is increasingly recognised by the guardians and the promoters of Spanish who are currently selling their product to a world-wide public whose attraction to Spanish is characterized, for instance, by a craze for Latino music, dance and fashion, by mass tourism to Spanish-speaking destinations, as well as by the recognition of the existence of growing Spanish-language economic markets.

The concept of *'disembedding'* referred to by Coupland (and following the well-known work of Giddens 1995a; 1995b) is apparent in the transfer of culturally specific speech items originated in one Spanish speech community to another and their consequent adaptation or re-embedding. Coupland (2003: 468) cites Giddens (1991: 18) in explaining this concept as 'the "lifting out" of social relations from their local contexts and their rearticulation across indefinite tracts of time-space'. In the case of Spanish, the twin effects of this are hybridity, on the one hand, and homogeneity, on the other. That is to say that Spanish created to address international or global audiences (for example, in films, the media, the internet) is characterized both by a tendency to bring together various regional or national varieties (often those considered 'non-standard', and frequently also peppered with anglicisms) or the opposite effect of aspiring to a exaggerated neutral, form of the language bereft of any regional or national traces. Neither form is 'owned' by their speech communities which leads to alarm and defensive action from those set to guard the 'pure' standard form of Spanish; above all those who support Castilian Spanish from central Spain as the model for the language.

In their attempts to respond to such features of globalization affecting Spanish these same guardians, such as the Spanish Government, the Spanish Royal Language Academy (*La Real Academia de la Lengua española*, the RAE), Spanish media outlets, academics and educationalists, seek to promote and extend the role and status of Spanish and to define the nature of the language. Insofar as the relationship between language and national identity has always been a significant and often contentious one throughout the history of Spanish nation-building (Mar-Molinero 2000), this defence is also to some extent a rearguard action against the forces of globalization in a world where the nation-state is losing its centrality. Furthermore, it is an example too of many Western European nations' desire to maintain control of their linguistic and political hegemony across the world. Globalization is, thus, both the cause of the perceived threat to the loss of dominance and control by former imperialist powers, but can also serve to further and retain this dominance, if its characteristics are fully grasped and exploited by European and Western elites.

In the final section of this chapter I would like to examine how, then, this deliberate global spread of Spanish is being realised by focussing on the teaching of Spanish as an international language (and through that the transmission of Spanish language culture), and how in particular this raises questions about concepts of 'standard' language. Lippi-Green has identified the link between language standardisation and cultural dominant groups as Standard language Ideology which she defines as 'a bias towards an abstract, idealized, homogeneous spoken language which is imposed and maintained by dominant bloc institutions and which names as its model the written language, but which is drawn primarily from the spoken language of the upper middle class' (1997: 54). In the case of much of the international Spanish promoted by the Spanish government across the world, we might also add that it is drawn too from the educated variety of Castilian Spanish from central Spain.

Today, Spanish continues to spread by the inter-generational transmission of the language amongst Spanish-speaking communities, including, by those created by recent migration (such as in the US and parts of Northern Europe). However, it has also spread through effective and popular teaching of Spanish as a foreign language in many parts of the world. The demand displayed for learning Spanish is based on a series of reasons mentioned above including those overtly promoted by the Spanish government as part of its aim to strengthen and enhance a pan-Hispanic community across the world. As already argued, part of this is the desire to strengthen Spain's sense of its own national identity in a world of increasing supranational identities, but it is also a desire to consolidate a power bloc with some claim to compete with the overwhelming march of global English. The Spanish language learning/teaching industry is thus a flourishing and expanding one. Whilst smaller in scale, in many senses it resembles the enormous EFL/ELT industry.

As with the British Council and its ELT provision, a significant agent in this delivery of Spanish language learning is the Instituto Cervantes. I will, therefore, in this section highlight some of the characteristics of the Instituto Cervantes and particularly of its language teaching programme. First, I will give some background information about the Instituto Cervantes as well as quoting extracts from some of its key documents, before discussing how far we can identify an ideological agenda underpinning this organisation – either consciously or unconsciously.

The Instituto Cervantes

Since its beginnings in 1991 the Instituto Cervantes has expanded the number of its centres across the world dramatically. Besides those in existence in Spain, there are now centres in Europe, North America, Brazil, Africa, the Middle East and Asia. Today there are over forty Instituto Cervantes centres around the world. On the Instituto's website its purpose is described as the following:

> The Instituto Cervantes is the public institution created by Spain in 1991 for the promotion and teaching of the Spanish language and for the diffusion of Spanish and Hispanoamerican culture. (www.cervantes.es)[2]

> (El Instituto Cervantes es la institución pública creada por España en 1991 para la promoción y la enseñanza de la lengua española y para la difusión de la cultura española e hispanoamericana)

'Spain' in this context includes a host of significant and influential people and groups, given that the Instituto is to be overseen by a '*Patronato*' (governing body) which includes the King and the Spanish President on its board, as well as representatives from the world of culture and letters in Spain and in Latin America (for example, from the Royal Academy/ies, universities and other institutions). Moreover, and significantly, its *Consejo de Administración* (management body) which will approve the general plans and projects of the Instituto is made up of representatives from the ministries of Foreign Affairs, Education, Culture and Sport, Treasury, and Home Affairs, as well as from the *Patronato* itself. A clear commitment and interest in the shape and direction of the Instituto and its activities are manifested by such high-profile membership. Indeed in the second edition of the Insituto's new in-house magazine[3] (January–February 2005) the speeches of King Juan Carlos, of the current Spanish President, José Luis Rodríguez Zapatero, and of the Spanish Minister for Foreign Affairs to the annual meeting of the *Patronato* are reported with the occasion clearly seen as a significant political event. Whilst the broad mission and aims of the Instituto are likely to be shared across the political spectrum in Spain, the policies and philosophy of the Spanish government of the day can be expected to be reflected in its work.

The website declares the Instituto's aims and objectives as:

- To organize general and specialized Spanish language courses;
- To accredit by means of certificates and diplomas the knowledge acquired by its students and to organize the examinations of its Official Diploma of Spanish as a Second Language (DELE);
- To ensure up-to-date teaching and teacher training methods;
- To support the work of Hispanists;
- To participate in programmes to promote the Spanish language;
- To provide cultural activities in collaboration with other Spanish and Hispanoamerican organisations and groups from the host nations;
- To provide public libraries equipped with the most up-to-date technological resources. (www.cervantes.es)

Objetivos y funciones:

- Organizar cursos generales y especiales de lengua española.
- Acreditar mediante certificados y diplomas los conocimientos adquiridos por los alumnos y organizar los exámenes de los Diplomas Oficiales de Español como Lengua Extranjera (DELE).
- Actualizar los métodos de enseñanza y la formación del profesorado.
- Apoyar la labor de los hispanistas.
- Participar en programas de difusión de la lengua española.
- Realizar actividades de difusión cultural, en colaboración con otros organismos españoles e hispanoamericanos y con entidades de los países anfitriones.
- Poner a disposición del público bibliotecas provistas de los medios tecnológicos más avanzados.

Clearly the teaching of Spanish is seen as the Instituto's most important role and activity. Since its creation the Instituto has translated this priority into the provision of language classes, and teachers' development and examinations venues throughout its many centres. It has developed its own second language teaching/learning methodology and set up an on-line Spanish language learning environment (the AVE, *Aula Virtual de Español*). It has also worked with Spain's national radio and television to deliver Spanish language courses. With its publications, on-line bibliographies, library holdings, and the hosting of major conferences on the state of the Spanish language, the Instituto aims to provide vast coverage of the needs of learners of Spanish as a Foreign Language.

In order, as it claims on its website, to give coherence and direction to its language curriculum, the Instituto Cervantes has developed a 'curricular plan' to serve as a blueprint for its courses across the many centres. The features characterizing this plan represent the Instituto's pedagogical philosophy and methods. These are described in the following list:

- It is an open plan, given that it works from a series of general assumptions which should be adapted to the concrete circumstances of the social, cultural and educational environment of each centre and to the particular characteristics of each group of students;
- It is a student-centred plan which considers as fundamental the dialogues between teacher and student over objectives, content and even the teaching methods;
- It is an integrated plan insofar as the different curricular components – objectives, content, methodology and evaluation – operate in a simultaneous and non-sequential way;
- It is an eclectic plan in the choice of information it offers and in its implementation;
- It is a flexible plan, given that working from the general lines of implementation that the plan establishes, each centre organizes the spread of courses and the type of timetable according to the needs of the students;
- It is a homogeneous plan in the way in which it establishes for different centres the same general objectives, distributed over the four levels – beginners, intermediate, advanced and higher – into which the teaching is organized. (www.cervantes.es)
- (Es un plan abierto, ya que parte de una serie de propuestas de carácter general que deben adaptarse a las circunstancias concretas del entorno social, cultural y educativo de cada centro y a las características propias de cada grupo de alumnos.

- Es un plan centrado en el alumno, que considera fundamental el diálogo entre el profesor y los alumnos sobre los objetivos, los contenidos e incluso la metodología de la enseñanza.
- Es un plan integrado, en la medida en que los distintos componentes curriculares – objetivos, contenidos, metodología y evaluación – actúan de forma simultánea y no sucesiva.
- Es un plan ecléctico en la selección de las informaciones que ofrece y en el planteamiento de las propuestas de actuación.
- Es un plan flexible, dado que, a partir de las líneas generales de actuación que el propio plan establece, cada centro organiza la distribución de los cursos y la oferta de horarios en función de las necesidades de su alumnado.
- Es un plan homogéneo, en la medida en que establece para los distintos centros unos mismos objetivos generales, distribuidos en los cuatro niveles -inicial, intermedio, avanzado y superior- en los que se organiza la enseñanza.)

The plan is thus described, on the Instituto Cervantes website, as student-centred, adaptable, flexible and at the same time homogeneous in its ultimate aims. However, of particular interest to this chapter are certain underlying principles concerning the *model* of language to be used by the Instituto and its centres when delivering Spanish language learning. To discover this we can note the criteria given for the materials and courses available on the on-line website, the *Aula Virtual de Español*, or AVE. Here we find an important statement concerning the choice of linguistic varieties to be used:

> The principal variety of the AVE and the corpus's norms which are presented to the students as a model of language for them to copy is central peninsular Spanish. (. . .) [C]entral peninsular Spanish was chosen because it is not in contact with other languages and has the fewest differentiating characteristics as regards the shared language. (. . .) The selection of this as the principal variety is based on the fact that central peninsular Spanish has sufficient demographic importance and status amongst the Spanish-speaking community through media and cultural expressions. (www.cervantes.es)

> (La variedad principal del AVE y norma del corpus que se propone al alumno como modelo de lengua para su reproducción es el español peninsular central. (. . .) se optó por el español peninsular central por no estar en interacción con otras lenguas y tener menos elementos

diferenciadores con respecto a la lengua común. (...) La selección de esta variedad como principal está fundamentada en que el español peninsular central tiene suficiente importancia demográfica y proyección hacia el conjunto de la comunidad hispanohablante a través de manifestaciones culturales y medios de comunicación.)

Furthermore we are told:

> (...) General or standard Spanish brings together the common features shared by all its varieties (...) The secondary varieties are present in the *AVE* through presenting and commenting on their features and/or through their use by their speakers. (www.cervantes.es)

> ((...) el español general o estándar recoge los rasgos comunes y compartidos por sus variedades. (...) Las variedades secundarias están presentes en el AVE a través de la presentación y comentario de sus rasgos y/o de la actuación de sus hablantes.)

Recalling the quotation by Lippi-Green earlier on about standard language ideologies, this particular position regarding language varieties taken by the Instituto Cervantes through its AVE materials suggests a very clear ideological position *vis-à-vis* a perception of standard Spanish. This standard form is conceived by the Instituto and promoted through its language courses and resources as being that of not only a Spanish from Spain variety, but also that of central Spain, uncontaminated, it claims, by such influences as other regional languages or dialects and accents. Moreover, the use of the term 'secondary' to refer to the varieties different from the 'central peninsula' one, implicitly or explicitly denotes a position of inferiority. It is claimed that this central variety has a certain demographic importance, which appears hard to justify. The current population of all of Spain is some forty million, of whom the 'central peninsula' variety speakers are only a part. Given that the figures for global Spanish speakers, on the other hand, are estimated at over 400 million, the claim, it would seem, is based rather on a perception of this variety's importance through its 'media and cultural expressions'. Herein lie further ideologically framed interpretations of the position of the peninsular Spanish variety.

By 'cultural expressions' we understand the Instituto to refer to those practices, activities and output that the AVE stress form an important part of the sociocultural content of their materials. Their website claims that

Knowledge of the culture of Spanish-speaking countries constitutes one of the main objectives of the *AVE*. The sociocultural content of the courses offers a true image of Hispanic culture and society in all its variety and richness through materials from diverse sources: press, literature, cinema, music. (www.cervantes.es)

(El conocimiento de la cultura de los países de habla hispana constituye uno de los objetivos básicos del AVE. Los contenidos socioculturales de los cursos ofrecen una imagen real de la sociedad y de la cultura hispanas en toda su variedad y riqueza a través de materiales de distinta procedencia: prensa, literatura, cine, música.)

However, the question must be asked as to what a 'true image' is and who decides it. The selection, interpretation and presentation of this Hispanic diversity is inevitably a subjective one, and one based therefore on the ideology, beliefs and agenda of those who guide the policy and the decisions of the Instituto Cervantes, identified previously as being at the heart of the Spanish Government. Significantly, the Spanish President said in his speech to the 2005 annual meeting of the *Patronato*: 'Language is not only words, but a faithful reflection of our conception of the world, and in it we incorporate our history.' ('La lengua no es sólo palabras, sino un fiel reflejo de nuestra concepción del mundo, y en ella se recoge nuestra historia.')

It is not just the nature of the cultural content of the materials used in language courses or of the selection of the quintessential Castilian central peninsular linguistic variety that suggest that the ideological baggage of the Instituto Cervantes reflects a world view of *Hispanidad* as having its centre in Madrid. The mission of the Instituto to promote 'widespread cultural activities', albeit in collaboration with 'Spanish and Hispanoamerican organisations', has meant that its centres across the world are hugely proactive in introducing cultural events, lectures, film showings, book launching, etc. all of which celebrate a particular Hispanic canon, one which whilst not necessarily only Spanish (from Spain) is nonetheless allocated its privileged position through the eyes of a Eurocentric/Western Hispanism.

In many ways we are reminded of the nature and structures of the British Council as described by Phillipson (1992) whose emphasis on the spread of (the English) language, government-led policies, funding mechanisms and largely elitist cultural activities are echoed, consciously or unconsciously, by the Instituto Cervantes. Similarly, I would suggest,

Phillipson's comments about ELT and the British Council can be applied to Spanish and the Instituto Cervantes,

> One may conclude that ELT has not been promoted globally as the result of a master-minded plan. It is in the nature of hegemony that it is not static and rigid (...) This means that at the ideological level it adapts dialectically to challenge and change. (Phillipson 1992; 307)

I would not necessarily argue that the Instituto Cervantes has set out *deliberately* to impose the Castilian language in its peninsular form with an elite Eurocentric set of cultural practices on all those learners of its language courses and visitors to its centres, and thereby to relegate other Spanish varieties and non-peninsular culture to a secondary position. However, it has, consciously or unconsciously, started from the premise that Spanish originated with the Spaniards and insofar as the Spanish language is a symbol of Spanish nationhood, any fragmentation into transnational or global configurations is a threat to Spanish national identity. The Spanish Government and the Instituto Cervantes understand the importance and strength of the high numbers of the global Spanish-speaking community and wish to consolidate this *Hispanidad*, but, it would seem, from a position of leadership and, moreover, from a position of economic gain, as Spain recognizes the profitability of the linguistic product that is the Spanish language today.

Notes

1. All demographic statistics about the number of speakers of languages should be treated with caution, and so this figure is only an estimate provided by one of the more reliable sources. For further discussion of this issue of language statistics and counting speakers of Spanish, see Mar-Molinero 2004: 8–9.
2. All translations are mine.
3. In October 2004 the Instituto launched the *Revista del Instituto Cervantes*, in order, according to the Instituto's Director, César Antonio Molina, to 'for the first time, to make known also in Spain, its [the Instituto's] work in promoting Spanish, the co-official languages [such as Catalan, Basque, Galician and Valencian] and Spanish and Hispanoamerican culture in the world' ('por vez primera, para dar a conocer, también en España, su labor de promoción del español, las lenguas cooficiales y la cultura española e hispanoamericana en el mundo').

Part II

New Formations in Europe: Language and Social Change

7
Why 'New' *Newspeak?*: Axiological Insights into Language Ideologies and Practices in Poland

Anna Duszak

Weighting the task

It is not an easy, nor a common job for a linguist to write about the future of language, let alone about the future of a continent. Normally, one would expect, a linguist's task is to describe and explain rather than predict. If dislocated from the present, the viewing angle is retrospective rather than prospective, as documented by an ample record of diachronic studies on language. On the other hand, an opposite under-current may have started already with the rise of macrolinguistics (see, for example, James 1980) and the steady growth of metalinguistic reflection on matters exceeding language structure and 'simple' form-meaning matching. This centrifugal tendency gained strength with new developments in various domains of linguistic theorizing, such as in various models of pragmatics (for example, Verschueren 1999), textuality (for example, de Beaugrande 1996) or cognitive semantics (for example, Lakoff and Johnson 1999). Today linguistics is increasingly being informed by insights, methods and motivations coming from other sciences, social sciences and the humanities in particular, that are more akin to theorizing on the future on the basis of available evidence than traditional linguistics ever was.

An important breakthrough in modern linguistics came with the legitimization of the concept of *ideology* as an inherent element of discourse structuring and functioning in society (cf the works of Martin, van Dijk or Fairclough). Within the last decade or so we have observed a steady increase of 'ideological topics' on the linguistic agenda. This led to an elevation of the status of language in how social issues should be interpreted, managed or resolved in a variety of social contexts. Even though many linguists today still question, if not negate, the sense of an ideological involvement in linguistics, many others acknowledge its role in the service of social issues. We witness a growing number of studies on minority discourses, media communications or language policies. A lot of such work is accommodated under the rubric of Critical Discourse Analysis (CDA), a flagship label especially for ideological discussions of modern media.

Still, 'political talk' in linguistics remains a delicate choice, weighted differently in different social and academic environments. Some stigmatization of authors and topics may follow as a result. I would venture, for instance, that the attribution of leftist ideologies to CDA could be partly responsible for the very modest presence of this framework on the domestic linguistic agenda in Poland (Duszak 2004a).

On the other hand, it is natural that linguistic expertise should strive for social recognition in areas beyond the restricted domains of language teaching and translation, and speak up on many other social issues. Such global relevance, it seems, linguistics could prove only by showing its validity in matters of immediate social concern. For that to happen, linguistic expertise will have to relate itself to judgements coming from other sciences, complement or verify them, and, if necessary, use them for a revision of its own positions. To ponder on language and the future of Europe could be a part of such a daring involvement. The task opens challenges that are worthwhile even though ultimately they can be met only selectively or tentatively, if satisfactorily at all.

The present author approaches the topic cognizant of the fact that her contribution can open more questions than provide answers. Right at the start some reservations are perhaps in order. The motto 'Language and the Future of Europe' begs for some ramifications in terms of scope, rigidity and relevance of what might be said. As Susan Gal (this volume) points out, the very concept of Europe is a fuzzy construct and admits of various perspectives, readings and valuations. Somehow naturally, Europe lends itself for attention in territorial terms, yet like any spatial conceptualization it invites psychological extensions that give rise to fuzzy mental concepts and attitudes. Europe cannot be seen as a bounded entity with clear-cut boundaries segregating between 'in' and 'out' or 'for' and 'against' on the level of denotational and axiological meanings. There are derivatives that are still poorly understood, let alone defined, such as the emergent construct of *European identity*. The future of 'Europe' will depend then on how various individuals, social groups and entire nations choose to co-construct their sense of European unity (in disunity?), and how they will implement it in social practice. Such non-linguistic considerations are of course inalienably linked to language even though they will remain beyond the scope of this discussion.

Similarly, we may ask what meaning of 'language' should be prioritized in addressing the task. The future of Europe will of course depend on language in the sense that language is an essential component of human social life. So, people will communicate somehow, no matter what the nature of the tool available to them or what the actual quality of their performance. On a narrower view, however, at least two major perceptions of language lend themselves to attention. One has to do with an invasive presence of English as global *lingua franca* and the way in which this disposition of English may bear on the integrity of other language systems. The other will be to focus on bridges and barriers in processes of linguistic 'unification' in Europe and to look into the mutual translatability of styles across languages and societies. This would be an extension of up-to-date work on congruities and incongruities with which various cultures find linguistic solutions to definite social goals. Admittedly, the two perspectives are not disparate in that 'leakage' of English affects many languages and mental lexicons. For a linguist it gives a new dimension to the distinction between 'a language for communication' and 'a language for identification' (see, for example, Joseph 2004).

More data is still needed on how individual discourse systems communicate 'on' Europe, its present and its future. For linguistic, social and cultural reasons some national systems may communicate 'better' and some 'worse'. The purpose of this chapter is to cast some light on the prerequisites for such dialogue 'with' Europe from the perspective of Polish. What is the historical baggage and what are the current dilemmas of the Polish discourse system that draw attention and demand answers in the years to come?

Ideologies and policies: redefining society

There are countries in Europe for which membership in, let alone identification with, Europe is now more of an issue than in the case of other states. This applies to the former Soviet-bloc countries of which Poland is an example. For Poland the best orientation point would be 1 May 2004, i.e. the date of her accession to the *European Union*, to refrain from the possible, yet controversial alternatives of 'entering' or 'reentering' *Europe*.

Throughout her history Poland's place in Europe was a 'matter of degree'. At various times this view was entertained both within and outside of the country, with positive as well as negative connotations. It was stigmatized by Poland's own sense of pride and of victimization. Thus, Poland was (seen as) a 'savage' borderland with Asia, a 'protective buffer zone for Christianity' or a prison behind the 'iron curtain'. In the 17th century Poland took credit for 'salvaging' (Christian) Europe from the (Muslim) Asian flood following King Sobieski's victory at Vienna. After World War Two Poland felt abandoned by Europe to the 'barbaric' Soviet regime. In the 1980s, in turn, Lech Wałęsa, the charismatic workers' leader, and the Solidarity movement initiated transformations that made it possible today to talk about a new sense of Europe.

Polish élites have always looked West for intellectual and artistic inspiration. They also 'went West', so that Paris for long epitomized the cultural Mecca of the rich and the cultured. At home Poland's Western roots had been traditionally cherished, and Latin and French were prestige varieties in the higher circles of society. At the same time, however, Polish society had always lived in a state of axiological dualism, caught between this fascination, if not infatuation, with French culture, and the domestic ethos of the gentry, St. Mary's cult and love of homeland. Criticisms of yielding to the foreign element go back centuries, and today's accusations of trading 'traditional' Polish values for foreign (European or American) symbols are nothing new. After the Second World War Polish society found itself caught in a particular form of axiological schizophrenia, with the official policies being overtly pro-Soviet, and the unofficial pro-Western. Many social practices and human relations were regulated by a covert pact of relativity – thinking one thing and saying another.

The recent debates over Poland's accession to the EU came on the wave of more general and hectic discussions over the costs and gains of Poland's radical turn to the West after the overthrow of the communist regime. Within the last decade or so Poland has been undergoing radical transformations: political, economic, social, demographic, cultural as well as linguistic. The construction of a new social order has been taking place under a mounting pressure of globalization and technological advancement. In Poland, like in many other post-communist European countries, this meant unprecedented change in people's material and mental spaces. As a result, society had to start learning how to reposition itself on a number of issues, and how to adapt its repertoires of new values and words.

Powered by an official fall of communist ideologies, the historical swing of the pendulum resonated in social enthusiasm and axiological consensus. What united people most was the denouncement of the communist past, a shared sense of national harm, of lost opportunities and of violations of human rights. All this boosted hopes for benefits associated with the democratic social order, and with freedom of speech and free markets, in particular. The 'return' to Europe was in fact stamped already in the late 1980s, so that any successive steps towards connecting Poland with NATO and EU institutions were interpreted against those breakthrough events that led to the fall of the Berlin Wall.

Today Poland has changed from a testing ground for peaceful political revolutions into a war theatre of old and new ideologies, old and new styles of living and of talking. Above all, Polish society has to cope with the spread of aggressive market philosophies across all domains of social life, including those that were traditionally guarded as shrines for national high-culture values (especially the church and academia). Sociologists and psychologists speak about the 'pragmaticization' of social consciousness in Polish society and the focus on profit (see, for example, Źiółkowski 1994). Linguists, in turn, as will be argued below, talk about radical changes in the national discourse system.

Still, following the initial phase of enthusiasm and indiscriminate readiness to accept the new, Poland has reached the stage when an account is being made of all the gains and the losses. The predominant pro-American orientation at the beginning of Polish transformation is giving way to a 'post'-American reflection, when Western values are accepted only selectively or cautiously, if not overtly rejected. Such scepticism follows from disillusionment with the free-market economy and the functioning of democratic mechanisms. It shows in nostalgia for the past (according to various public opinion polls) or in the rise of populist movements that take steam from the growing dissatisfaction with the present, especially among peasants and the unemployed. As a result, we witness a growing polarization of society as to what is right and what is wrong. Somewhat paradoxically perhaps Polish society today has found itself again in some state of axiological schizophrenia with values that are relative and increasingly divisive.

Ideologies and policies: redefining language

Ideologies, whether invited or imposed, normally come – and go – with a language. That was the situation of Russian in Poland, and so is the case with English at the moment. Poland's turn to the West, and her ensuing 'new' Europeanization is inalienably linked to the growing use and acceptance of English among wide sections of Polish society.

To some extent ideologies define, and are defined themselves by attitudes to language. This interaction of linguistic and non-linguistic values manifests itself in particular in asymmetrical power relations between languages (and cultures) in contact. As a regional, not to say a minority language, Polish has found itself on many occasions under the impact of a dominant language, to recall here the 'globalizing' spread of Latin and French or the administrative imposition of Russian during the tsarist occupation and then under the Soviet regime. In some sense the recent invasion of English is therefore only a new form of linguistic 'imperialism', so it is perhaps natural that it should reinvigorate the traditional protective attitudes to the Polish language.

At its very core Polish linguistics has always been more on the conservative, if not the purist side, when it comes to evaluations of language change and linguistic borrowing in particular. Such policies prevailed and persevered not without a reason. Poland had lost her independence at the turn of the 18th century and fought it back as late as in 1918 only to 'lose' it again under the Soviet domination in Eastern Europe. For a long time the protection of the native tongue was elevated to the rank of a national imperative in Poland. Guarding the integrity of the linguistic system meant attending at the same time to the unity of the nation. For long language policy in Poland has been epitomized as *language culture*, sometimes also called *culture of the word* (see, for example, Buttler *et al.* 1971; Pisarek and Zgółkowa 1995; cf. also the term *Sprachkultur* in German), and exercised as a form of standardization policy with a 'high' mission. As a result, it was always vested in ideational and rhetorical values of prestigious written texts, the propagation of which was done on the verge of a prescriptive rigour. Due to such priorities, language culture was effectively limited to issues of grammatical correctness and stylistic coherence. Within this framework interlingual borrowings were always severely scrutinized for rational use (cf. Daneš 1987, on the distinction between rational and non-rational motivations behind linguistic borrowing), and preference was normally given to revitalization through native resources (see, for example, Walczak 1995). Quite naturally, therefore, this language policy was also exercised towards English loans and it still persists today even though a more lenient orientation is on the increase (see, for example, Miodek 1996; Pisarek 1999).

Today Polish discourses thrive on innovations that blend English and Polish patterns of talk and writing. The nature of such hybridization processes is part and parcel of a general 'recontextualization' of discourses that is taking place today in Europe in general, and in Eastern Europe in particular (see Duszak 2004b for more discussion).

There are, it seems, two major currents of discoursal innovation in the ongoing evolution of the Polish discourse system. First we are dealing with new types of genres that seek accommodation within the local system (for example, legal instruments of the EU, new legal documents, PR discourses, promotion discourses, advertisements and commercials, talk shows, customer services, etc.). Secondly, the new element comes less overtly with an osmosis of new ideologies into the traditional generic structures. Such leakage erodes the existing practices, redefines them and often tailors to new 'globalizing' formats and meanings (especially changing formats of news, academic papers, CVs or public interviews). The two funnels of linguistic change are in practice inseparable in an intertextual flow of discourses – a connected network of dependencies, ideologies and practices.

It may be due to the scope and the intensity of language change that many communicative practices in today's Poland are estimated as having ambivalent axiological loading. Furthermore, and quite importantly, the ongoing change-in-progress seems to invite ideologies of criticism, scepticism if not negation both among linguists and in the media. It is argued, for instance, that Poles are not able (any longer?) to communicate. Opinions of this kind, whether justified or unfounded, could be a bad indicator for the future of Poland's societal life (in Europe). To what extent is such pessimism justified in a society in transition struggling for a new style of communication in new political and social realities? In order to get a better understanding of what is going on it is necessary to sketch the frame of reference against which the ongoing developments and controversies can be gauged. The style of public communication is the domain most affected by the ongoing change and, at the same time, most heavily criticized.

High- and low-context communications in Poland

Prior to the changes initiated in the late 1980s, Poland had her own version of 'high'- and 'low-context' communication, to invoke here the familiar distinction used in studies of cross-cultural communication (especially in the tradition of Hall). That is to say, for centuries Poland was a country with a dichotomous linguistic culture: the high style of public and formal exposition, and the low style of everyday colloquial interaction. On the one hand, discourses that were written, official and formal represented the high standard, and were regulated by implicit relations of power, status, respect and distance. On the other hand, casual speech was governed by implicit relations of equality, solidarity and affection. This division of labour had its reflection in specialization of contexts and rules of social conduct. On the linguistic level, it found its expression in the distinction between strategies of *indirect* and *direct* communication. Only recently the vernacular, once merely a 'tolerated' variety of Polish (Gajda 2000: 22) has earned a better reputation among linguists.

The high variety, an 'official variant' of Polish (Walczak 1994), always had a prestige function connoting the possession of appreciable social, intellectual and communicative skills of the user. However, low-context practices were also highly valued in the social consciousness by implementing the ideology of 'involvement' (on 'culture of involvement' see, for example, Wierzbicka 1991). We may say therefore that in Poland, despite the 'official' prestige of 'high' values, the axiological vectoring in social life was always *away from* psychological distance and communicative indirectness and *towards* psychological proximity and verbal directness. For example, a rite of passage was celebrated in a drinking ritual comparable to the German *Brüderschaft* tradition. It involved a change of address forms from the pronouns of power (*Pan/Pani*) to the pronoun of solidarity (*ty*), and heralded the onset of a new mode of communication between the partners concerned.

High-context varieties of Polish included first of all the language of science with its 'idealization' of knowledge and the imperative of a 'difficult' text. Some form of intellectualization was also characteristic of the language of politics and of institutional discourses in general, including here the typical bureaucratic jargon. Bralczyk (2003: 18), for instance, argues that political texts of the communist epoch resembled academic texts: the use of difficult language, terminology and syntax was intended to show the writer's competence and claim credibility. The language of politics was placed towards the 'official' pole, next to such prestigious varieties as the language of science or the language of the law (Walczak 1994: 20), even though it was often described derogatorily as *newspeak* (the Polish term *nowomowa* attributed to Głowiński, for example, 1990) and denounced as pompous, ceremonial, schematized and evaluative, with axiology replacing semantics.

Challenges to the language of politics came in the 1980s along with a challenge to the political system itself. The overthrow of communism was celebrated as a possibility to create a new political reality and a new 'real' tool for social dialogue. Quite naturally therefore people were eager to remove the old political jargon. The desired direction of change was to make the language of politics more dialogic, direct, expressive and open. Attempts were made to create a new form of public orality patterned after the vernacular of direct interactions between equals. People would see the new style as a manifestation of freedom of expression in contexts that once required constraint and caution.

This style shifting has been described as *colloquialization* or *vernacularization* (cf. *conversationalization* in Fairclough 1992). Such tendencies, originating in politics, escalated soon into other public domains, including academia. With time, the course of change came under the influence of American communicative patterns and general '*mediatization*' of discourses (Fairclough 1992). In Poland today we may talk about a spreading activation of a new orality in public discourses, including genres traditionally associated with the 'high' language variety and embedded in formal institutionalized contexts. In place of high-context communication we receive then a version of low-context style that tries, but largely fails to capitalize on the good reputation of 'straight talk'. What Polish society faces now is the question of how to strike a proper balance between the old and the new while setting new standards for public being and talking.

Why *new* newspeak?: an emerging 'uni-style' under fire

Under 'uni-style' I understand the new style of public communication in Poland, indicating, as it were, its midrange position between high- and low-context behaviour patterns. The new format is supposed to convey the ideology of a democratic society and of an egalitarian communication system, in which ideations are more transparent and interaction routines are based on solidarity rather than distance. Its credibility, however, is losing ground. Today the new style faces mounting criticism among the public and in various domains of scholarly life, including linguistics. The main target of such attacks is media communications, and, especially, the language of politics (cf Bralczyk and Mosiołek-Kłosińska 2000, 2001). Some linguists talk about a *new newspeak* (for example Lubaś 1996:156–7). That such analogies should be made between the communist jargon and the post-communist (?democratic) language of today is indicative of a negative assessment of the changes that have taken place in Poland since the early 1990s. Discussing the language of politics at the end of the 1980s, Głowiński (1990: 144) says: 'new epoch – old language'. Following up on Bralczyk, Kochan (1994: 86) argues that 'in place of one' relatively coherent language of communist propaganda there came numerous, idiosyncratic languages of various political parties, fractions and groupings, and that those 'small totalitarian worlds' grew their own '*newspeaks*' and styles of propaganda.

Among the major sins of the new political jargon the following are enumerated most often. Colloquial expressions infringe upon the ideals of high culture and bring communication down to the level of commonalities, if not trivialities. By analogy to the old newspeak, the semantics of the new jargon dwells on connotations rather than denotations, and thus builds its ideology on slogans, such as *normality, Christianity* or *traditional Polish values*. As a result, it leads to a simplified view of the world and can be as manipulative as the artificially intellectualized jargon of the communist era. Various 'language games' are played in order to provoke, shock at any price, or attain superficial expressiveness. Furthermore, the spread of colloquial interaction patterns often goes hand in hand with verbal violence and vulgarization of speech. As argued by Markowski (2000: 102), the negative valuation of the Polish adjective *agresywny* (*aggressive*) has recently changed to connote a positive meaning, as in an *aggressive journalist*, where the word *aggressive* became synonymous with *dynamic, eager, skilful* or *enthusiastic*. Other linguists (for example, Satkiewicz 2000: 28) talk of a growing emotional stupor in a society that is increasingly exposed to aggressive behaviours and aggressive language. In a similar vein Gajda (2000: 26) speaks about the removal of taboos in self-expression and a growing tolerance to loss of self-control.

The media is not the only locus of language change in today's Polish. The 'uni-style' is escalating within and across various social and discursive domains. The thrust of the change can be seen in the growing (excessive?) use of colloquial register and direct strategies of being and talking. Such tendencies enhance the ideology of egalitarian 'phatic bonding' and the dominance of the phatic function in communication (cf. Pisarek 2000: 16). That is to say, pressure for spontaneous expression encourages informality, levity and (fake) intimacy. As already mentioned, Polish is a *Sie – du* (*vous – tu*) language in its pronominal and politeness systems, which explains its traditional sensitivity to social and contextual variables. This distinction is being seriously eroded now in a variety of social and textual environments. Still for many people the spreading use of the *ty* (*du/tu*) form (instead of the honorific *Pan/Pani*) is controversial. Some consider it impolite and still others see it as disrespectful if not plain rude in formal settings (Grybosiowa 2000: 61).

The swing of the ideological pendulum takes its share of criticisms too. The Western values in communication become targets of a new 'axiological revisionism'. Criticisms are directed at what is seen as a negative Western influence on traditional Polish values. One of the major issues is the apparent 'trivialization' of Polish culture, of public topics and of rules of social conduct (for example, the regime of *infotainment* in the media). 'Pragmatization' of social and linguistic values takes its toll in the steady erosion of high culture, including political and academic culture, and in a steady lowering of (public and private) norms of speaking (Lubaś 2000: 86).

Many linguists are concerned about the emergent levelling of styles. They fear a loss of standards and a drop in the social sensitivity to core values, such as truth and falsehood, if not a general 'decomposition' of the Polish language. In political discourse, as Bralczyk implies (2003:70), this produces a 'catch-22 situation'. On the one hand, politicians may be talking in a 'regular' language and, on the other, people may start talking the way politicians do. The new language of politics may be closer to the person in the street type of talking. At the same time, however, it falls short of the social expectation that public discourses create norms and standards. Gajda (2000: 22, 24), in turn, speaks about a 'linguistic terrorism of the media', in which he sees a threat to the balanced co-existence of language and culture. According to him the media constitute a stylistic 'melting pot' of contemporary Polish that 'erodes' the language through the dissemination of careless, common and vulgar patterns of speech. In summary: the former criticisms of a totalitarian ideology assume a new format and zero in on a new target. What was seen before as a remedy for the communist regime now comes under fire. Democracy has its costs in a society that all too easily interpreted it as a right to unconstrained action and speech. The new behaviours make an even stronger impact under mediatization and information technologies. Somewhat ironically, perhaps, the sharpest edge of criticisms turns away from politics and gets at the media and its role in disseminating the new 'evil' and 'superficial' patterns of communication. By dwelling on political scandal and enhancing showmanship, the media are responsible for a new social dynamics in the relations between the élites and the public.

The media may add to what is described as low discourse awareness or poor comprehension skills among Poles (functional illiteracy). Yet the reasons for that social condition, if well-diagnosed at all, may actually be more complex. They may follow from poor teaching of practical language skills in schools. The current outcry about the degenerating style of communication could have a positive effect by showing that more attention is needed to teaching critical interpretation of texts and practical skills of self-expression. For a long time Polish linguistics had focused on language and not on communication (that is on system rather than use). To talk of discourse is a relatively new thing. Under the imperative of scientificness Polish linguistics cherished theory more than practical observation, as a result downgrading empirical discourse studies, or the social teaching of verbal skills, for that matter.

Conclusions

Poland is a culture of spontaneity verging on unruliness; it is a culture of complaint with a strongly developed sense of self-victimization; it is a culture with a sense of pride and a sense of guilt, a ceremonial respect for high values and a natural inclination for cordiality and simplicity. The post-communist realities have repositioned the traditional values, sentiments and practices, leaving some spaces in disarray and in need of revaluation. In many public and academic discussions the new changes resonate with a low tone of ambivalent, if not critical judgement (cf. Duszak 2005).

For many the attitudes of negation grew from thwarted expectations that people linked, somewhat naively perhaps, with the rebuilding of the social order. Freedom and democracy did not cleanse political discourses from manipulation and 'small totalitarian worlds' took the place of 'the old big one'. In post-war communist Poland attitudes to politics and attitudes to the language of politics resided in a simple distinction: *us* (society) and *them* (the communist regime). Talking politics was a ritual of solidarity, a part of which was to hint (imply) rather than verbalize. Under a covert pact of agreement it was clear what was good (and meaningful) and what was wrong (and meaningless).

Disillusionment is a form of self-victimization, of playing down the responsibility for what is (or is not) happening. Even leading critical linguists resort to this kind of socially accepted argumentation. Głowiński (1990: 145) talks about the lack of appropriate rhetorical patterns for a new language of political debating. Bralczyk (2003: 72) makes the same point, complaining about the 'difficult realities' for the creation of a real democracy in Poland. The heritage of the communist past is evoked as a possible obstacle to the development of a new style of public communications.

Linguistic criticisms go on a par with mounting attitudes of scepticism, if not outright negation and withdrawal. Already in 1996, a popular weekly *Wprost* – following Pentor's opinion poll – wrote that after a period of fascination Poles show signs of weariness with politics (*Wprost* 18 April 1996). In the same vein, and much later, another weekly *Polityka* argues that all political groupings have adopted the policy of complaint, negation and pessimism (*Polityka* 13 March 2004).

Some positive postulates are needed. First, to relativize the current (negative) evaluations of what is going on by extending the frame of reference. This includes a diachronic internal view. A rare voice to that effect can be found in Bralczyk (2003: 78–9), who says in passing that the negative picture of the Polish political scene might change after comparisons with the style of parliamentary debating in Poland in the Second Republic (between the two World Wars). A book by Kamińska-Szmaj (1994) would be a relevant contribution here. The author shows that Polish political discourse in the years 1919–23 was full of vulgar epithets and emotional accusations. Secondly, comparisons with political discourses in more stable democracies are also needed to put the Polish political squabbles in perspective.

On the whole, I would argue for a *cross-cultural* and a *discourse analytical view* as a most promising way of relating the Polish data to the evidence coming from other languages and cultures. It is another issue how to remove scepticism towards the study of such 'low' or *non-serious* communications (the term *non-serious* after Clark 1996) in a linguistic culture not used to indulging in critical discourse analyses. It is still a separate matter how speakers of Polish will funnel their 'third way' – a style of communication that places itself midrange between deferential formality and imposing informality.

8
Language Planning and National Identity in Sweden: A Performativity Approach

Tommaso M. Milani

Introduction

Much of the existing body of literature on language planning and national identity in Sweden has underscored the absence of language planning and a sense of a 'traditional' national identity until the mid-1990s (for example, Teleman 2003; Teleman and Westman 1997). This was followed in the late 1990s by the flourishing of a series of debates on the Swedish language both among academics and politicians. The new overt interest in language planning issues in Sweden has been interpreted in the light of social identity theory and language attitude theory as the manifestation of a budding ethnonationalist revival, which puts great emphasis on the Swedish language as a symbol of national identity in order to counteract the increasing pressure of globalization (Oakes 2001).

The present paper aims to explore the relationship between language planning and national identity in Sweden from a different perspective. By adopting a poststructuralist approach, the paper seeks to illustrate that language planning in Sweden was present even when it was said to be absent, and that national identity is a dynamic reality that is produced, rather than mirrored, in language debates and depends on the interplay of a set of historical, ideological and socio-political conditions.

As several studies within diverse poststructuralist frameworks have demonstrated (Pavlenko and Blackledge 2004; Blommaert 1999; Woolard 1998), language debates are not ideologically neutral discussions about language alone. They are historically situated and ideologically loaded battlegrounds where power and identity relations (be they social, gender, or national identity relations) are enacted, negotiated and contested in the interaction between different actors who struggle for the recognition and legitimization of certain language varieties. Thus, a poststructuralist perspective focuses on the dynamic aspect of the language–identity link. As far as national identity is concerned, language is not viewed as a mirror or marker of a given national identity, nor is national identity studied as a construction around a given language. Rather, both language and national identity are treated as interrelated *discursive* constructions within specific historical and socio-political contexts. In other words, language planning is viewed as a discourse on language and society, that is, as the sum of innumerable language debates which contribute to producing and tying together language and national identity (Blackledge and Pavlenko 2002; Blommaert 1999). What needs to be investigated are the mechanisms that underlie this production. In accordance with Pennycook (2004), the present paper claims that performativity theory (Butler 1990, 1993, 1997) gives us an adequate theoretical framework to explore the dynamic relationship between language, identity and change.

Performativity theory consists of a set of conceptual tools developed by the American philosopher Judith Butler to analyze issues of language and gender. The term *performative* was originally coined by the British language philosopher J. L. Austin in *How to Do Things with Words* (1962). Austin drew a distinction between two types of utterances: constatives and performatives. A constative is an utterance that conveys information. A performative, on the other hand, is an utterance that 'is, or is a part of, the doing of an action' (Austin 1962:5), as in the case of 'I name this ship the Queen Elizabeth'. Drawing on Austin, Butler applies the notion of the performative to gender, and inaugurates performativity as a mode of analysis to issues of language, culture and society. Performativity aims to illustrate that categories such as subject, gender, and identity are not pre-existing entities, the *cause* or the *origin* of certain social practices, but rather the *effect* of practices and discourses within grids of power relations. Whereas most sociolinguistic scholarship is concerned with actual, observable performances and their indexical relationship to one or several given subjects, performativity theory shifts the focus from language as the mirror of gender, age, and ethnicity to language as generative of categories and practices (Butler 1999 [1990]: xxix). Moreover, performativity theory does not treat the subject as a pre-given entity. Rather, it seeks to unveil the process through which the subject comes into being, by pointing to the link between what is observably performed and what is not or cannot be performed (Butler 1993).

Performativity theory is used in the present paper to explore language debates in Sweden 1970–2003. Particular attention will be paid to: (1) the conditions that regulate language planning in a specific socio-historical context, and (2) the relationship between language planning and national identity. It will be argued that these two issues can be understood by way of reference to three semiotic processes which constitute the core of performativity: censorship, interpellation and iterability.

In the following section I will present a historical overview of language planning activities in Sweden between 1970 and 2003. In this attempt to reconstruct a genealogy of language debates it is nearly impossible to set a rigid time span of analysis. The choice of the period 1970–2003 is motivated by the availability of an extensive corpus of documents in paper and electronic format which cover that period. However, it has been necessary in some cases to backtrack to earlier years in order to understand better the conditions underlying the emergence of language debates. The corpus contains: (1) government directives, legislative proposals, laws and official reports related to home language teaching, second language teaching and status planning; (2) the essays in *Språkvård* (Language Cultivation), the official publication of the Swedish Language Council, and the essays in *Språk i Norden* (Languages in the Nordic Countries), the official publication of the Nordic Language Council. Policy documents and the official publications of the Swedish and the Nordic Language Councils have been chosen in order to shed light on both political and academic language debates. The next section goes on to discuss the corpus data in the light of performativity theory, with particular focus on the production of a Swedish national identity through the processes of censorship, interpellation and iterability. Moreover, building on the Swedish data, I call for a slight modification of performativity theory in order to account for the interplay between multiple parallel discourses.

Language planning in Sweden

Absence (1970–90)

A review of Swedish legislation shows that the Swedish language is never explicitly mentioned as the official or national language. Furthermore, there are few regulations concerning the status and use of Swedish in official domains. According to Vogel (1999), an explicit reference to the Swedish language can be found in the Patents Act (patentlag 1967: 837) and in the Patents Decree (patentkungörelse 1967: 838). They both require public documents concerning patents to be drafted or translated into Swedish. An implicit reference to the Swedish language can be found in

the Administrative Procedure Act (förvaltningslag 1986: 223). According
to paragraph 7 of this act, a public authority 'should endeavour to express
itself in a comprehensible way'[1]. No mention is made of what language
the authority should use. As Vogel (1999: 360) points out, the assumption that Swedish is the *de facto* language of public authorities emerges
implicitly in paragraph 8 of the same act, which prescribes the aid of a
translator or an interpreter if the authority 'is dealing with someone
who does not have a command of the Swedish language'. Similarly, the
Administrative Court Procedure Act (förvaltningsprocesslag 1971: 271)
and the Code of Judicial Procedure (rättegångsbalk, chapter 33, paragraph 9) allow translations of documents that the court receives or sends
out (Vogel 1999: 361). The interesting aspect that emerges from these
documents is not only the implicit presence of the Swedish language, but
also that this presence is made possible by way of reference to 'someone
who does not have a command of the Swedish language', namely the
'ethnic Other'.

Immigration and immigrants represented two of the major topics in
the academic and political debates of the 1970s and 1980s. Although
immigration was not a new phenomenon to Sweden, in the 1970s and
1980s, it was different in nature and volume to previous periods. While
in the 1950s immigrants were numerically limited and were welcomed
as foreign labour to sustain Swedish economic expansion, in the 1970s
immigration rates increased considerably. Moreover, immigration was no
longer required to meet the needs of Swedish industry. Rather, immigrants were fleeing their countries for political, personal, and economic
reasons. While immigrants were expected to be assimilated into Swedish
society in the 1950s and 1960s, the nature of the new wave of immigration
brought the abandoning of assimilationism in favour of multicultural
policies in the late 1970s (Hyltenstam 1996a, 1999a).

As far as language is concerned, in the late 1970s Swedish academics
became interested in the field of bilingualism, second-language acquisition, language acquisition planning, and language contact. Debates
emerged on the immigrant's right to maintain and develop their 'home
language', on the instruction of Swedish to adult immigrants, on the
instruction of Swedish as a second language (Hyltenstam 1996a), and
on *Rinkeby* Swedish, an ideologically charged label used to define the
varieties of Swedish spoken by teenagers of immigrant background in
the Stockholm suburb of Rinkeby (Stroud 2004).

Another aspect that characterized the academic language debate of
the 1980s was the relationship between English and Swedish. In 1981
the project 'English in Sweden' (EIS) was started with the aim of

exploring the use of and attitudes towards English loanwords in the Swedish language (Ellegård 1989; Ljung 1986). Some of the results of the project were presented at a conference held in 1985 entitled *Engelska i svenskan som språkvårdsproblem* (English in Swedish as a language cultivation problem). The conference gathered together representatives of Swedish language planning agencies, academics, journalists, and translators, and its proceedings were published in an issue of *Språkvård* in 1986. As the title highlights, the focus of the conference was exclusively on issues of corpus planning (in Swedish *språkvård* means language cultivation). In fact, the papers dealt with the influence of English on Swedish vocabulary (pronunciation, spelling and grammar), in different areas of language (translation, the mass media and the school system). Catharina Grünbaum alone made mention of status planning issues. Grünbaum, who at that time worked as a research assistant at the Swedish Language Council (*Svenska språknämnden*), pointed in her talk to the problems which may occur when entire linguistic domains (for example, the natural sciences, trade and industry) 'become permeated with English'. However, when referring to the fear that Swedish would become a 'sort of semi-English', she assured her audience that 'it is not a real danger for our linguistic identity' (Grünbaum 1986: 24).

Presence (1991–2003)

After the fall of the Berlin Wall in 1989, Sweden regarded membership of the European Community (European Union from 1991) as compatible with its policy of neutrality. After submitting its application in July 1991, Sweden officially became a member of the European Union in January 1995.

Sweden's accession to the European Union generated anxiety among Swedish academics about the destiny of Swedish in an integrated Europe. In October 1992, Ulf Teleman, Chairman of the Swedish Language Council, delivered a lecture at the annual meeting of the Council, where he examined the possible linguistic scenario following closer European integration. According to Teleman, there are four factors that are crucial to understanding why Swedish might lose functional domains to English: the internationalization of higher education, the weakening of national autonomy, the Europeanization of the private sector, and the internationalization of popular culture. Moreover, drawing on the assumption that there is a formal equality but an actual inequality between the official languages of the EU, Teleman envisaged the possibility of a development towards an even stronger dominance of English, French and German in the EU institutions at the expense of 'smaller' languages such as Danish and Swedish. In sum, as Teleman puts it, '[...] from a perspective of European integration we will be more vulnerable' (1992: 16). It is relevant to point out here that two ground-breaking works on the spread of English as a global language and on language endangerment also appeared in 1992: *Linguistic Imperialism* by Robert Phillipson and the article 'The world's languages in crisis' by Michael Krauss published in *Language*, the journal of the Linguistic Society of America.

Whereas the discussion about English and Swedish revolved around problems of corpus planning in the 1980s (see above), in the 1990s academics shifted their focus to status planning issues, namely the *threat* of English as a global language, and the loss of functional domains (Hyltenstam 1996b; Phillipson 1992; Teleman and Westman 1997). Two concerns emerged among Swedish academics which are relevant to the discussion below. First, English as a global language, conquering functional domains, may represent a threat to the future and the existence of Swedish. Second, Swedish became one of the official languages of the EU, as a result of Sweden's membership. However, Swedish came to occupy the position of a *de facto* minority language in comparison to other larger EU languages, for example, English, French and German (Hyltenstam 1996b; Teleman 1992).

Politicians also became concerned about the status of Swedish in the European Union. Only five months after Sweden's official membership of the EU, the Swedish government commissioned an official inquiry which resulted in a report entitled *Svenskan i EU* (Swedish in the EU) (SOU 1998). The aim of the inquiry was to explore 'the measures that need to be taken in the Swedish public administration and in the EU, in order to secure the quality of Swedish EU texts' (Dir. 1995: 81). Further-more, the inquiry should propose 'what claims should be made for the use of Swedish as a working language in the institutions of the EU' (Dir. 1995: 81).

The language issue acquired even more salience in the political debate in 1997, when the Swedish government decided to give the Swedish Language Council the task of drafting an action plan for the promotion of Swedish (Regeringsbeslut 30 April 1997). At the heart of the decision lay the very concerns expressed by academics about the future of Swedish in relation to the impact of 'increased European and global integration' (Regeringsbeslut 30 April 1997). In the draft action plan (Svenska språknämnden 1998), the Swedish Language Council identified two main goals for Swedish language planning: (1) Swedish should be a 'complete'[2] language, serving and uniting Swedish society;[3] (2) Swedish should remain an official language of the European Union.

Through an analysis of the history and the organisation of the language planning authorities in Sweden, the Language Council pointed out that the status of Swedish as the principal national language has always been taken for granted. However, the Language Council underlined that the status of Swedish is no longer obvious as a consequence of strong Anglo-American influence. Therefore, the Language Council recommended that the status of Swedish as the principal language (*huvudspråk*) should be ratified by law, in order to guarantee its use in all official domains.

On the basis of the Language Council's proposal, the Swedish government recognized the necessity to continue the work of promoting the Swedish language (Prop. 1998/99: 1). In October 2000, a parliamentary committee was appointed with the aim of formulating a concrete action programme for the promotion of Swedish based on the Swedish Language Council's proposals to ensure that everybody in Sweden, irrespective of their social and linguistic background, should be given equal opportunities to learn Swedish (Dir. 2000: 66). After two years' work, the committee, called the Committee on the Swedish Language, published a report entitled *Mål i mun*[4] (SOU 2002). In their report, the committee presented a series of recommendations to guarantee three conditions: (1) Swedish should be a complete language, serving and uniting Swedish society, (2) Swedish in official and public use should be correct and function well; (3) everyone should have a threefold 'right to language': Swedish, their mother tongue, and foreign languages.

Discussion: the performativity of language planning

Censorship

It has been argued that during the second half of the 20th century 'the negation of traditional nationalism grew as a specific Swedish form of nationalism' (Teleman 2003: 28–29). According to several authors (Herlitz 1995: 54–6; Löfgren 1993: 28; Oakes 2001: 69–71) this is the result of the almost uninterrupted rule of the Social Democratic Party since the 1930s and evidence of the effects produced by nationalism during World War II. While toning down Swedishness in the national arena, Social Democratic governments promoted the image of Sweden as an active and modern country in the international arena (Dahlstedt

1976; Oakes 2001; Teleman 2003). As Daun (1996) points out, Swedish-ness and its symbols became more or less taboo.

However, this does not mean that Social Democratic governments imposed a straitjacket on Swedish society, prohibiting discourse about Swedishness and the Swedish language as a symbol of national identity. Rather, the taboo on Swedishness can be interpreted in the light of Butler's notion of *censorship*. Butler (1997) defines censorship as a specific form of power that generates 'discursive regimes through the production of the unspeakable' (Butler 1997:139). In other words, what is and can be said in a given historical context is determined by what is not or cannot be said. In the case of Sweden, the social democratic taboo on Swedishness determined the conditions of language discourses by establishing that Swedish, as a symbol of national identity, constituted the domain of the unspeakable. Swedishness was not repressed. It assumed a different manifestation. In fact, Swedishness emerged in language debates in a *covert* and *implicit* guise, enabled by way of reference to the ethnic Other, i.e. immigrants and/or ethnic minorities.

As was argued in a previous section, much of the political and academic debate in the 1970s focused on immigrants. In Foucault's terms (1998 [1978]: 28), one could claim that immigrants in Sweden became a 'public problem' to be investigated, a category to be defined, a 'disorder' to be systematized. Immigration and immigrants became the object of a series of parliamentary inquiries (SOU 1974) and the 'object of knowledge' of several disciplines. As far as language is concerned, debates in this period revolved around Rinkeby Swedish, Swedish for immigrants, and Swedish as a second language. By pointing out phenomena related to immigrants, these very categories contributed to drawing a boundary between what is Swedish and what is not. In this way, in a context where the overt manifestation of Swedishness was taboo, Swedishness was defined implicitly through the description of the ethnic Other.

One can take as an example the former Swedish for immigrants (SFI) syllabus (in force until July 2002), where it is stated that:

> SFI is not only a source of language knowledge and language develop-ment for immigrants, but it is also a *bridge* to life in Sweden. There-fore, various aspects of Swedish social life, culture and social organisation shall be integrated in language teaching, to enable students to share attitudes and traditions which characterize the country in which they now live (Kursplan för svenska för invandrare, my emphasis)

The subtext here is that of integrating newly arrived immigrants with no knowledge of Swedish. Immigrants are portrayed as if they stand in no man's land. The Swedish language is imagined as an instrument, a bridge – in other policy documents the metaphor is that of a 'key' (Motion 1997/98: Ub18; Prop. 1997/98: 16) – that allows immigrants entry into life in Sweden. In this text immigrants are defined by a set of differences to 'Swedes' (attitudes and traditions), and by their lack of knowledge of Swedish. At the same time, immigrants represent what Derrida calls the 'constitutive outside'. As Butler puts it:

> [constitutive outside] is the defining limit or exteriority to a given symbolic universe, one which, were it imported into that universe, would destroy its integrity and coherence. In other words, what is set outside or repudiated from the symbolic universe in question is precisely what binds that universe together *through its exclusion* (Butler 1997:180, emphasis in the original)

In other words, the presence of the ethnic Other enables the emergence of Swedishness through an act of identification. Identification is a concept borrowed from psychoanalysis that defines the process through which a subject comes into being, by internalizing an aspect or property of another. Identification is partly unconscious and is structured not only by affirmations, but also by rejections, foreclosures, refusals and disavowals (Cameron and Kulick 2003). As in the case of Rinkeby Swedish described by Stroud (2004), by defining immigrants through differences and deficiencies, Swedishness emerges in the above text through a process of identification with what it is not (that is, 'immigrantness') and through the lack of deficiency (that is, a knowledge of Swedish).

Interpellation

By joining the European Union in 1995, Swedish became one of the official languages of the EU institutions, as is stated in Council Regulation 1 (also called The European Union's Language Charter). Regulation 1 recognizes the equality of all EU languages as both official and working languages of the EU institutions. However, what is not and cannot be said explicitly – because it would go against the EU policy of multilingualism – is that some languages are *de facto* 'more equal' than others (Phillipson 2003).

   The proclamation of Swedish as one of the official and working languages of the EU is an example of what Austin (1962) calls a performative. In fact, Council Regulation 1 is not merely descriptive of a state. Instead, it enacts Swedish as a legitimate language to be used in the EU. While Austin focuses on the conditions that guarantee a performative, Butler argues that the performative needs to be rethought as 'one of the powerful and insidious ways in which subjects are called into social being from diffuse social quarters, inaugurated into sociality by a variety of diffuse and powerful interpellations' (Butler 1997:159ff). *Interpellation* is a concept which was originally used by the French philosopher Louis Althusser (1971) to explain the way in which ideology 'hails' individuals, thereby transforming them into subjects with specific ideological and social positions.

By appropriating Althusser's notion of interpellation – as Butler does – one could claim that, by 'hailing' Swedish as an official and working EU language, Council Regulation 1 is a performative which functions as an interpellation. Based on the assumption that the contexts of an interpellation are not determined in advance, interpellation 'is not descriptive, but inaugurative. It seeks to introduce a reality rather than report on an existing one' (Butler 1997: 33). Similarly, Council Regulation 1 brings to the surface the category of official language, which was previously *covertly* and *implicitly* defined. At the same time, it inaugurates a new reality with a number of practical implications that Swedish as an official EU language entails, for example, the establishment and management of translation and interpretation services. In this way, Council Regulation 1 interpellates and makes salient a variety of actors in the social field who respond to this interpellation: academics (for example, Teleman, Hyltenstam) and politicians (for example, those involved in the Committee for the Swedish language). Thus, accession to the EU inaugurates a new regime of discourse, characterized by an *overt* debate on the status of Swedish.

While Butler accounts for the authority of a single and isolated performative by its potential to break with previous contexts, this does not take into consideration the presence of other parallel and/or competing discourses. As Foucault states: 'we are dealing [...] with a multiplicity of discourses produced by a whole series of mechanisms operating in different institutions' (Foucault 1998 [1978]: 33). The overt debate on language in Sweden is not exclusively the effect of Sweden's accession to the EU. Rather, it is the effect of the interplay of different concomitant discourses. Swedish became the *de jure* official language through Sweden's accession to the EU. However, Swedish came to occupy the weaker *de facto* position of a 'minority' language (in relation to English, French and German) (Hyltenstam 1999b). In Swedish policy documents, European and global integration is described as a common phenomenon characterized by the high status of English and by the loss of domains of use for Swedish (Regeringsbeslut 30 April 1997; SOU 2002: 47–8). As is clearly stated in the draft action plan to promote the Swedish language: 'when we joined the EU, we became incorporated into a political, administrative and judicial organisation, where other languages, especially English and French, play the major role' (SOU 2002: 52).

The actual position of Swedish as a weaker language in the EU stressed the element of threat exerted by English, already present in the academic debate on English as a global language (see above). In other words, accession to the EU played a major role in amplifying and extending into the political arena a debate generated in academic circles.

Iterability

The claim that Sweden and other countries are experiencing a new awareness and a nationalist revival as a response to globalization (Oakes 2001) fits within an academic tradition that interprets the struggle for independence in certain parts of the world as 'the return of the repressed' (Ignatieff 1993: 2). In the case of Sweden, it has been argued that a 'traditional' national identity has returned after having gone 'underground' since the 1960s (Oakes 2001: 71). Accordingly, national identity is treated as a pre-existing reality – a thing one possesses or a psychological state – whose presence or absence is mirrored in discourse.

By contrast, the present study views national identity as the product of social practices within a context of power relations. Social practices include (but are not exclusively) ways of using language to think and talk about the self and the community (Billig 1995). In the case of Sweden, in the 1970s and 1980s the discursive regime was regulated by the taboo on Swedishness (Daun 1996). While the Swedish language, as one of Sweden's symbols, constituted the domain of the unspeakable, the academic and political debate focused on immigrants. As far as language was concerned, the domain of the speakable included Swedish as a second language, Swedish for immigrants, semilingualism, and Rinkeby Swedish and so on. As was argued above, this did not mean that Swedishness was absent. Rather, Swedish national identity was implicitly produced and reproduced (among other things) through those very categories that were connected to immigrants. At the same time, academics were interested in the relationship between English and Swedish only from a corpus planning perspective. The conditions of discourse then changed in the 1990s. In fact, the debate on accession to the EU brought to the surface the category of official language and underscored, together with the debate on English as a global language, the status of Swedish as a weaker language in the EU. By acting as interpellations, these two debates inaugurated a new regime of discourse.

However, the force of interpellation in generating an overt debate on the status of Swedish is not in interpellation *per se*. As Butler (1997) claims, the performative force of interpellation lies in repetition and citation. Drawing on Derrida (1991 [1972]), Butler does not view repetition as a static process of replication. Rather, repetition implies change through breaking with an original context and the inauguration of new contexts, and hence of new meanings – that which Derrida calls *iterability*. Iterability, together with censorship and interpellation, helps to explain the reasons and conditions that contributed to a shift from a covert and implicit to an overt and explicit definition of Swedishness and the Swedish language. As an example, one can take the lecture given by Teleman in 1992. Teleman claimed: 'I find the influence on Swedish, mostly through loanwords, still rather innocuous. The interesting and important consideration is what will happen with the functional domains of Swedish' (1992: 12). He went on to declare that: 'English will be the language – together with French and German – in which the political and administrative problems in an integrated Europe will be discussed' (1992: 14). Teleman here cites the previous debates on the influence of English on Swedish, and ties them to the possibility of Swedish accession to the EU. Through repetition and citation, Teleman opens up a new context, and thereby resignifies, the debate on English and Swedish. In turn, the government decision (30 April 1997) which entrusted the Swedish Language Council to elaborate a draft action plan for the promotion of Swedish cites the fears expressed by the Swedish Academy and the Swedish Language Council about 'what can happen to the [Swedish] language in future. It regards in particular [...] what an increased European and global integration may imply for the Swedish language' (Regeringsbeslut 30 April 1997). Similarly, in other policy documents, by citing the draft action plan elaborated by the Swedish Language Council, the link between nation and language became explicit by referring to the Swedish language as 'our most important upholder of culture' (Bet. 1997/98: Kru05) or as a 'symbolic resource and upholder of national identity' (Bet. 1998/1999: Kru08). Policy documents, through repetition and citation, resignify and contribute to extending the academic fears into the political field.

Conclusion

By means of the Swedish example, it has been possible to illustrate three interrelated *discursive* processes (censorship, interpellation and iterability) by which national identity is produced. Censorship has shown how the grid of multiple and dispersed power relations regulates the domains of the unspeakable, and thereby the production of the speakable in specific socio-historical contexts. Through interpellation, it has been possible to illustrate how power relations and identity are dynamic and changeable. In the case of Sweden, this has meant a shift from a covert and implicit to an overt and explicit definition of Swedishness and the Swedish language. Finally, in the light of iterability, national identity emerges as the product in process, which is embodied in the iteration of social practices, i.e. the never-ending chain of repetition and resignification operated by different social actors within a grid of discursive conditions. By paraphrasing Butler's definition of gender identity, one could claim that national identity is 'a set of repeated acts within a highly rigid regulatory frame that congeal over time to produce the appearance of substance, of a natural sort of being' (Butler 1999 [1990]: 43–44).

Acknowledgments

Many thanks to Kenneth Hyltenstam and my colleagues at the Centre for Research on Bilingualism at Stockholm University, as well as the editors of this volume and an anonymous referee, for excellent suggestions on earlier versions of this paper. Thanks also to Christopher Stroud (National University of Singapore) and Don Kulick (New York University) for precious discussions on performativity theory.

Notes

1. Quotations of Swedish laws and policy documents, together with academic texts written in Swedish have been translated into English by myself.
2. *Komplett språk* (complete language) refers to the possibility of a language being used in all domains.
3. The adjective *samhällsbärande* poses translation problems. Literally it means 'society bearing'; in the English summary of *Mål i mun* it has been rendered 'serving and uniting our society'.
4. In the English summary, *Mål i mun* has been translated as *Speech. Draft action programme for the Swedish language.*

Primary sources

Bet. 1997/98: Kru05, Kulturutskottets betänkande, Språkfrågor.

Bet. 1998/1999: Kru08, Kulturutskottets betänkande, Bibliotek, litteratur och kulturtidskrifter.

Dir. 1995: 81, Kommittédirektiv. Svenskan i EU.

Dir. 2000: 66, Kommittédirektiv. Handlingsprogram för det svenska språket.

Förvaltningslag, 1986: 223.

Förvaltningsprocesslag, 1971: 271.

Kursplan för svenska för invandrare, http://www.skolverket.se/vux/dokument/kurspl_sfi_020103.pdf.

Motion till riksdagen 1997/98:Ub18 av Britt-Marie Danestig med flera (v)

Patentkungörelse, 1967: 838

Patentlag, 1967: 837

Prop. 1997/98: 16, Sverige, framtiden och mångfalden från invandrarpolitik till integrationspolitik.

Prop. 1998/99: 1, Budgetpropositionen för 1999.

Regeringsbeslut 30 April 1994, Uppdrag till Svenska språknämnden att utarbeta förslag till handlingsprogram för att främja svenska språket (Stockholm: Riksdagen).

Rättegångsbalk.

SOU (1974) Invandrarutredningen. Invandrarna och minoriteterna. Huvud-betänkande av invandrarutredningen. Stockholm.

SOU (1998) Svenskan i EU. Hur vi kan främja kvaliteten på de svenska EU-texterna. Statens Offentliga Utredningar (SOU) 1998: 114 (Stockholm: Fritze).

SOU (2002) Mål i Mun. Förslag till handlinsprogram för svenska språket. Statens Offentliga Utredningar (SOU) 2002: 27 (Stockholm: Fritze).

Svenska språknämnden (1998) *Förslag till handlingsprogram för att främja svenska språket* (Stockholm: Svenska språknämnden).

9
The Macedonian Standard Language: Tito–Yugoslav Experiment or Symbol of 'Great Macedonian' Ethnic Inclusion?

Christian Voss

Introduction

The Macedonian issue has to be seen in the context of the anthology edited by Michael Clyne in 1997, *Undoing and Redoing Corpus Planning*. The languages which are the topics of this book (among others Ukrainian, Hungarian, Chinese, German, Vietnamese, Bosnian/ Croatian/Serbian, Moldavian, Turkish) have all been profoundly affected by socio-political change, mostly following the end of the Cold War. In many cases, therefore, undoing corpus planning means restoring the language to its state before the end of the Second World War. Clyne's collection focuses on the political situation concerning both the original corpus planning and the rebuilding of these languages. Our case study of Tito–Yugoslav Macedonia fits Clyne's typology of language planning (mostly in totalitarian regimes) that aims to impose a new consciousness on the population. Beside the question of the durability of communist language projects raised by Clyne I shall focus on the relationship between the ex-Yugoslav Republic of Macedonia and the ethnic minorities in the regions beyond the state borders, that is to say geographical or historical Macedonia (see Map 1). By dealing with the reconceptualization of Macedonian national, ethnic and linguistic identity after 1991, I hope to contribute to a differentiation of the complex role of language in processes of ethnification, nationalization and assimilation.

Current international borders

Historic Macedonian boundary (Bulgarian claim)

Approximate Serbian claims

Approximate area claimed by both Greece and Serbia

Approximate Greek claims

Source: D. P. Hupchick and H. E. Cox, *The Palgrave Concise Historical Atlas of The Balkans* (New York, 2001), Map 30. Reproduced with the permission of the publisher.

Map Macedonia.

Levels of 'Macedonianness'

To overcome the semantic ambiguity of the name Macedonia, it is necessary to contrast the historical development in Greek Macedonia (Aegean Macedonia) with the situation in ex-Yugoslav Macedonia (Vardar-Macedonia). In Ottoman Macedonia until 1912–13, as is typical for borderland identities, a local Macedonian consciousness developed which tried to avoid (Bulgarian–Greek) national bipolarization – the same can be observed in Alsace or in Silesia (where the local movement avoided French or German and Polish or German claims respectively).

Macedonian identity before 1913 was synonymous with indigenity and the inherited Ottoman local autonomy, understanding the village as a microcosm and thus an antonym to local and social mobility and to every extended horizon. In the overall picture of the 20th century, the distinguishing feature of the Slavic-speaking community in today's Greece is the oscillation between Greek, Bulgarian, Serbian and Macedonian orientation as a result of four different irredentist discourses claiming northern Greece. Individual identification with one of these ethno-national entities before 1912 depended simply on whether the speakers concerned had attended a Bulgarian or a Greek school and should be seen as a political act, not as the result of ethnic self-ascription. This nationalization process of rural areas 'Peasants into Greeks, Peasants into Bulgarians' (cf. Weber's *Peasants into Frenchmen*, 1976) was guided and controlled by the respective consulates in Bitola and Salonika, who were allowed to organize national networks (churches and schools) within the borders of the Ottoman Empire.

In one part of the historical region of Macedonia, in Vardar-Macedonia, a very successful process of *nation-building* was realized on the basis of the widespread regional consciousness just described, with the codification and implementation of a new standard language after 1944: until 1991 Macedonia was governed by a pro-Serbian elite and represented the most peaceful republic in Tito–Yugoslavia.

Concentrating on Vardar- and Aegean Macedonia, I will propose the following two-part thesis:

First, the standard language codified and implemented after 1944 in Tito–Yugoslav Macedonia bears the hallmarks of Tito–Yugoslav ethno-politics even today and therefore is unfamiliar and strange to the minorities beyond the state borders, and this to a higher degree than in the normal case of 'roofless' borderland minorities. This has to explained by the conditions of the supra-ethnic ideal '*bratstvo i jedinstvo*' ('Brotherhood and Unity') which exposed standard Macedonian to heavy Serbocroatian interference expressing the Macedonians' devotion to Tito – in the end it functioned as a mechanism for the exclusion of all ethnic Macedonians living outside Yugoslavia.

Secondly, even in Yugoslav times we notice the coincidence of *national* language ideology and *ethnic* identity ideology. This contradiction becomes even sharper after 1991 and remains unresolved today. A language policy corresponding to the recent ethnification of Macedonian national identity would imply a rapprochement to the Bulgarian standard. This would mean a radical break with Macedonian culture under Tito because its 'de-Bulgarizing aspect of Macedonian culture has been one of the principal forces behind Belgrade's encouragement of culture' (Palmer and King 1971: 154).

Five stages of divergence

The linguistic divergence within the historical region Macedonia took place in several steps and helps to explain the *almost diglossic situation* of Tito–Yugoslav times, with Serbocroatian as H-variety and Macedonian as L-variety, as a phenomenon of 'longue durée' in the sense of Braudel's structural view on long-term history: Belgrade, as the political and economic centre of gravity, gave the same high prestige to Serbian in socialist as in monarchist Yugoslavia, thus neutralizing Tito's principle of linguistic equality.

First, after 1870, the Slavic population of Ottoman Macedonia was exposed to the diverging and increasingly aggressive attempts at nationalization by the Greeks, the Bulgarians and later the Serbs, who according to their 'mental maps' shaped discourses of Macedonia as their genuine national landscape, thereby deconstructing and ignoring the demographic realities in the region. Before the Balkan wars of 1912–13, marking the end of European Turkey, Vardar–Macedonia was characterized by Serbian-Bulgarian national antagonism, whereas the South, that is Aegean Macedonia, was affected by Greek-Bulgarian national rivalry (Aarbakke 2003).

Secondly, the new national borders drawn in 1913 cut through old Slavic dialect continua: the dialects in the North had Serbian, in the South Greek as their overarching 'umbrella language' and thus the only source for lexical enrichment. The local Slavic-speaking population in Serbia and Greece, as well as in Bulgarian Pirin-Macedonia, was exposed to strong internal colonization and assimilation measures denying regional disparities. This belated integration into existing nation-states led to the ethnification of the regional identity patterns of the local population. The Macedonian issue during the 1920s and the 1930s was exploited by the Bulgarian Communist Party and the Komintern to destabilize Greece and monarchist Yugoslavia, but then it was Tito who transformed regional Macedonianness into a sufficient predisposition for a nation-building process as a part of Tito-Yugoslavian ethnostatistical experiments after 1944.

Thirdly, the Tito-Yugoslav 'Third Way' was politically and economically attractive for the Macedonians. The *nation-building* process of the Macedonians was accomplished by the codification and implementation of a new standard language after 1944. The *subordinate Serbocroatian–Macedonian bilingualism*, developed during the interwar period in

Yugoslavia, from now on reflected the subordination of Macedonian national identity to the new supranational Yugoslavian identity.

Fourthly, the Tito-Yugoslav experiment influenced not only the language, but also the shaping of ethno-national affiliations. Whereas Vardar-Macedonia lived the nationally pluralistic *'bratstvo i jedinstvo'* experience, which forced the ethnification of all nations and nationalities and through ethnic quotas (for example, for the allocation of public sector jobs) made ethnicity a central feature of everyday life in Yugoslavia, minorities in Greece until today are affected by the discourse of inclusion and the assimilationist programme that began with Rhigas Feraios' attempt to convert Christian-Orthodox *millet*-identity into Greek national consciousness: in Ottoman times, ethnicity had been defined on the basis of denomination, thus gathering all orthodox Christians within the 'Greek' *millet rum*. That is why in Greece the most ardent enemies of minority languages, such as Aromunian, Arvanitika or Slavic, are often the speakers themselves. Whereas the Greek situation until recently has been characterized by prohibition, Tito–Yugoslavia gave strong support to ethnic and minority languages. In this respect, Yugoslavia reflected the Soviet ideology that the simple codification of small and minor languages would be an irreversible step towards language maintenance.

Finally, after 1991, cultural policy became a tool in the rivalry of post-communist elites: the neo-nationalists interpret the Tito–Yugoslav period as a dead end for Macedonian nationalism and even put Yugoslav times in the same category with Ottoman occupation. This tendency reached its peak between 1998 and 2002, when the neo-nationalists came to power. With the dissolution of Yugoslavia former diplomatic taboos were abolished; the inner-Yugoslav taboo concerned Serbian–Macedonian relations: no Serb should continue the Great Serbian discourse of the interwar period denying the existence of Macedonian nationality. Therefore Macedonians were obliged to define their national identity exclusively within the Yugoslav borders. This corresponded to the second taboo, mutually respected by Tito–Yugoslavia and Greece: since Macedonia was the weakest flank of Tito–Yugoslavia, Tito never put the topic of the many thousands of political refugees from Greece in 1948–49 on his political agenda, and as a countermove Greece conceded the name of Macedonia until the collapse of Yugoslavia. After 1991 and the breaking of these taboos, it was somehow logical that the Macedonian diaspora came to exert a strong influence, namely in the choice of the new Macedonian coat of arms: the central symbolization of the heritage of Macedonian antiquity and the myth of descent from Alexander the Great was imported to Skopje by the Canadian and Australian diaspora descending from northern Greece. It clearly breaks with the national identity policy of Yugoslav times and is openly irredentist.

As can be seen from this short overview, Macedonian identity is not an artefact coined by Tito, as Bulgarian and Greek scholars continue to claim (cf. Kofos 1992, Dimitrov 2000). Rather, as I argued in the previous section, it has to be explained as indigenism typical of borderland identities trying to avoid national bipolarization. The complicating factor in the Macedonian case is that the name 'Macedonia', initially designating the non-belonging of nationally indifferent rural populations to the Greek, Bulgarian and Serbian national parties, after 1944 was used in Tito-Yugoslavia for the *nation-building* process: this has led to what might be called a homonymic conflict over the name 'Macedonia'.

The role of Aegean Macedonia in the Macedonian national doctrine

The osmotic processes between Aegean and Vardar Macedonia have to be considered on two highly contradictory planes: first, the level of language planning and secondly, the level of national ideology and identity management.

Reducing this relationship to a simple formula, I repeat my initial opinion on the synchronicity of a national language ideology and an ethno-national identity ideology. The Macedonian national doctrine coined after 1944 in Skopje includes Aegean Macedonia as one, if not the, central component of Macedonian national history, and this for several reasons. First, the most famous Macedonian heroes acted and died in Aegean Macedonia: this holds true for the anti-Ottoman terrorists of the 'Inner-Macedonian Revolutionary Organization' founded in 1893 (VMRO), as well as for the martyrs during the Greek Civil War of 1946–49 who fought as Macedonians in the communist lines. Secondly, the discourse of victimization presenting Macedonian history as the history of a suppressed, divided nation has to concentrate on Aegean Macedonia, since the clash of Greek and Bulgarian nationalism was at its peak here. Thirdly, the Greek Civil War is interpreted in Skopje as an integral part of the Macedonian struggle for national liberation, which totally ignores the dynamics of Greek society during the 1940s. In the absence of a sizeable number of resistance partisans against the Bulgarian occupation from 1941 to 1944, the Greek communist cause produced an alibi for Skopje to participate in the crucial Tito-Yugoslav foundation myth of *'narodnooslobodilačka borba'* ('People's Liberation Struggle'). Finally, the central role of Aegean Macedonia in the Macedonian national doctrine is also in part accounted for by the strong personal input of political refugees at the end of the Greek Civil War, who today are overrepresented in the academic elites of historians and linguists in Skopje. To counter with the aggressive negations of Macedonianness by Greek and Bulgarian nationalism treating Macedonians like 'ethnic zombies cloned by Tito' (Troebst 1994: 218), Macedonians during the last 50 years have tended to prove their existence *beyond* the Yugoslav borders. Since there was no migration movement from Bulgarian Pirin Macedonia to Vardar Macedonia during the 19th and 20th centuries, there is no personal input and consequently no knowledge to serve as the material basis for work on Pirin Macedonia.

In this way, Aegean Macedonia has become the repository for collective memory in Skopje, a function that Vardar Macedonia cannot fulfil since it was easily brought under the jurisdiction of the Bulgarian national church, the Exarchate, and was therefore not exposed to merciless Bulgarian terrorism at the beginning of the 20th century when the Greek and Bulgarian church took up arms to conquer the villagers' souls in Macedonia. This explains why – in contrast to Pirin and Aegean Macedonia – there was no strong anti-Bulgarian potential among the population in the interwar period in Vardar-Macedonia.

The inclusive and exclusive functions of the Macedonian standard language

Does this relationship between the South and the North of historical Macedonia find any expression on the linguistic level? Just the opposite is the case: since 1944 planning the Macedonian standard language has been a constant process of excluding all non-Yugoslav Macedonians – in this way it strictly fulfils the criteria of Macedonian *nation-building* within Vardar-Macedonia. Although until the Komintern conflict in June 1948, with the split between Tito and Stalin, the political project of a Great Macedonian federation was not given up by Tito supporting the communist side in the Greek Civil War, Serbocroatian was the most important umbrella language, which has to be seen in terms of the continuity of Serbian–Macedonian diglossia after 1913 in Vardar-Macedonia. Without this specific bilingualism, developed over a period of 30 years, it would not have been possible to declare as the official state language in 1944 a language that had no written dictionary or grammar.

To explain the position of Macedonian between Serbocroatian and Bulgarian, we should bear in mind the historical circumstances of South Slavic language codification: during the 19th century the linguistic identity of the South Slavs was determined by the political rivalry between the Habsburg Empire (propagating Austroslavism) and Russia (propagating Panslavism). Whereas the Serbs surmounted the intralinguistic diglossia (with the archaic Slaveno-Serbian as H-variety) with the help of Vuk Karadžić's (1787–1864) model radically upgrading the vernacular (and his famous imperative *'piši kao što govoriš'*: 'write as you pronounce'), the Bulgarians overcame the interlinguistic diglossia (with Greek as H-variety) by a model oriented towards Russian and Church-Slavonic. This historically developed dichotomy was politically sanctioned by the split between Tito and Stalin in June 1948: whereas the Bulgarian lexicon was affected by a second wave of russification, Macedonian radically began to avoid Church-Slavonic and Russian elements (especially in word formation: suffixes like *-tel*, *-stvo* and *-nie*). The following synonyms may illustrate the Bulgarian-Macedonian differentiation resulting from the diametrically opposed use of Church-Slavonic elements:

Russian/Bulgarian	*Serbocroatian/Macedonian*	
dokazatelstvo	dokaz	proof
izrečenie	rečenica	sentence
namerenie	namera	purpose
opisanie	opis	description

Another specific feature of Serbocroatian are calques based on German and developed during the puristic Croatian Illyrism in the 19th century. Through Serbocroatian lexical roofing, this model of loans, which is not autochthonous in the Macedonian region, reached the Macedonian standard, for example dvopek ('rusk' < German 'Zwie-back'), padobran ('parachute' < German 'Fall-schirm'), putokaz ('road sign' < German 'Weg-weiser'), oblakoder ('skyscraper' < German 'Wolken-kratzer').

Semantic condensations and univerbizations (that is, the reduction of semantically transparent compounds to one stem expressions omitting the *explanandum*), developed in the 19th century by Croatian for the same puristic reasons, found their way (slightly adapted phonologically) into the Macedonian standard as well. For example:

Serbocroatian	*Macedonian*		*derived from*
grudnjak	gradnik	brassière	grud (grad)
dokolenica	dokolenica	knee sock	koleno
otrovnica	otrovnica	poisonous snake	otrov
padavica	padavica	falling sickness	padati
ulaznica	vleznica	(admission) ticket	ulaz (vlez)

The irreversible turning point in the Serbianization of standard Macedonian took place in the late 1950s. What had happened? The political refugees from Greek Macedonia scattered in the Eastern Bloc were under the control of the Moscow-oriented Greek Communist party, which undertook considerable efforts to foster a style of Macedonian identity that was anti-Yugoslav by printing books and newspapers in a language heavily influenced by Bulgarian. This cultural policy of Macedonians in exile 'threatened the very fabric of Yugoslavia' (Brown 2003: 32). Although the authors of these newspapers were not willing to accept – in their own words – the 'Vardar language', in 1956 they were forced to give up their ethnolinguistic experiments within the framework of destalinization and political thaw. The Macedonian issue – once the bone of contention between young nation-states – in the 1940s–50s took on the same role in the rivalry of the Communist parties of the Soviet Union, Yugoslavia, Bulgaria and Greece.

The end of Moscow's support for the contestation of standard Macedonian's legitimacy from abroad coincided with the preparation period for the Macedonian dictionary of Blaže Koneski published between 1961 and 1966. This dictionary marked the end of the initial period of implementation of the standard, which was characterized by a strong indigenous impact trying to nativize the lexicon and to avoid Serbian and Bulgarian loans as well. During the 1950s there had been a slight tendency to coin loan translations, like for example:

Serbocroatian	*Macedonian*	
potražnja	pobaruvačka	demand, market
pronalazak	pronajdok	invention
zapremnina	zafatnina	cubic contents, volume
zaposlenost	vrabotenost	employment

The fundamental change undergone by the language planners in Skopje during the late 1950s can be seen in the most popular source of linguistic advice, the 'Language corner' (*Jazično katče*) by Blagoja Korubin during the 1960s, 1970s and 1980s. Korubin never openly attacked traces of Serbocroatian interference, which was not seen as damage to the norm but interpreted as politically opportune and connoted with social progress. Reacting to letters to the editor from Macedonians abroad who criticized Serbocroatian elements, Korubin several times literally answered that only 'the last Mohicans' were opposed to Tito-Yugoslavia. Linguistic interference was inseparably linked with the political experiment. This explains why the Serbocroatian influence has become an integral part of Macedonian vocabulary and shows its sustainability even after the dissolution of Yugoslavia and the end of Serbocroatian-Macedonian bilingualism.

Linguistic and ethnic identities in northern Greece

Doing fieldwork in Greek Macedonia, I often heard sentences like 'Over there, they mixed the language with Serbian', or 'They speak in a different way from us', or 'They have forgotten their own language. They have given up their own language' (Voss, forthcoming). Even radical Macedonian ethnic activists in Greece are very reserved and distant towards their potential 'mother nation' language: high-ranking leaders of the 'RAINBOW-party of national Macedonians in Greece' (a member of the 'European Free Alliance') showed their annoyance by telling me that for them it is easier to buy cigarettes in Plovdiv (Southern Central Bulgaria) than to start a conversation with a young waiter in Bitola, 15 km beyond the Greek–Macedonian border in the vicinity of Florina.

This sharp feeling, shared by the older generation, of being excluded from a standard language their relatives in Bitola are speaking has recently come to be offset by a new pragmatic position of legitimacy for the ethnic language. In order to participate in a newly opened Balkan market, Slavic speakers can take advantage of their access to multiple linguistic and cultural resources. Young Slavic-speakers learning English at school and making contact with standard Macedonian, will quickly discover that due to internationalisms, the abstract vocabulary of both languages is to a high degree identical. This new insight is about to replace the widespread prejudice among minorities that bilingualism from childhood is very harmful and detrimental to social advancement. Many people told me that they were painstakingly trying to learn standard Macedonian by watching Macedonian television from Skopje.

Since the beginning of the 20th century, Greek nationalism has tried to convince Slavic-speakers that their dialect is just an inferior variety of Greek, as the Arvanite or the Aromunian community in Greece even today frequently believe. Parts of the minority have even lost the sense of speaking a dialect that does *not* belong to the Greek diasystem. As part of the Greek national propaganda in the 1900s leaflets were distributed in the Slavic-speaking villages written in Greek characters trying to convince them that they had lost their 'real mother tongue' during the Ottoman times on the grounds that Bulgarians and Russians have 'piggy faces', whereas the Greek race is as pretty as the Macedonians. In an astonishing way this parallels the so-called 'Windischentheorie', a theory developed by German nationalism in the 19th century claiming that Carinthian Slovene dialects are more closely related to the Germanic than to the Slavic family of languages. This categorization by the majority of speaking a 'Slavic-like idiom' (in Greek: *to slavofanes idioma*) continues to exert a powerful influence on identity patterns of the (still unrecognized) Slavic-speaking minority in Greece, since the absence of any official language ideology exposes the minority to the one-sided influence of the dominant language group through the Greek ethnocentric discourse. After 1945 the Greek state persecuted communist partisans more than former collaborators with the Germans (Karakasidou 2002: 135). This general assessment holds especially true for the Slavic-speakers, who were punished for communist tendencies (in the western region of Aegean Macedonia) as well as for pro-Bulgarian tendencies (in the eastern region). The experience of social exclusion and open or covert discrimination has hampered a successful assimilation and has led to a subjective perception of otherness, which is not articulated openly.

Borderland minorities like the Slavic-speakers in Greece use the term 'national homeless' (Karakasidou 2002: 149). The terminology of self-ascription is symptomatic in this regard: they call themselves '*dopii*', the Greek term for 'locals' (in Slavic: '*tukašni*'), their language is called '*po naše*' ('our language'). The non-locals are simply labelled '*madžiri*' (from Turkish *muhaceri*), that means 'the refugees'. All these terms possess an exclusively local frame of reference without any ethnic semantics.

What the outsider tends to consider as an ethnic conflict between ontological entities is in fact a conflict between locals and refugees, the strongest persistent identity-rendering opposition in the region. Both groups lay claim to deserving more rights than the other, one side on the basis of indigenity, the other on the basis of the appropriate nationality. The Greek–Turkish treaty of Lausanne 1923 set a precedent in European history by sanctioning waves of ethnic violence. As a result, Aegean Macedonia (together with post-war Poland) is a low point in European ethnic cleansing policy: on a territory of ca. 35,000 square kilometres, which in 1912 had 1.2 million inhabitants, 600,000 Greek Pontic and Asia Minor refugees were settled, while approximately 90,000 Slavs went to Bulgaria. The political goal of this colonization was to stabilize the northern border region with loyal Greek nationalists, but this led to the minorization and marginalization of the indigenous Slavic-speaking population. These social tensions are still at the very core of the ethnic movement.

Language death in Greek Macedonia?

Fieldwork conducted in northern Greece between 2000 and 2003 allows the following answer to Fishman's question 'How threatened is threatened?' (Fishman 1991: 81) in relation to this context. In the diagram of overt and covert minority rights (Phillipson and Skutnabb-Kangas 1995: 490) leading from one extreme (that is, prohibition), via toleration, non-discrimination, prescription, permission, to the other extreme (that is, promotion), the Slavic dialects in Greece are obviously situated under the category 'overt prohibition', with a slight tendency towards 'overt toleration' after the liberalization starting in the late 1990s. This teaches us that language suppression does not automatically lead to language death. Therefore it is not appropriate to equate suppressed languages with threatened languages, because language loyalty and prestige are important factors for language maintenance. The strong pressure exerted on the Slavic-speakers has rendered the so-called 'covert prestige' (Labov 1972: 192; Trudgill and Tzavaras 1977: 178) of the Slavic vernacular attractive, especially for men. The dialect has become a kind of subcultural code that constitutes group solidarity.

Sometimes, villages with traditionally Greek national consciousness make more active use of their Slavic dialect: This makes it clear that language does not inevitably have to function as a central symbol of ethnic boundaries. The non-congruence of ethnic and linguistic group membership has already been pointed out by Trudgill (1983) for the Arvanites in Greece, as well as by Minnich (1988) for Slovene-speakers in Austria and Italy.

In general, the loyalty of minority members towards their ethnic language is low; women in particular are trying to escape from their villages by linguistic exogamy (Gal 1978). Whereas up to the 1960s women were excluded from the labour market and did not have command of the Greek language, their role has totally changed: for the sake of better integration at school and career opportunities, they are not willing to teach the Slavic dialect to their children. Slavic varieties are now spoken almost exclusively by men with their parents and grandparents. On Fishman's 'graded intergenerational disruption scale' (1991: 112–114) the situation in northern Greece corresponds to degree 7: 'most users of Xish are a socially integrated and ethnolinguistically active population, but they are beyond child-bearing age' (1991: 89). In households with almost monoglot Slavic-speaking grandparents, bilingual parents, and monoglot Greek-speaking children with a passive knowledge of Slavic, the young generation imposes Greek at home

In a way that is typical for transition periods in the life cycle of minority languages on their way to language shift the elder generation makes use of all sorts of code-switching which can be seen as an 'act of non-identity' to distinguish themselves from different linguistic out-groups, namely the monolingual nations on both sides of the border.

The absence of any kind of Slavic lexicographical tradition, as well as the 80 years of Greek influence, have led to various techniques of linguistic interference. After any Slavic lexical influence had been stopped in 1912–13, numerous relexifications from Greek have been integrated into the Slavic dialects as borrowings or so-called nonce loans. Within three-generation families we notice situational code-switching (that is, switching that takes place when the addressee or the setting changes), whereas the degree of conversational code-switching (that is, within the same speech exchange), always representing expressive discourse strategies in comparison to monolingual speech, depends on the ethno-political self-identification of the speaker. Code-switching as well as borrowing is often introduced by comments such as 'as we used to say...', or 'in our language...': this indicates that the speakers have a very affectionate relationship to their mixed linguistic practices. Their multiple and shifting identities are negotiated through the linguistic interplay of codes. Due to transmigration, open borders and especially the global ethnic networks, linguistic roofing and linguistic competence have become a highly personalized and individual affair. The prototypical idea of monolingual speakers never changing their place of residence is not appropriate for the Balkans of the 1990s and 2000s. 'Ethnic middlemen' play important mediating roles within their village communities. The summer visits of relatives from the Canadian or Australian diaspora, where the Macedonian standard language enjoys high prestige, could potentially contribute to ethnic pride and new language attitudes.

Language policy of ethnic activism in Greek Macedonia

The ethnic revival in the Florina region started officially in 1989 as a product of the ecological movement in Greece and leftist groups. It is a late consequence of the Greek liberalization after the fall of the Colonels' junta in 1974, allowing Slavic-speakers access to higher education and in general increased upward social mobility. Although this process began two years before the independence declaration of the Republic of Macedonia, the ensuing Greek anti-Macedonian campaign directed against Skopje was, all in all, a very strong support for the success of the native Macedonian movement. It is important to stress that the

articulation of Macedonian identity in Greece was not simply a consequence of the Yugoslav development, but had its own dynamic. As a
typical indigenous movement, the agenda was local, anti-centralist and
anti-racist without any national content: its first aim was the legaliza-
tion of prohibited Macedonian songs for village festivals. The ethnic
activists started printing local folklore in Greek characters. The first
newspaper, *'Ta Moglena'* ('The Moglen Region'), referred exclusively to
the local history of the Almopia region (in the north of Edessa). The
attempt to edit a journal in standard Macedonian (*'NOVA ZORA'*:
'New Dawn') in 1996 failed and was stopped two years later. This
indicates the non-acceptance among the members of the minority of
the minority-engineering and identity-management of the local elites
and their dependence upon the role of Vardar Macedonia as referential
nation. This misunderstanding between the rural dwellers and the
(urban) ethnic activists can partly be explained by the fact that most of
the latter studied in Belgrade or Skopje during the 1970s and 1980s
and master the Macedonian standard.

The failed language policy of the 'RAINBOW PARTY of national
Macedonians in Greece', using the Cyrillic alphabet and standard
Macedonian as symbols of their national belonging, will contribute to
language death in Northern Greece, since the Slavic-speakers' complex
that they speak a dialect of very poor quality is intensified by the fact
that the standard language which goes hand in hand with their potential ethnic identity is a closed book to them: the propagation of an
unfamiliar, new standard 'denigrates and reproves those who *do* use
the dialect' (Vassberg 1993: 178). The content of the newspaper *'LOZA'*
('Grapes'), published in Saloniki since 2000, has been brought into line
with the press of the Canadian- or Australian-Macedonian diaspora,
sharing its sharp anti-Albanian undertones. In many cases the articles
are simply translated into Greek.

Conclusion

The study of borderland minorities after the transmutation of the Iron
Curtain into a 'melting border' shows that cross-border cohesion of
ethnic groups is not primarily dependent on linguistic features – in
our case it even hampers the self-identification with the referential
nation. This indicates that at grass-roots level, language nationalism,
that is the equation of language and nation propagated by 19th
century political romanticism, is still not at home in the Balkans. The
fluid and multioptional identity patterns of small ethnic groups in

the Balkans and their ethnic mimicry sharply contradict Western stereotypes defining Balkanhood as 'powder-keg' and 'ancient hatreds' (Goldsworthy 2002: 26–7).

The 'European Charter for Regional or Minority Languages' (1992) is directed explicitly at 'national minorities', a label in no way applicable to the Slavic-speakers in Greece, who are not identifiable as one ethnic group, and are to a high degree detached from ethnic loyalties and prioritize economic success and material prosperity. A language policy ignoring the strong emotional attachment toward the usual mode of code-switching and borrowing and neglecting to cultivate the local vernacular to the benefit of standard Macedonian denigrates and reproves those who do use the dialect (cf. for the situation in Alsace: Vassberg 1993: 178) and only adds to the number of the Slavic-speakers who make use of a socially extremely negatively marked dialect who now realize that the standard language, which goes hand in hand with their potential national identity, is unavailable to them.

The distinguishing feature of the European minority policy in the Balkans is the misconception of ethnicity as a constant that inevitably determines and even predestines human thinking and social action. This primordial idea that equates ethnic and language group member-ship ignores the transitional identities typical of the Balkans. Minority protection that leads to the ethnicization of society along the contours of cultural identities, tends to create new ethnic identities and leads the minority to catch up on a *nation-building* process of their alleged co-nationals, and in the long run it is not in the minority's interest. If we take into consideration the fact that Bulgaria will become a member of the EU in 2007, whereas the stability of the Republic of Macedonia is still threatened by interethnic tensions and Albanian ethnic extremism, we should expect to see radical changes in the identity patterns of the Slavic minority in Greece with the abolition of the Bulgarian–Greek border. Therefore, the phenomenon of cross-border cohesion at the Macedonian–Greek border should not lead the Western European observer to the conclusion that the Slavic-speakers in Greece represent a group with homogeneous ethnic, national and linguistic identity.

10
Language Loyalty in the Baltic: Russian Artists and Linguistic Nationalism in Estonia

Rémy Rouillard

Introduction

Heie Treier (2001: 216), an Estonian art critic, reported that multicultur-alism and the relation to the Other were widely discussed throughout the 1990s in Estonia, but that

> in the Estonian context this does not relate to communities of other races, but to coping with ourselves as a small nation, in whose collective psyche there is an ingrained fear of being assimilated, of losing our identity.

This excerpt underlines the Estonian preoccupation with the survival of their nation, in the aftermath of their Soviet experience and at the dawn of their entry into the European Union (EU). Treier, however, does not mention Russians or other non-Estonians, who compose more than a third of Estonia's population, even in a discussion of multi-culturalism.

It was during its occupation by the Soviet Union, which began in the Second World War and lasted until 1991, that the Estonian Republic saw the arrival of a great number of immigrants, mostly from the Russian Soviet Federated Socialist Republic (RSFSR). While in 1934 Russians were only 8.2 per cent of the Estonian population, they made up 30.3 per cent of the 1.5 million inhabitants of the Estonian Soviet Socialist Republic (ESSR) by 1989 (Lieven 1993: 434). Although most of them came to work in the industrial sector that was being imple-mented by the Soviet state, many were attracted to the ESSR because of its freer atmosphere, particularly in the cultural sphere. This was due to the authorities of the Baltic republics, who often manifested a greater tolerance towards artists whose works more or less opposed the canons of Socialist Realism than did authorities in other regions of the Soviet Union (Feinstein 1977: 31; Svede 1995: 192; Andriuškevičius 1995: 221).

The present chapter is based on research that was conducted in Tallinn in the fall of 2002, which examined twenty-six Russian authors' and painters' feelings of belonging to Estonia, to Russia, and finally to Europe, of which they are now a part, via the European Union, as of 1 May 2004.[1] We will see that the multiple senses of belonging held by these individuals reflect indissociable facets of their ethnic identity. Before tackling this issue directly, we will try to understand the situation of Russians and other non-Estonians in relation to two policies of the Estonian state, the citizenship and language laws, which are related to the issue of loyalty.

The Estonian language and the question of loyalty

In his chapter in this volume, Patrick Stevenson illustrates well how a language issue – in his case it concerns German in both Austria and Germany – can be ideological when its knowledge is associated with the right to belong to a community. As we will see, the situation in post-Soviet Estonia shows similar characteristics.

Soon after proclaiming independence in the turmoil following the failed coup that took place in Moscow in August 1991, the Estonian government updated the citizenship law of 1938, which became the cornerstone of the Estonian nationalization policy. Only those who had been Estonian citizens prior to the Soviet occupation, along with their offspring, were recognized as legitimate citizens. Thus, the vast majority of Russians and non-Estonians[2] were excluded from the right to citizenship. As a result, 500,000 of the 600,000 non-Estonians were not allowed to vote for the new constitution in June 1992, as non-citizens may not vote at national elections (Chinn and Kaiser 1996: 100).[3] Others who wanted to become citizens had to show that they had been residing in Estonia for at least five years and prove sufficient knowledge of the Estonian language (the only official language), history and constitution. Since until then Estonia had been a bilingual republic, in which Russians needed less than Estonians to speak both Russian and Estonian, the vast majority of Estonia's Russians were not generally able to fulfil the linguistic requirements of citizenship, and this is still the case even today. Among the members of the arts community that I met, 14 affirmed that they spoke little or no Estonian; 11 felt that they can have (at least simple) conversations with native speakers in Estonian, and only one person claimed to have mastered it.

The decision of the Estonian state to associate the right to citizenship so directly with knowledge of the official language cannot be separated from the issue of loyalty of non-Estonians. As Estonia had been part of the Russian and then of the Soviet Empire, both the Estonian state and people seem to have doubts about the loyalty of the large minority of non-Estonians who arrived during the Soviet occupation. According to Kruusvall (2002: 132), even in 2000, only 37 per cent of Estonians were confident of the loyalty of non-Estonians towards the Estonian state.[4] For Marika and Aksel Kirch (1997: 157), it is the possibility that Estonian Russians may not identify strongly with Estonia that creates doubts about their loyalty to the country:

> For Estonians, although Russians may identify themselves with Estonia and may even prefer the Estonian and European cultural context to the Russian one, their perceived inability or unwillingness to contrast themselves sufficiently with Russia or the Russian state raises concerns among Estonians. To the extent that Estonians do feel this threat, it creates doubts among the Estonians as to the Russians' loyalty.

Klara Hallik (2002: 79) has noted that the non-Estonians' knowledge of the official language does not only represent for the Estonians 'an instrumental ability that enables one to be more successful in life, but [is also seen] as an existential category that shows one's principal attitude towards the Estonian state'. And this attitude should, of course, be loyalty. This insistence on the mastering of Estonian as a proof of loyalty is reflected in the policy of integration of non-Estonians, adopted by the Estonian parliament in 1998. This policy was in fact implemented after the country was pressured by the European Union to improve its relations with its national minorities. According to the Estonian state, 'the central objective of integration is the formation of a population loyal to the Republic of Estonia and the reduction of the number of persons without Estonian citizenship' (Integration Foundation 2002: 4). This statement clearly illustrates how discourses of language and nation are now expressed as a question of 'good faith' on the part of non-Estonians (who should demonstrate 'willingness to relinquish or at least diminish their otherness and acknowledge the legitimacy of the majority') and of 'good governance' ('democratic practice requires equal ability to participate in processes of public discussion and debate' through their knowledge of the state language) (see Stevenson, this volume).

In this chapter we will see that, although the majority of painters and authors have not mastered the Estonian language, they have a strong sense of belonging to Estonia that is expressed in different ways. This, however, should not be looked at separately from other attachments of those individuals, who have a sense of belonging to Russia and Europe as well. These attachments reflect indissociable facets of their ethnic identity. This then calls into question policies that closely associate loyalty to the Estonian state with mastering of the official language. To begin, I shall discuss briefly how non-Estonians and the members of the arts community that I interviewed perceive the citizenship and linguistic policies and how they oriented their decisions towards them.

Citizenship and language issues

In 1999, 71 per cent of Russians in Estonia wished to be citizens of the Republic of Estonia (Pettai 2000: 83). In 2000, about 40 per cent of non-Estonians had Estonian citizenship, generally because their ancestors had been living in Estonia prior to the Soviet occupation, because they had supported the Estonian Congress,[5] or they had passed the state language exam (Hallik 2002: 73). Among the artists interviewed, half had become Estonian citizens through these various methods.

Others had two options: to adopt the Russian citizenship that was offered to those who 'were born on the territory of the Russian Federation, or where either parent at the moment of their birth was a citizen of the USSR and was in permanent residence on the territory of the Russian Federation', or remain aliens in Estonia[6] (Gelazis 2003: 56). According to the census of 2000, 20.4 per cent of Russians living in Estonia were citizens of Russia (Hallik 2002: 73). Sociological research from 1996 showed that two out of three Russian citizens had chosen their citizenship because it allowed them to visit their relatives and friends in Russia without a visa (Pettai 2000: 78). For five of the six participants in my research who had Russian citizenship, the choice of the Russian passport was related to their desire to be able to visit Russia easily and/or to their fear of finding themselves without citizenship and thereby without the protection of any state.

In 2000, 38.4 per cent of Russians living in Estonia were still without citizenship, placing them in the 'alien' category (Hallik 2002: 73). According to Klara Hallik (2002: 80), it is the 'lack of solidarity with

Russia' that made them choose alien status over Russian citizenship. On the other hand, between 50 and 70 per cent of alien adults are of the opinion that they could not fulfil the linguistic requirements necessary to obtain Estonian citizenship (Hallik 2002: 77). It must be mentioned, however, that collectively non-Estonians seem to have made progress in their knowledge of Estonian in the last decade, as the percentage of non-Estonians who claim to speak Estonian fluently rose from 13 per cent to 29 per cent between 1993 and 1999 (Proos 2000: 108).

Nationalism has often been studied in light of language, as in the major works by Benedict Anderson (1983) and Eric Hobsbawm (1990). One of my interests in working with both authors and painters is that while writers have to use their language, Russian, in order to create, the painters do not in principle need to access the realm of language, whether Russian or Estonian, to create their art. Therefore, it is relevant to compare briefly their attitudes toward the language issue in Estonia.

Two main positions are observed, with no significant difference between the authors and painters. Five artists and three writers shared the opinion that is expressed well by the painter Denis (60, Russian):[7]

> We must have an education [system] that teaches Estonian well enough, but it is also necessary to preserve the language of each minority. Then there won't be conflicts, because language is an instrument of balance. If people understand each other, they can agree on something.

Seven authors and six painters – half of my informants – expressed the opinion that it is important to know Estonian, but that one ought not to experience discrimination if one does not have a sufficient knowledge of Estonian, especially if one does not really need it in daily life. This is probably the case for many people who live in regions like the north-eastern part of Estonia, where most inhabitants are Russian speakers.

My informants' opinions and decisions concerning the Estonian language and citizenship policies show different senses of belonging. Although the majority of painters and authors generally recognize the importance of knowing the language of their state, they feel that their language, Russian, should also be preserved in Estonia. In the following section, we will see that the relationship to Estonian territory can also reveal multiple senses of belonging.

Estonia, land of roots and compromise

Triin Vihalemm (1999: 18) has argued that instead of having a strong political loyalty to the Estonian state, Russian speakers identify strongly with the Estonian territory. And this is being said when more than 60 per cent of non-Estonians were born in the Russian Federation or in a former Soviet Republic other than Estonia (Hallik 2002: 70).

My informants have different ways of expressing their sense of belonging to the Estonian territory. For three of them, this link is conceived in terms of historical rootedness. The essay-writer Ruslan (50, Estonian) often tackles the rootedness of Russians in Estonia in his works, which trace the relationship of members of the Russian intelligentsia to Estonia. It is in virtue of these ties that he considers Russians at home in Estonia:

> When one says to a Russian that he has no roots here, that he is an immigrant, an occupant, that he is a foreigner, that he comes from the moon or from Mars [...], by reading my book, he will begin to understand that he is not a foreigner. This is his land like it is that of Estonians, a land he should love, for it is his. I am doing something that is very positive for Estonian society. I would like it if Russians loved this soil as if it were their own. If they defended it if something were to happen. [...] Through this, these Russians, feeling that it is theirs, will find their identity. This question is not only 'who am I?', but 'what is the relationship I have to the world'?

One can notice in this excerpt that the necessity of defending one's land presents emotional ties to the soil as a proof of loyalty towards a territory, towards a nation, which, in this case especially, has its doubts about the loyalty of a third of the population (Malkki 1997: 56). The painter Nikolai (40, Alien) was born in Estonia, but has no citizenship yet. He perceives the rootedness of Russians in Estonia by the ancient presence of the Orthodox religion in Estonia.[8] One can thus see, as Liisa Malkki (1997: 58) points out, that 'culture has for long been conceived as something existing in "soil" '. Another way of expressing one's sense of belonging to the Estonian territory situates it in a broader territorial context. But this context is not only territorial, for it concerns the political, economic and social situation of Estonia, Russia and Europe. As Gupta and Ferguson (1997b: 40) have remarked, '[p]laces, after all, are always imagined in the context of political-economic determinations that have a logic of their own'.

The impossibility of travel to EU countries without a visa is a preoccupying factor for the majority of non-Estonians who do not have Estonian citizenship (Pettai 2000: 77). This can lead us to believe that there exists, on the one hand, a sense of belonging to Europe, but on the other, a desire for access to a better quality of life and to resources comparable to those of northern and continental Europe. Two of my informants who have alien status are bothered by the difficulty of access to Europe. One of them, the painter Mikhail (55, Alien), wishes to obtain an Estonian passport in order to get in contact with European colleagues easily, without which he has the impression of being stuck in the local artistic scene: 'If I cannot, it is a whole part of my creativity that suffers; I feel stuck in this circle.'

The attachment to Estonia in relation to its geographical location was also expressed as the Estonian Republic constitutes some sort of a compromise between Russia and Europe, a place where it is pleasant to live, in particular because of the access it offers both westwards and eastwards. What the poet Kyril (30, Russian) says illustrates this opinion well. Though he arrived in Estonia at the age of one, he chose to be a Russian citizen in order to facilitate visits to his parents now living in Russia:

> My parents live in Kuban [a region of Russia that lies near the Black sea, north of the Caucasus]. Nowadays, although I am Russian, I could not live there. I am closer to Europe. I understand better the European mores [...] Estonia is a compromise. For all the information that nourishes me comes from the East, from Russia. There, life is something else, but I need it as well. There, it is tough (жесткий). In Europe, it is softer. Here it is in the middle.

One can thus see that a sense of belonging to Estonia does not only concern its territory, but the prevailing mores of Estonians and Estonian Russians.

Russian artists with Estonian mores

Recently, 60 per cent of Estonians and non-Estonians expressed the belief that they were becoming more similar to each other in their way of life and attitude (Kruusvall 2002: 129). Although most painters and authors interviewed in my study do not seem to have much contact with Estonians (excepting three who come from mixed families or who have Estonian partners), 18 of my informants had only positive words about the manners and customs of Estonians. Only four persons had derogatory opinions about the temperament and way of life of Estonians, for they considered them difficult to communicate with, cold, indifferent and passive. What seems to be most enjoyed about Estonians, as mentioned by 12 informants, involves various closely related qualities: quietness, restraint, respect for others, absence of extremism. The icon painter, Peter (40, Russian) affirms that he shares his temperament with Estonians, despite the fact that he grew up in Russia:

> I like Estonians' temperament. They are calm and restrained, and the structure of society corresponds to this. There is no agitation, it is very close to my temperament. This corresponds to my vibes. [...] They are good. They are not in a hurry, everything is in order, they are able to organize their lives and their business. All this pleases me.

Peter alludes to the organization of Estonian society, to the ordered aspect that is, according to him, characteristic of Estonians. Ten informants also mentioned that they appreciate the reliability of Estonians, their capacity to be organized and orderly, especially compared to Russians in Russia.

The research conducted by David Laitin (1998: 165) among the Russian-speaking populations of four post-Soviet republics, including Estonia, shows that those people have 'two contradictory lines of thinking' about Russia: Russia is seen as 'foreign' and as 'homeland'. The artists who were interviewed in my research also generally expressed such paradoxical opinions. Ten out of 12 informants born in Russia and who consider Russia as their homeland see it in this contrasted way. Corruption, dirtiness, disorder and danger are the characteristics of Russia that they seem to have difficulties coping with. The author Anton (75, Russian) has lived in Estonia, where he raised a family, for more than 40 years. Although he feels at home in Estonia, he still 'is on Russia's side'. But he says:

> Sometimes, I feel like crying for Russia, but I do not know how to cry. I do not accept the Yeltsin period. I think he has caused a lot of harm to Russia. [...] It is a paradox that the world's richest state is not able to stand up. [...] Nevertheless, I am happy that culture is being preserved. Although contemporary literature is not my thing, the other aspects of culture, music, ballet, operas, visual arts are still as before despite the difficult context. They are being preserved and are popular everywhere in the Western world.

The great majority of the 14 informants who were born or who grew up in Estonia show similar contradictions in their view of Russia. Their external homeland is appreciated for the vastness of what it has to offer to the world, for its culture and history, but its unstable and chaotic aspect worries them. In the next section, we will see how the producers of culture relate to both Russian and Estonian arts and literatures.

The nationality[9] of culture[10]

The great majority of painters and authors that I have interviewed are unable to read in Estonian, which limits their access to Estonian culture. However, in the Soviet days, Estonian literature, translated into Russian, aroused great interest among Soviet readers, for it presented a different conception of the world, one that was more European.[11]

Nineteen artists express opinions that are rather positive about the art and literature of Estonians, either in general or concerning one or some painters/authors they like. However, only three informants feel that the Estonian cultural sphere has been influential for them in their works. One of them, the Estonian born novelist Natalia (50, Estonian) says:

> Estonian literature has certain characteristics that could not but influence someone living here, including me. [...] I always answer that my homeland is the Russian language, that my homeland is Russian culture. But the absolute freedom of form of Estonian writers has always been a model for me. I write like I want. It is the non-fear of a school or rigour. [...] The intellectual construction in their works [of Estonians] which is rational and precise has always pleased me, and of course, influenced me.

Three painters and two authors express a more negative opinion about Estonian art or literature. All five insist that since it is the culture of a numerically small people, Estonian culture cannot have much originality. The essay writer Ruslan (50, Estonian) comes from an ethnically mixed family and considers himself as a bearer of the two cultures and languages, Estonian and Russian. It is, according to him, not only because Estonian literature is that of a small nation that he talks negatively about it, but because the Estonian language itself is limited:

> A great literature can only be based on a great language. You might exclude some historical cases, like *Kalevala* or *Kalevipoeg*.[12] Great literatures are the French, British, Russian, German, Italian [...] Russian

language in itself is a language of science. It masters the categories and concepts with which the human being in fact thinks. In Estonian, this does not exist.

Most of my informants show a profound sense of belonging to Russian culture. This is of course related to their education. In the Soviet days and still today, the Estonian school system has two different programmes, one in Russian and one in Estonian, which will merge in 2007. Nevertheless, the three informants who are currently students had their first teaching related to Russian artistic traditions, which put a strong emphasis on the mastering of drawing and painting techniques. One should not be surprised then that even those students do not really appreciate the current Estonian art scene, which is more oriented towards Western contemporary art. A few professional painters, who studied at the State Art Institute of the ESSR in the Soviet times, are actually worried about what is now being taught in the Estonian Academy of Arts. One of them is the painter Mikhail (55, Alien):

Nowadays, they are not teaching how to draw anymore. Those who are completing their studies absolutely do not know how to draw. We at least had to learn some drawing because Moscow had its requirements. I fear that they are now trying to get rid of everything that existed in the USSR and in Russia, as they are doing in politics, with the pretext that everything that has to do with Russia is bad. So, learning how to draw would be bad. I have the impression that they are not learning anything. They are being told: 'think by yourself'. But what can you imagine or think if you do not even know how to achieve it?

Mikhail and some other informants thus believe that the reorientation of Estonia toward the West and the detachment from Russia can be perceived in art as well. In this point of view one can see the attachment these people have toward Russian culture. What they consider to be reorientation also shows that the sphere of cultural production can be related to the political sphere. Ernest Gellner (1983: 57) affirms that in a nationalist context, an 'alien high culture' which previously enjoyed a privileged status may be eliminated and replaced by a new 'high culture' which would be partly invented, partly related to local popular culture. So if in Soviet Estonia Russian culture had a particular status reflected in the requirements that Moscow had set for arts institutions both in and outside Russia, nowadays it is being replaced by what is considered to be local culture, a new local culture that is influenced this time by the West.

Although they are deeply attached to Russian culture, there are disagreements among my informants as to what can be considered paradigm examples of Russian literature and art. Certain individuals that I have interviewed feel more intimate with authors of the Golden Age[13] of Russian literature or to classical painters, whereas others feel closer to Russian literature of the Silver Age and to avant-garde artists of the early 20th century. Following Fredrik Barth (1969), it appears to be relevant to look at culture not as a content but more in terms of a difference marker. In that sense, Arjun Appadurai (1996: 13) proposes

> that we restrict the term *culture* as a marked term to the subset of these differences that has been mobilized to articulate the boundary of difference. As a boundary-maintenance question, culture then becomes a matter of group identity as constituted by some differences among others.

Despite different 'contents' associated with Russian art or literature, the fact that my informants generally seem attached to what they consider to be 'Russian culture' and little to Estonian culture may demonstrate how culture can serve as a difference marker vis-à-vis Estonians. In the last section of this chapter, we will see how the painters and authors that I interviewed perceived Estonian Russians to be different from Russians in Russia, thereby showing a sense of belonging to Estonia's Russian community.

'We're not those Russians, we are Russians living in Estonia'

Among the 26 informants, 23 feel that Russians living in Estonia are distinct from Russians in Russia. This is perceived and explained in different ways. The first is in quasi-evolutionary terms, moving from Russians in Russia to the Russians in Estonia towards Estonians/Europeans. On a trip to Russia, the young poet Sergey (30, Estonian), who was born in Estonia, found himself surprised at having thought of himself as more advanced than Russians in Russia:

> One could see Russia as a nostalgia for his own youth. Not a nostalgia for the Soviet past, but for youth. The term Soviet has nothing to do with it. It was a mix of eurocentrism and 'centrism' of the contemporary: I, as a European, modern and more experienced,

came to a backward Russia. But how can you see your own youth in such a lofty way? In fact, I envy my youth.

For the novelist Vladimir (45, Estonian), it is the influence of the Estonian soil and climate that makes Russians in Estonia become like Estonians. One poet and one painter think that Russians in Estonia are different from those in Russia because they are living at the meeting point of two cultures.

If most of my informants find that Russians in Estonia are different from Russians in Russia, this also concerns the language that they in principle share. Triin Vihalemm (1999: 21) refers to research conducted by Anu Masso in Tartu, which revealed that many Russians from that Estonian city now believe that the Russian language is a factor distinguishing them from Russia's Russians. There were six participants in my project who thought that way. Two authors, the most prolific of my informants, are very critical when they talk about the Russian spoken in Estonia. One of them, the novelist Natalia (50, Estonian) cannot stand the use of Estonian words in Russian, although she speaks Estonian. She says:

> The Russian language here, especially that of the middle class, I can't stand. It is a language of conjuncture, a language that is adapting to new life conditions. A sales language. A language that introduces Estonian words in order to reach some sort of compromise.

Three informants prefer the Russian spoken or written in Estonia for it is, in their opinion, either less vulgar, or somehow more pure, less influenced by other Slavic languages (like Ukrainian) than in Russia. This leads us to think that the border that was established between Estonia's and Russia's Russians has had linguistic effects in the perception of some informants. Or as Hobsbawm (1990: 63) puts it, 'languages multiply with states; not the other way round'. Despite this, the vast majority of the participants in my study did not mention such differences between the Russian spoken by these Russian communities.

Conclusion

The 26 members of the Russian arts community that I interviewed still have links to Russia, links that seem to make Estonians and the state have doubts about their loyalty. However, almost all of my informants consider Estonian Russians different from those living in Russia, which is explained in different ways. Although they generally have a weak knowledge of Estonian, most painters and authors interviewed are deeply attached to Estonian mores, which probably explains in part why they are so attached to the Estonian territory.

For a few years now, the Estonian state has undertaken the immense process of the integration of non-Estonians. In its definition of integration, the state still associates citizenship – an important condition to participation in society – with the knowledge of language, showing how the language issue is related to the question of loyalty. Thus, most of my informants express in different ways a strong sense of belonging to Estonia, which seems to reflect certain facets of their ethnic identity which cannot be dissociated from their attachments to Russia, and to a certain extent, to Europe. This leads me to think that the Estonian state might benefit by taking into consideration forms of expression of loyalty other than solely the knowledge of the Estonian language. At a time when integration is a major preoccupation of Estonian society, it might also be desirable for institutions which have a cultural character, public or not, to help non-Estonian producers of culture reach the Estonian public. This would permit Estonia to look at itself through the representations of its inhabitants, be they Estonian by citizenship or by heart.

Notes

1. During the field research, which lasted for nearly half a year, I interviewed 13 individuals whom I will refer to as authors (poets, novelists, essay-writers) and 13 individuals who will be referred to as painters (graphic artists, painters, students). 20 of them are men, six are women. These informants belong to different circles, different organizations, different generations, the youngest being 20, the oldest 75.
2. In this chapter, I will refer to 'non-Estonians', 'Russian speakers' and 'Russians'. These categories, which are used by different actors, are all problematic in some way. I will therefore refer to them depending on the sources I take my information from. Here, it is only important to say that 80 per cent of non-Estonians are Russians and other non-Estonians generally speak Russian in public life (Pavelson and Luuk 2002: 91).
3. Non-citizens who are residents of the Estonian Republic may now vote at municipal elections.
4. It must be mentioned that in Estonia as in many other post-Soviet republics, there is a tendency in social sciences to rely mainly on quantitative methods. Although my research involved solely qualitative methods, the results of research projects conducted by Estonian social scientists were very helpful in my research despite the different paradigm in which they were realized.

5. In 1993, the Estonian government decided to offer Estonian citizenship to all those who had supported the Estonian Congress, without having to fulfil the linguistic and residential requirements (Everly 1997: 110). The Estonian Congress, an informal representative organ of citizens of Estonia created during perestroika whose goal was the restitution of independence to Estonia, was replaced by the Estonian parliament – the Riigikogu – once independence was re-established.

6. In 1994 an identification document was created for the residents of Estonia who were still aliens, the alien passport.

7. Throughout the chapter, I refer to research participants by a pseudonym. Before agreeing to participate in this project, the informants were assured that their identity would never be revealed. After their pseudonym, I put in parentheses two important characteristics of the informants (age, citizenship).

8. Although most Estonians belong to the Lutheran church, a considerable number of Estonians are of Orthodox faith, which arrived in Estonia from Russia around the 11th century (Maltsev 2000: 112).

9. In 1932 the notion of 'nationality' ('национальность') was introduced in official documents as a key element of personal identification for Soviet citizens. For Rogers Brubaker (1996: 31), 'Ethnic nationality (natsional'nost') was not only a statistical category, a fundamental unit of social accounting, employed in censuses and other social surveys. It was, more distinctively, an obligatory and mainly ascriptive legal category, a key element of an individual's legal status.' Although nationality is not an official element of identification in Estonia anymore, many Russian speakers still use the term 'nationality' to discuss what might be called 'ethnic identity' in the Western world, a terminology widely used by the Estonian state and in social sciences.

10. I must clarify that I use the term 'culture' here to mean 'intellectual and artistic aspects of a collectivity' and not in the more broad sense that anthropologists normally use it. However, when I refer to different authors' conception of culture, this term will take the meaning given by the person in question.

11. Bassel (2002: 171) reports that between 1940 and the mid-70s, more than 1000 works of Estonian authors were translated into 45 languages with a total printing of more than 31 million copies. Half of these books were translated into Russian.

12. In Finland, Elias Lönnrat published *Kalevala* between 1835 and 1849, based on ancient Carelian poems. In 1861, Friedrich Kreutzwald published *Kalevipoeg* ('The Son of Kalev'), an Estonian epic narrative, inspired by Lönnrat's work, which became an important element of the Estonian national awakening in the 19th century.

13. In Russian literature, the term 'Golden Age' is commonly used to refer to the authors of the 19th century, (like F. Dostoevsky, L. Tolstoy, N. Gogol, and the one who is probably the most important for Russians, A. Pushkin). The 'Silver Age' comprises the authors who were writing shortly before the Russian Revolution and until the 1930s (of whom one of the most important figures is the futurist poet V. Mayakovsky).

11
'National' Languages in Transnational Contexts: Language, Migration and Citizenship in Europe

Patrick Stevenson

Introduction: language, migration and anti-cosmopolitanism

In the literature on language policy and language planning in modern nation-states, language is seen to be central both to the practical, instrumental processes of nation building (for example, in relation to citizenship) and to the symbolic, integrative processes of developing a national 'culture' (for example, in relation to national identity) (Wright 2004: 42). Standard languages, in particular, are seen as both a vehicle for articulating and achieving common political goals and a manifestation of a common purpose and singular identity. While these processes are sometimes cast as political and ideological issues respectively, I want to argue that discourses of citizenship are not separate from, but rather subsumed in, discourses of national identity, and that recent public debates and national policies on the relationship between language and citizenship in western European states are not merely issues of political 'management' but part of a larger ideological process and constitute a classic example of what Blommaert (1999) calls a language ideological debate.[1]

This process has, of course, to do with challenges to national sovereignty (in economic, political and cultural terms) in the context of social and political change in Europe and in particular in relation to perceived threats to national integrity posed by large-scale migration. The movement of people brings with it the movement of languages, and this arguably most salient item in the baggage of migrant individuals and groups confronts most immediately what Blommaert and

Verschueren (1998: 194–5) call the 'dogma of homogeneism': 'a view of society in which differences are seen as dangerous and centrifugal and in which the "best" society is suggested to be one without intergroup differences'. For, as the literature on language and nationalism has repeatedly shown, the fundamental paradox on which the dominant discourse in most European nation-states is still constructed is that these manifestly multilingual societies are conceived as essentially and irrevocably monolingual (see, for example, Billig 1995, Fishman 1989, May 2001).

But post-1989 the processes of rapid social transformation and increasing population flows in Europe have reinforced a growing instability of beliefs in and understandings of 'national' integrity: for example, debates in the UK on regionalism, 'Englishness' (see, for example, Blunkett 2005) and the popular image of the 'disunited kingdom'; the recent debates in Germany on multiculturalism, patriotism and the concept of the *Leitkultur* (see Manz 2004); and ruptures in the political culture in Austria over social and ethnic inclusion. Governments of radically different colours in Germany and Austria (as well as, for example, the Netherlands) have reacted simultaneously by introducing new legal instruments to control the flow of migrants, which include the statutory requirement to demonstrate proficiency in the 'national' language.[2] It therefore no longer appears to me possible to regard the question of the relationship between language and citizenship exclusively as a matter of principle in liberal democracies. Rather we have to acknowledge the historicity of discourses on language and citizenship and analyse them in the context of the national histories of the states in which they occur. From this perspective, overtly political (nationist) activities promoted as pragmatic management measures may be revealed as tacitly ideological (nationalist) operations intended to salvage the integrity of the nation based on the myth of a stable mono-lingual norm that is increasingly at odds with, and under assault from, multilingual realities.[3]

For the denial of societal multilingualism underpins and reinforces discourses that reject the status of (particularly) Germany as an *Einwan-derungsland* (country of immigration). For example, the insistence of the Süssmuth Commission on Migration that

> It is a fact that Germany has been a country of immigration for a long time.... The assertion that 'Germany is not a country of immigration' used to be a defining political principle but has become untenable as the cornerstone of migration and integration policy.

(Faktisch ist Deutschland seit langem ein Einwanderungsland.... Die in der Vergangenheit vertretene politische und normative Festlegung 'Deutschland ist kein Einwanderungsland' ist als Maxime der Zuwanderungs- und Integrationspolitik unhaltbar geworden.) (*Zuwanderung gestalten – Integration fördern* 2001: 1)

has not eliminated the counter-discourse, as represented, for example, by Jörg Schönbohm (Christian Democrat member of the Berlin Senate):

Ideological maxims – Germany is there for all! – are inflated into demands that are imbued with the irresistible appearance of humanist ideals.... One of these maxims is the oft repeated mantra that Germany is a country of immigration and that it should develop its policies accordingly. It is claimed that we are obliged to do this for historical reasons and because we live in a prosperous region. Since the numbers of foreigners coming to Germany have been high for decades, so the argument goes, Germany is de facto already a country of immigration. But this very argumentation is not only problematic but superficial and simply wrong.

(Ideologische Maximen – Deutschland ist für alle da! – werden zu Maximalforderungen erhoben, die sich mit dem unwiderstehlichen Schein humanistischer Ideale umgeben.... Eine dieser Maximen ist die gebetsmühlenartig wiederholte Behauptung, Deutschland sei ein Einwanderungsland und müsse seine Politik konsequent daran ausrichten. Dazu seien wir aus historischen Gründen und weil wir in einer Wohlstandsregion leben, moralisch verpflichtet. Da es in den letzten Jahrzehnten hohe Zuwanderungszahlen von Ausländern nach Deutschland gegeben habe, sei Deutschland bereits, so wird argumentiert, faktisch schon ein Einwanderungsland. Doch bereits diese Argumentation ist nicht nur problematisch, sondern in ihrer undifferenzierten Oberflächlichkeit schlicht falsch.) (Schönbohm 1998)

And even having reached an apparent consensus on the 2004 Immigration Act, members of the German parliament clearly disagreed in the closing debate on what they were giving their approval to. On the one hand, Volker Beck, a Green MP, declared categorically:

Germany is a country of immigration (*Einwanderungsland*). With the passage of this Immigration Act (*Zuwanderungsgesetz*) this fact is now recognized and will be given the official seal of approval today in the Bundestag and next week in the Bundesrat.

(Deutschland ist ein Einwanderungsland. Mit der Verabschiedung des Zuwanderungsgesetzes wird diese Tatsache anerkannt und heute vom Bundestag sowie in der nächsten Woche vom Bundesrat amtlich besiegelt.) (Deutscher Bundestag 2004: 10707)

On the other hand, Peter Müller, a leading Christian Democrat who had worked on the final compromise, insisted:

This act is an act for restricting immigration (*Zuwanderungsbegrenzungsgesetz*). It puts an end to the idea that Germany can be transformed into a multicultural immigration society.

(Dieses Gesetz ist ein Zuwanderungsbegrenzungsgesetz. Es macht Schluss mit der Vorstellung, Deutschland könne zu einer multikulturellen Einwanderungsgesellschaft umgestaltet werden.) (ibid.: 10723)

In this chapter, I shall explore these competing conceptions of the nation in relation to the new policies on migration and integration in Germany and Austria, focusing on two principal questions: first, why is proficiency in a single 'national', 'legitimate' language invoked as the touchstone of social cohesion and integration in these societies, and secondly, what do the language requirements enshrined in these policies represent? I shall begin by outlining briefly the main relevant features of the two policies, and then discuss the ideological effects of these measures in terms of the respective official discourses of migration in the two states.

Regulating migration through language: the German *Zuwanderungsgesetz* and the Austrian *Integrationsvereinbarung*

The new Immigration Act in Germany – which came into effect on 1 January 2005 – was preceded in 2000 by the reform of the law on citizenship rights (*Staatsangehörigkeitsgesetz*), which introduced a qualified version of the *jus soli* (principle based on place of birth) in addition to the more restrictive *jus sanguinis* (principle based on descent). According to the new law, children of foreign parents born in Germany after 1 January 2000 automatically qualify for German citizenship as long as at least one of their parents has been living legally in the country for eight years or more. Adults are now entitled to apply for citizenship after eight years' residence in Germany, instead of after 15 years as had previously been the case, but they must have an 'adequate knowledge of German' and declare their allegiance to the German constitution. Following debates at the drafting stage on the possibility of dual citizenship, a compromise formula was established, according to which anyone holding citizenship of another state in addition to German citizenship must choose one or the other by their 23rd birthday. The liberalization of the law was intended not to facilitate, let alone encourage, further immigration, but rather – in the words of the Interior Minister Otto Schily – as 'a contribution to internal peace in Germany' (einen Beitrag zum inneren Frieden), since 'for us, it is above all about integration' ([u]ns geht es vor allem um die Integration) (quoted in Fietz 1999). What is meant by integration, though, is not always clear and I shall come back to this: it has become a key but hotly contested concept in discourses of migration and citizenship in Germany and Austria in recent years (see, for example, Gould 1998).[4]

There were repeated calls at the time from the conservative opposition parties not to relax the conditions for entry into Germany but rather, on the contrary, to restrict further immigration and at the same time to develop a clear integration policy for those foreigners already in the country. Jürgen Rüttgers (Christian Democrat), for example, insisted in an article in *Die Welt*:

We must ensure that those who live here speak German. We must make sure that there are no classes in schools in which more than 50% of the children are foreigners. We must see to it that young foreigners in Germany receive training. We must make sure that there are no ghettoes in our cities, which lead to social conflicts.[5]

(Wir müssen dafür sorgen, dass diejenigen, die hier leben, die deutsche Sprache sprechen. Wir müssen verhindern, dass es in den Schulen Klassen gibt, in der mehr als 50 Prozent Ausländerkinder sind. Wir müssen dafür sorgen, dass ausländische Jugendliche in Deutschland eine Lehre machen. Wir müssen verhindern, dass es in unseren Städten Ghettos gibt, die zu sozialen Konflikten führen.) (Fietz 1998)

A report on the position of families of foreign origin, prepared by an independent commission and delivered to the government in October

2000, stressed the same themes but emphasized what its authors saw as the positive contributions of the families to the process of integration. The government's commentary on the report concludes with the following declaration:

> The Federal Government considers the targeted support of language learning an important means of achieving integration. It is planning for all immigrants who hope to attain the right to stay here a programme of language learning that is suited to their needs.... Integration is a long-term task and its success also depends on whether the German population helps foreign families to identify with the country and to find a new homeland (*Heimat*) here.

> (Die Bundesregierung sieht in der gezielten Sprachförderung ein wichtiges Mittel zur Integration der Zugewanderten. Sie plant für alle Zuwanderinnen und Zuwanderer mit Aussicht auf dauerhaftes Bleiberecht eine bedarfsgerechte Sprachförderung.... Integration ist eine dauerhafte Aufgabe und das Gelingen hängt auch davon ab, ob die deutsche Bevölkerung ausländischen Familien hilft, sich mit dem Land zu identifizieren und hier eine neue Heimat zu finden.) (Bundesregierung 2002d)

In later statements relating to the planning of the new immigration law, the principal objective of improving integration continues to be stressed and language proficiency identified as a major issue. For example, the Minister responsible for *Aussiedler* (ethnic Germans migrating to Germany from eastern Europe and the former Soviet Union), Jochen Welt, identified the key problems affecting the integration of *Aussiedler* as:

- Insufficient[6] or no knowledge of German amongst accompanying family members (in the case of more than 75 per cent of new arrivals)
- cultural distance from the indigenous population
- the difficult job market situation

(• unzureichende oder keine Deutschkenntnisse der mitreisenden Familienangehörigen (bei mehr als 75 Prozent der Neuankömmlinge)
- kultureller Abstand zur einheimischen Bevölkerung
- die schwierige Arbeitsmarktlage.) (Bundesregierung 2002a)

and set out a 4-point plan to tackle the causes of these problems, the first of which was the provision of substantial financial support for language learning (859 million DM in 2001). However, the new policy included a stick as well as a carrot: the new immigration law was to specify a language test for the families of *Aussiedler*, and Welt made it clear that he anticipated this would act not only as a means of improving integration for those already in Germany, but also as a deterrent for those who might be contemplating applying for entry to the country (see also Bundesregierung 2002b). Language proficiency was therefore to be at the heart of the twin-track policy: 'Whoever demands better integration of *Aussiedler* must say yes to immigration control and to the support of integration' (Wer eine bessere Integration der Aussiedler fordert, der muss ja zur Zuwanderungssteuerung und Integrationsförderung sagen) (Bundesregierung 2002a).

The original version of the law was not entirely new, but rather a radical rewriting of existing law, introduced according to government statements to address three main aims (Bundesregierung 2002b):

- to control and restrict immigration in relation to the integration capacity of the Federal Republic;
- to meet Germany's economic and job market interests but also to meet our humanitarian commitments and our obligations under international law;
- to recruit highly qualified personnel for jobs that in spite of high domestic unemployment cannot be filled at the moment; this will create new jobs and increase the competitiveness of the German economy and German science.

(• um Zuwanderung unter Berücksichtigung der Integrationsfähigkeit der Bundesrepublik Deutschland zu steuern und zu begrenzen;
- um den wirtschaftlichen und arbeitsmarktpolitischen Interessen Deutschlands gerecht zu werden, aber auch unseren humanitären und völkerrechtlichen Verpflichtungen nachzukommen;
- um hochqualifizierte Arbeitskräfte für Arbeitsplätze zu gewinnen, die trotz hoher Arbeitslosigkeit im Inland derzeit nicht besetzt werden können; dies schafft neue Arbeitsplätze und erhöht die Wettbewerbsfähigkeit der deutschen Wirtschaft und Wissenschaft.)

The decisive factors guiding the new policy were the concept of the 'capacity for integration' (*Integrationsfähigkeit*) on the one hand, and Germany's economic interests and the demands of the labour market on the other. The overall aims were to reduce the absolute number of immigrants while giving priority to highly skilled personnel required to plug the skills gap in the German job market. Language is again identified as one of the key issues in the current circumstances; among the problems the law was expected to address were these (Bundesregierung 2002b):

- young foreigners up to the age of 16 join their family members in Germany without linguistic knowledge or useable training;
- many foreigners have little or no knowledge of German;
- supporting measures for integration, such as language learning, are neither sought nor adequately provided.

(• Jugendliche Ausländer ziehen ohne Sprachkenntnisse und verwertbare Ausbildung bis zum Alter von 16 Jahren zu ihren Ange-hörigen nach Deutschland;
- Zahlreiche Ausländer verfügen über keine oder unzureichende Sprachkenntnisse;
- Integrationsleistungen, wie Spracherwerb, werden weder gefordert noch hinlänglich gefördert.)

The Immigration Law was passed by the Bundestag and ratified by the second chamber, the Bundesrat, in March 2002. It was due to come into effect on 1 January 2003, but on 18 December 2002 the Constitutional Court declared it null and void due to incorrect voting procedures in the Bundesrat. It was only after protracted negotiations in the Mediation Committee (Vermittlungsausschuss) of the Bundestag that a revised version was finally agreed and re-presented to parliament in July 2004. It was announced as Interior Minister Schily's 'flagship project', which he hailed as representing 'the most modern immigration law in Europe' (das modernste Zuwanderungsrecht Europas) (Bundesregierung 2002e) and which he declared to be 'a historic turning point' (eine historische Wende) because 'we recognize that we have, and will continue to have, immigration'[7] (weil wir anerkennen, dass wir Zuwanderung haben und weiter haben werden) (Schily 2004). It contains statutory provisions for language instruction and so-called orientation courses, the costs of which are largely to be borne by the government. Basic and advanced language courses will last approximately 300 hours each and in each case the course is to be completed within one year. The orientation courses, covering aspects of Germany's legal system, culture and history, will last 30 hours and will be taught in German following completion of the advanced language course. All foreigners who intend to take up permanent residence in Germany have an *entitlement* to participate in these courses. However, they will be *obligatory* for all those who do not know German, and 'sufficient' knowledge of German and of the legal and social system will be a condition for the granting of the right of permanent residence. As the government statement puts it: 'Failure to participate will have consequences for the right to stay in the country' (Der Verstoß gegen die Teilnahmepflicht hat aufenthaltsrechtliche Auswirkungen) (Bundesministerium des Innern 2002).

One of the most contentious issues in the negotiations over the redrafting of the new law concerned questions of national security in the wake of the Iraq War and terrorist attacks in Spain and elsewhere in the early months of 2004. Not surprisingly, therefore, the Government came under increasing pressure from the opposition parties to impose tighter constraints on migration into and through Germany. Although in this context the question of language proficiency may seem marginal, its potential as an instrument of social control brought it back to prominence in the negotiations. One clear consequence of this, for example, is the extension of the requirement to take the language and orientation courses to migrants who have been living in Germany for some time already (so-called *Bestandsausländer*) if they are deemed to be 'in particular need of integration' (*besonders integrationsbedürftig*).

Integration is also the key concept in the official discourse of migration in Austria, where the so-called 'Integration Agreement' (*Integrationsvereinbarung*) came into force on 1 January 2003. Here too the professed aim is 'to build a bridge between all people who live in Austria in order to enable them to live together in peace and understanding' (ein Brückenbau zwischen allen in Österreich lebenden Menschen, um ein friedliches und verständnisvolles Zusammenleben zu ermöglichen) (Austrian Government statement cited in Migration Online Austria 2002) and it is confidently asserted that:

> Through the creation of an integration agreement the provision of language learning opportunities in the educational sector will be reinforced, cultural and social cohesion will be promoted, fear and anxiety in the indigenous population will be reduced, social abuses will be contained, and opportunities for occupational development will be improved.

> (Mit der Schaffung einer Integrationsvereinbarung werden die Angebote zum Spracherwerb im Bildungsbereich verstärkt, das kulturelle und soziale Zusammenleben gefördert, Ängste und Sorgen der heimischen Bevölkerung abgebaut, sozialer Missbrauch eingedämmt und Chancen für eine Weiterentwicklung im beruflichen Bereich verbessert.) (ibid.)

These remarkable effects are promised on the basis of a 100-hour language course, that will cover the following areas:

- simple, basic knowledge of the German language for the purposes of communication and reading simple texts;
- everyday topics, bureaucratic procedures, knowledge about the country and citizenship, and
- basic values of the European value community.

(• einfache Grundkenntnisse der deutschen Sprache zur Kommunikation und zum Lesen einfacher Texte
- Themen des Alltags, Verwaltungsabläufe, Landes- und Staatsbürgerschaftskunde sowie
  Grundwerte der europäischen Wertegemeinschaft.) (Bundesministerium für Inneres 2002)

The course is obligatory for all new migrants (unless they can prove adequate knowledge of German), who will have to pay 50 per cent of the costs themselves (the other 50 per cent will be paid by the state or, in the case of so-called 'key workers', by employers). Furthermore, as in Germany, the requirement is backdated, so that it applies to all migrants seeking extension of their residence permits who have been legally in Austria since 1 January 1998. Again, as in Germany, the acquisition by foreign migrants of (a limited degree of) linguistic proficiency in German is regarded as critical for the achievement of social integration, and the emphasis of the new measures is clearly determined by economic and labour market requirements. The right to temporary residence, for one year, is granted only 'if a quota place is available and in response to demand in the regional job market' (im Falle eines vorhandenen Quotenplatzes und eines regionalen Bedarfs des Arbeitsmarktes) (Bundesministerium für Inneres 2002); and key employees of international organizations, amongst others, are exempted from the language course requirement (see: http://www.bmi.gv.at/downloadarea/fremdenwesen/Ausnahmen_Integrationsguide.pdf).

However, apart from the much shorter duration of the language course (100 hours, as opposed to 300 or 600 hours in Germany), there has from the outset been a significantly greater emphasis on enforcement in the Austrian policy, as sanctions apply if the courses are not completed within a strict schedule. Migrants who are required to take the course must do so within one year of receiving their temporary residence permit. If they fail to complete it successfully in this time, their permit will be extended, but if they do not complete the course within the next 6 months the state's contribution to the costs will be reduced from 50 per cent to 25 per cent. State support will be completely withdrawn if the condition has not been met by the end of the second year, and if the course has not been started by this stage a fine of 100 Euro will be imposed. This fine will be increased to 200 Euro if the course has not been completed after 3 years, and if it has not been *started* the residence permit will not be renewed. The final deadline is the end of the fourth year, when the permit will not be renewed unless the course has been completed (Bundesministerium für Inneres 2002; see also Smit 2002).

The Integration Agreement proposed by the centre- and far-right coalition government aroused widespread protest, not only on the part of the opposition in parliament but also amongst academic experts in language learning and many groups fighting discrimination and racism (see, for example, ' "Integrationsvertrag"? Nicht mit uns!' 2002; Boeckmann *et al.* 2003; ver*bal* 2002). And Eva Linsinger, in an article with the Foreigner Talk headline 'Du müssen integrieren' published in *Der Standard* (9 February 2002), argues:

> True to the tradition established by SPÖ [Socialist] interior ministers, 'integration' is defined only in terms of limitations for migrants, not also as a duty for Austria. Of course: linguistic knowledge is an important pre-requisite for integration, inadequate German is a serious barrier to integration. But it's not the only one....The ÖVP [the conservative Austrian People's Party] and the FPÖ [the far right Freedom Party] have failed to dismantle barriers to integration [e.g. lack of voting rights, restricted access to welfare rights and social housing] which the state had erected – and require foreigners to overcome the barrier of language.

> (Getreu der von SPÖ-Innenministern eingeführten Tradition wird 'Integration' nur als Beschränkung für Zuwanderer definiert, nicht auch als Pflicht für Österreich. Keine Frage: Sprachkenntnisse sind eine wichtige Voraussetzung für Integration, mangelndes Deutsch ist eine gravierende Integrationsbarriere. Aber eben nicht die einzige....ÖVP und FPÖ haben [aber] Integrationsbarrieren, die der Staat aufstellt, unverändert stehen gelassen – und verpflichten Ausländer, die Integrationsbarriere Sprache zu beseitigen.)

The ideological effects of language policies

Both the similarities and the contrasts between the German and Austrian laws are striking. Their motivation and principal purpose appears to be (the perceived need) to redefine the scope and scale of immigration. However, my interest here is not to evaluate the relative merits and demerits of the two policies, but rather to explore what seems to me to be a common underlying theme, which might be referred to as the 'post-nationalist' ideology of national languages (again, see also Piller 2001).

The issue I am concerned with, then, is not the importance of having access to the linguistic resources that are necessary for participation in political processes and engagement with social institutions: this I take to be axiomatic in any liberal democracy. What I want to focus on is the naturalization in political discourse of ideas about what constitutes legitimate forms of communication and expression. In this case, what this involves is the exposing of the established, 'common-sense' position that social integration depends on a unilateral effort of the incoming minority to learn the 'national' language of the state, as – in Gal and Woolard's term (2001b: 4) – a particular 'régime of representation'. This is, as they argue, especially important when 'the establishment of a "natural" phenomenon ... authorizes political programmes' [scare quotes added].

Recall here the repeated emphasis on achieving integration, above all through the acquisition by incoming migrants of a certain degree of linguistic proficiency in German. Whatever else may be understood by integration, therefore, it seems reasonable to assume that it is taken to mean 'the integration of migrants *into* the "host" community' and not the 'integration *of* migrants and the indigenous population', for the burden of action is placed solely on individual migrants – and little, if anything, is said about rights that may accrue to the individual, only the obligations imposed on them. Furthermore, if a particular degree of linguistic proficiency is essential for integration, why does this apply only to some migrants and not to others? Either it is, as official discourses appear to insist, a fundamental principle or it is not.

There is an alternative interpretation of these policies, however, that may account for their apparent contradictions. According to this view, reducing the observable evidence of otherness (as an irritant or affront to the singularity of the dominant monolingual majority) and re-asserting the authority of the majority through the sole legitimacy of 'its' language are more important than enabling or empowering the multilingual minority and fostering social integration based on recip-rocal accommodation of indigenous and immigrant populations: in other words, Otto Schily's apparent faux pas in an interview with the Süddeutsche Zeitung (Prantl 2002) – 'the best form of integration is assimilation' (die beste Form der Integration ist die Assimilierung) – may actually have revealed the real intention (and the appeal of this objec-tive to large parts of the German – not to mention Austrian – electorate probably helps to explain the rapid and vehement rebuttals from his SPD colleagues and Green Party members). This reading seems to me to be supported by at least three arguments.

First, in official statements relating to migration policy, such as those already referred to above, there seems to be a link – not explicit but implied through the collocation of comments on linguistic proficiency and other requirements for citizenship – between public commitment to German monolingualism and what Milroy (2001: 242), with some irony, calls 'democratic ideals and generally proper and civilized behav-iour': multilingualism is then not so much a hindrance to the social welfare of minority populations as a threat to the prevailing monolin-gual order. Secondly, the limited nature (especially in Austria) of the required language programmes has been attacked by teaching profes-sionals and others as inadequate and unrealistic (see verb*al* 2002), but it could be argued that a minimal proficiency is sufficient to meet the implicit aim of the policy: to embed in law and in the public conscious-ness the principle that knowledge of German is a necessary condition for citizenship – the ability of migrants to use German in order to exer-cise their rights as citizens (or even merely as residents) is of secondary importance. Even if the level of support for language learning in Germany is more realistic than in Austria, the recent emphasis on using linguistic proficiency as a tool for policing migration seems to lend weight to this view. Thirdly, the requirement to 'learn German' is specified in such a way as to emphasize the (written) standard variety. This reinforces the 'dogma of homogeneity' rather than promoting the purported objective of assisting integration into the practices of everyday life. At the same time, the migrants themselves are homogenized as a one-dimensional social category ('non-German-speakers'), which disregards their highly disparate linguistic starting points (for example, different degrees of literacy in their first language, different writing systems), and of course the new rules do not apply to EU citizens. Furthermore, while the legislation is silent on migrants' needs and desires to maintain their other languages there is an implication by omission that *this* kind of language loyalty is of no importance and maybe even suspect.

Conclusions

Postulating a necessary relationship between a 'national' language and citizenship seems anachronistic at a time characterized by moves away from the fixity of categories of nationhood and so forth. However, strong undercurrents of national forms of identification have not abated even in a time dominated by economic, political and cultural globalization – or rather, perhaps, precisely for that reason. This contemporary manifestation of linguistic nationalism operates at a more covert level than earlier forms: the converse of the 19th century project of constructing or legitimating nations, this seems to be a defensive reaction to the 21st century emergence of transnational and cosmopolitan communities.

In this context, of course, the discourse of English as *the* global language plays a key role. But English may be accepted as an instrument of policy in non-English-speaking countries (for example in university programmes or in multinational companies) to the extent that it is not perceived as a threat to national cohesion, because English is deemed to have been deracinated from any territorial *Heimat* and released from any national or cultural ties (see Brutt-Griffler 2002a). The incursion of other languages, however, is resisted precisely because they are inextricably associated with other national, ethnic or cultural traditions. What seems to be happening here, therefore, is the application of the subsidiarity principle to language: the claiming by national governments of the right to impose (a particular quality of) proficiency in a 'national' language as a form of resistance to the loss of national sovereignty. In the context of the turbulence and flux of contemporary social and political relations in Europe, it represents an attempt to preserve (rather than construct) a public (Gal and Woolard 2001b) that will remain strong and intact only so long as it is conceived as inherently monoglot.

Discourses of language and nation have then not been abandoned but rather recontextualized and reformulated in terms of the relationship between language and citizenship. The requirement to demonstrate competence in the 'legitimate' language of the majority population is represented in official discourses as a question of 'good faith' on the one hand (a sign of non-native speakers' willingness to relinquish or at least diminish their otherness and acknowledge the legitimacy of the majority), and of 'good governance' on the other (democratic practice requires equal ability to participate in processes of public discussion and debate). However, I have tried to outline an argument which claims that the underlying purpose of these representations is to re-assert an idea of the integrity of the nation still based on a stable monolingual norm that is increasingly contradicted by dynamic multilingual realities, and that they are more likely to hinder social inclusion than to promote it.

Notes

1. Ingrid Piller (2001) argues along similar lines in her critique of naturalization language testing in a range of contexts (including Germany). For a recent critical analysis of debates on language testing régimes in relation to citizenship in Britain, see Blackledge (2004).
2. In German texts, the term *Landessprache* is now frequently used to avoid unpalatable connotations of the conventional term *Nationalsprache*. In its exclusivity, however, it is no less debatable.
3. This distinction between 'nationism' and 'nationalism' was coined by Fishman (1968).
4. However, giving substance to the concept of integration has now been identified as a key objective of the newly founded Ministry for Migration and Refugees (see http://www.bamf.de/template/index_integration.htm).
5. Note the collocation of arguments, and especially their sequence, here – how linguistic proficiency heads the list that leads to social conflict via inadequate education and insufficient training posts.
6. No definition is offered of what is meant in this context by 'insufficient'.
7. Note that he uses the term *Zuwanderung*, now preferred in official migration discourses, rather than the older term *Einwanderung*: as Robert Gould (this volume) argues, *Zuwanderung* implies (temporary) migration while *Einwanderung* is taken to mean (permanent) immigration. The terms are therefore indexical of radically divergent discourses and political positions.

Primary sources

Integrationsvertrag? Nicht mit uns!" ' (2002) http://www.illegalisiert.at/ANAR/ integrationsvertrag/index.htm

Bundesministerium des Innern (2002) Übersicht der Neuregelungen des Zuwanderungs-gesetzes http://www.bmi.bund.de/dokumente/Meldung/ix_m76106.htm

Bundesministerium für Inneres (2002) Integrationsvereinbarung http://ln-inter1.bmi.gv.at/web/bmiwebp.nsf

Bundesregierung (2002a) Stärkere Integration von Aussiedlern http://www.bundes-regierung.de

Bundesregierung (2002b) Fragen und Antworten zum Zuwanderungsgesetz http://www.bundesregierung.de

Bundesregierung (2002c) Bundeskabinett beschließt Integrationskurse im Rahmen des Zuwanderungsgesetzes http://www.bundesregierung.de

Bundesregierung (2002d) Familien ausländischer Herkunft in Deutschland http://www.bundesregierung.de

Bundesregierung (2002e) Bundesregierung wird Zuwanderungsgesetz erneut in den Bundestag einbringen http://www.bundesregierung.de

Deutscher Bundestag (2004) Stenografischer Bericht. 118. Sitzung. Plenarprotokoll 15/118. http://dip.bundestag.de/btp/15/15118.pdf

12
The European Paradox: Swiss Discourses of Identity Between Dependence and Xenophobia

Robert Gould

The goal of this chapter is to demonstrate how the discourses of globalization and security have invaded that of identity and immigration, how foreigners are presented and operationalized within this mingling of discourses, and finally to comment on some of the implications of the overlapping of these different discursive practices.

Introduction

Although interlingual (dealing with material in both French and German), the following analysis is intrathematic in that it will analyze examples of the discourse of identity and immigration in the official political sphere in Switzerland. By 'official political' I mean written texts issued by political parties or a minister of the federal government. Thus they represent material which is not 'deniable' and which forms, as the case may be, an important link or a starting point in a chain of communication seeking to influence the outcome of a referendum and a federal election within a three-year period. The analysis will concentrate exclusively on a small corpus of Swiss texts; however, as language and discourses cross political boundaries in Europe, and as many of the social, economic, and political circumstances related to identity and population movements experienced by Switzerland are not particular to that one country, occasional references to similar linguistic phenomena in neighbouring countries will be made.

The texts in question are, first, the written text of a speech by Ruth Metzler-Arnold, the Federal Minister of Justice and Police (Cheffe du Département fédéral de justice et police). It was given in French at her party's congress (Parti démocrate-chrétien/Christlichdemokratische

Volkspartei, PDC/CVP) in Delémont, six weeks before the referendum of 24 September 2000 proposing a constitutional amendment to restrict the proportion of foreigners in the country to 18 per cent of the total population. Secondly, the chapter will examine the election manifestos for the 2003 federal elections issued by the four political parties represented in the Federal Council (i.e. the collective executive of the country, the cabinet). The parties are the Parti démocrate-chrétien/Christlich-Demokratische Volkspartei, Schweizerische Volkspartei/Union démocratique du centre (SVP/UDC), the Freisinnig-demokratische Partei/Parti radical-démocratique (FDP/PRD), and the Sozialdemokratische Partei der Schweiz/Parti socialiste suisse (SPS/PSS). The statements are important and authoritative components of a widespread discourse at the national level and concern questions in the forefront of political and popular discussion not only in Switzerland, but also in many of the countries of Europe. To examine this discourse more broadly even for Switzerland is not possible within the scope of this chapter, but by their very nature the texts selected are coherent on at least two planes: they are drawn from the mainstream of political life in Switzerland representing parties which together have the support of a significant majority of the electorate, and they demonstrate efforts by the same parties to influence electoral behaviour by linking their appeals to common topoi.

As part of the pragmatic background it is important to recognize that both the Office fédéral de la statistique and the business-oriented foundation Avenir Suisse have, among others, publicly stated the necessity of immigration to maintain the economic viability of Switzerland (Office fédéral de la statistique 1996, Münz and Ulrich 2001). In addition to the occasional trans-border references to be mentioned, two further European discourse dimensions have to be incorporated in order to be able to provide a fuller picture of the elements at play. I shall refer to changes recently observed in the post-cold-war security discourse of NATO and to the Europe-wide discourse of globalization and competition in the business sphere, which also influences the way in which the state is conceptualized. It will not be argued that there is a direct cause-and-effect relationship between the shifted security discourse emanating from NATO. However, the topoi observable in connection with non-citizens are such that the view will be presented that there is now an interpenetration of the new security discourse with the migration and foreigner discourse.

One fundamental point to be made clear, is that the discourse is really not about immigration in the normal English sense of the term. In my view what is present here is a labour-market and foreigner management discourse, underlined by its being based on the idea of the commodification of workers frequently, or even normally, referred to in terms of their abilities rather than as persons, e.g. 'die besten Köpfe', 'Arbeitskräfte', 'des personnes hautement qualifiées (dont on a un urgent besoin)', or as 'Zuwanderer' (the best brains, members of the workforce, highly-qualified persons (whom we urgently need), (im)migrants) in purely economic terms for the benefit of the autochthonous in-group.[1] The negative results of the two referenda on 26 September 2004 on proposals to place the naturalization process under federal (rather than cantonal or local) control in order to facilitate the acquisition of citizenship by 'foreigners of the second and third generation' demonstrate the extent to which the population as a whole is unwilling to consider even Swiss-born and permanently-resident foreigners as immigrants with facilitated access to citizenship.[2]

The post-Cold-War security discourse

What I wish to argue first is that elements in the Swiss (and European) foreigner-management discourse of the early twenty-first century reflect important features of the new European security discourse of the 1990's. NATO is a community representing shared European and North-American values which has come together to defend these values against whatever is perceived as threatening them. Its statements on its defensive mission in the circumstances at the end of the twentieth century are therefore part of a pan-European identity discourse. And one of the things I wish to suggest is that the national identity discourses within individual states (as represented by their political parties) are also becoming, in some measure, more pan-European – even when the parties are anti-EU, as in the case of the SVP/UDC, somewhat essentialist, as in the case of the CDU/CSU, or strongly pro-EU, as represented by the ÖVP.[3]

In the new NATO discourse the following elements are to be found (Schäffner 2002):

a) there is a 'danger'/'problem'/'challenge' which comes solely from outsiders, their values and their activities;
b) foreigners bring (organized) crime – and control the drug trade;
c) there are complex new risks arising from ethnic conflicts, economic breakdown, and political collapse;
d) there is the strong possibility of unchecked population movements; above all the movement of refugees, and these movements endanger internal social, financial, and political stability;

e) there is a direct security threat, i.e. open violence;
f) the danger/problem/challenge is now multi-polar.

Globalization discourse

The globalization discourse arose in the 1990s. On the surface, the globalization model represents an overcoming of the bi-polarity of the world present in the cold-war rhetoric. But underneath, there is also a competition model, multipolar – like that of the new security discourse, but here it is business against business, country against country. It contains such foundation concepts as 'competition', 'competitivity'[4] (Danthine n.d.; Teubert 2000; Wodak 2000) 'innovation', and in German 'Wirtschaftsstandort' or in French 'la place économique' (place for/of business) and the notion of unrestricted trade and movement of financial services across borders.

It contains also the representation of the state in business terms, by which I mean the repeated use of expressions such as 'la place industrielle et économique suisse' (Switzerland as a place of business) or the collocation of 'Schweiz' (Switzerland) (or 'Deutschland' or 'Österreich' (Germany, Austria) in the other countries) with 'Standort', 'Wirtschaftsstandort', 'Finanzplatz', and even 'Forschungsstandort' (place of business, economic centre, financial centre, research centre), where the latter refers particularly to research from a business perspective. One thus has a startling synecdoche of state and business, and, I would argue on the basis of some German party statements, even of nation and business.[5]

First I shall examine Ruth Metzler-Arnold's speech which, while given at a party congress, is aimed at the electorate as a whole. She was speaking as a representative of the Federal Council, presenting its viewpoint and recommendations to the country. Her speech clearly reflects the consensual political and business discourses of the period on this issue.

Switzerland in Business Discourse

The paramount point here is the naming of the country in purely business terms. The minister refers to 'la place économique suisse' (twice) 'la place économique et industrielle suisse', and 'notre place économique' – (Switzerland as a place of business, the Swiss business environment, our business environment). Business is the unifying feature which covers the disparate regions, languages, traditions, and confessions of Switzerland. The conflation of business environment for country in this speech is a particular example of a systematic practice on the part of the Swiss Government in public documents and pronouncements.[6]

The frequent use of the first person plural 'nous', 'notre' (we, our) in connection with the area of the Swiss economy and business activity confirms and reinforces the phenomenon just mentioned: business and the resulting prosperity are the principal and common characteristics of the confederation and the nation.

It is therefore fully consistent with the presentation of Switzerland predominantly as a business unit and through the conflation of party, people, and government resulting from 'nous' and 'notre', that the vast majority of *positive* references to non-Swiss are made in economic terms; and of these a significant number of references also uses the first-person plural: for example, 'ouvrir *nos* frontières à des personnes hautement qualifiées' (opening our borders to highly-qualified people) , and, *three times*, with only slight variations 'les étrangers hautement qualifiés dont *nous* avons un urgent besoin' (the highly-qualified foreigners we need badly). This repeated statement that 'we need...' with the implication that 'we' will permit them to enter, places the foreigners in the service of the controllers and beneficiaries of 'la place économique suisse'. The specific mention that non-EU and non-EEA nationals will be allowed in only if their presence is 'indispensable' makes the relation very clear. They are a group from whom economic advantage is to be gained.

A significant element in this business discourse is the mention of multinationals. Their presence in Switzerland is to be protected and their implantation encouraged. There is an unquestioning acceptance of a direct link between prosperity and multinationals, and consequently there is also an implicit argument that the more of them there are, the higher prosperity will rise. An *explicit* argument is that of the absolute flexibility of multinationals: they will go wherever labour market conditions suit them. This situation is presented as if it were a natural law. Consequently, the Swiss government has no choice but to obey this 'law' and to submit itself to the pattern of behaviour of the multinationals. The 'omnipotence' of multinationals is constructed as matched only by the 'impotence' of the nation state when faced with them. This view is not defended or argued. It is asserted as a fact. Consequently the explicit threat-topos (the multinationals will leave if you vote 'yes') is all the stronger. But to keep the multinationals in the country, there must be an adequate supply of skilled labour which Switzerland itself cannot provide.

The argumentation implicit in the speech is the following: a victory of the 'Yes' vote in the referendum will harm business and prosperity;

business and prosperity are the central and unifying characteristics of Switzerland; therefore to vote 'Yes' is an anti-Swiss act. This demonstrates the potential power of the conflation of the discourses of business (which is now inevitably global) and of national identity for an individual or party who knows how to use it. At first sight this might appear paradoxical, as it is often stated that globalization is leading to a reduction in the importance of individual nation states and that the discourse of business deconstructs these states (e.g. Wodak 2000). But on the level of rhetoric the reverse is the case.

Foreigners in Switzerland

The positive presentation of non-Swiss in the workforce is inseparable from the presentation of Switzerland as a prosperous business entity. Four other aspects need particular mention: refugees, anti-foreigner topoi, the terms for the presentation of non-Swiss, including the use 'étranger', and the discourse of 'integration'.

Refugees

These are presented in a discourse of a national humanitarian tradition and of international humanitarian responsibilities. However, on each occasion that refugees are mentioned, the statement is made that their stay is temporary and that, after the emergency has passed, they *will be* returned home (the passive voice is used, with all its implications). On one occasion a term is used drawn from the discourse of business: 'réinsertion'. Implicit in the argument is the view that refugees as a class cannot possess the qualities needed to be useful members of the Swiss population and workforce.

Anti-foreigner topoi

These are to be found at the beginning, the middle, and the end of the speech. The minister begins by referring to 'frequent' media reports of criminal acts committed by foreigners and continues with references to schools with a high proportion of foreign children, and to workplace insecurity resulting from the presence of foreign workers. By stating that the government (le Conseil fédéral) is aware of these 'fears and complaints' and takes them seriously, she gives governmental approval and credence to the reports. Similarly, the references at the end of the speech to the same topoi as were mentioned initially and to 'abuses of existing legislation' (which the government is curbing through the new Foreigners' Act, for which this minister is responsible) reinforce a negative image of foreigners. In addition, it must be noted that this is based on an *uncontested* negative representation of others and the exploitation of hostile topoi in the popular and media discourse on foreigners.

Foreigners

At the same time, it emerges that there are two classes of non-Swiss. The positively loaded group are those who are already contributing, or who in the future will contribute, to national and individual prosperity and the model of Switzerland as a prosperous business environment. It is clear that potentially these include *all* citizens of the European Union (and of the European Economic Area), to whom the right of abode and work in Switzerland will be granted after a transition period provided for in the treaties linking Switzerland to the EU and its member states. Only selected persons from other countries belong to this group if they fill an 'urgent need' in 'la place économique et industrielle suisse'.

This leads to the question of when is a non-Swiss not a 'foreigner'.[7] What I argue is happening here is a reduction of intra-European marks of distinction along lines which conform to the discourse of business and prosperity. The minister systematically makes a terminological distinction between 'étrangers' (foreigners) and 'ressortissants de l'UE' (nationals of the EU). Twice she says these 'EU nationals' will be admitted without further formalities or checks. Immediately following the second of these two examples, the term 'ressortissant' is employed for non-EU/EEA citizens, but in a context of significant positive representation: 'L'admission de *ressortissants* d'États non-membres de l'UE et de l'AELA sera strictement limitée à la main-d'oeuvre hautement qualifiée, dont l'engagement se révèle indispensable' (The admission of nationals of countries which are not members of the EU or EFTA will be strictly limited to a highly-qualified workforce whose employment is absolutely necessary). It appears that 'ressortissants' (nationals) with its accompanying social and economic upgrading is employed here because of these individuals' being 'hautement qualifiés'. Earlier, the minister had referred to '*personnes* hautement qualifiées recrutées dans des pays non-membres de l'UE ou de l'Aire Européenne de Libre échange' (highly-qualified *persons* recruited in countries not members of the EU or the European Free-Trade Area). Here, as they are 'highly-qualified' these foreigners become 'persons' or 'nationals', rather than 'étrangers' (foreigners). In this positive evaluation of their contribution to Swiss business and prosperity it is as if highly-qualified people from outside the EU become honorary EU or EEA citizens.

Integration

It is necessary to add to these analyses a brief consideration of the discourse of integration. 'Étranger(s)' (foreign, foreigner) is, with a total of 41 occurrences for 'étranger' and 6 for 'étrangère', after the plural pronouns 'we', 'us', 'our' (62 occurrences in total : 'nous' 38, 'notre' 15, 'nos' 9), the single most frequent word in the speech. The minister builds the whole speech round the structural opposition of 'them' and 'us'. One strand of the European identity- and foreigner-discourse is that of 'integration', a term without which no European political party (including those on the extreme right, who reject it) can function at present.[8] In this speech 'intégration' – used twelve times – is presented as a guarantee of social stability and harmony through the reduction of difference. Very briefly, its functions are the following:

1. It is intended to communicate the ability of the federal government to deal with the social tensions and problems arising from the presence of so many non-Swiss in the country;
2. It is central to the process of constructing an in-group and an out-group;
3. Although possessing a positive connotational function, it nevertheless also indicates that the established order and values shared by the in-group are threatened;
4. It is a legitimizing agent in a discourse in which difference and the primacy of the economic advantage of the in-group are central, as was also the case in Germany in the elections of 1998 (Gould 2000);
5. At the same time, it distracts from the issues arising from the admission by the minister that the federal government is not in control of population movements which are, she says, subject to the irresistible demands of the economy and the multinationals.

At the same time, one is able to see in this appeal to the public by the minister features of the shifted security discourse which had evolved in the 1990s, as also evidence of the globalization discourse. The former is represented principally by the representation of the threat to Swiss stability and identity coming not from foreign states but from foreign persons, who are linked to crime and who present problems arising from their alien values and behaviour patterns. And while a major part of the speech focusses on the labour market and its needs for the inward movement of skilled workers, it also incorporates xenophobic statements on foreigners, who in turn are linked to assertions of threats to domestic stability and wellbeing. The globalization discourse is present in the linking of Swiss identity to the business environment and the competition topos within the globalization discourse, and particularly to the mobility of large multi-national corporations which, it is asserted, will leave if their competitive position is threatened by a lack of sufficient highly-skilled labour. Thus the inward migration of labour is simultaneously both a necessity and a threat.

The Election of 2003

Migration

I am considering only the four parties already represented in the Federal Council and which were also likely to continue to form (and did continue to form) this joint executive at the pinnacle of the state. In the discourse(s) of migration and identity within the official party platforms, two general groupings are perceptible: the SVP/UDC on the one hand, and the remaining parties on the other. However, all parties accept the obligations of the existing treaties linking Switzerland to the EU, which, among other things, provide for free movement of labour after a transition period. Information will be drawn and evidence will be given from the German-language or the French-language versions of the manifestos indifferently, as there is no divergence between the two. This phenomenon indicates that, despite differences in attitudes and voting patterns in the target audiences, on the level of these written statements the discourse was uniform, at least for these two language groups which make up approximately ninety percent of Swiss citizens.

For the SVP/UDC the basic conceptualization contains two sharply opposed categories: Swiss and foreigners. 'Ausländer' and other terms relating to non-Swiss occur virtually exclusively in strongly negative collocations linked to the notion of their being a 'problem', to crime, to drugs, to their abuse of Swiss legislation (including that concerning asylum), and to their undesirability. This latter is expressed in repeated statements, particularly in the section 'Ausländerpolitik' (policy towards foreigners), that their numbers and proportion in the general population have to be reduced. And although the treaties guaranteeing free movement of people between Switzerland and the European Union are not contested, it is nevertheless stated that the development of inward movements of EU citizens has to be closely monitored (p. 13). This is consistent with the overt hostility to the EU by the party, particularly manifest in the section 'Cela fait longtemps que la Suisse brade sa liberté et son indépendance!'/'Der Ausverkauf von Freiheit und Unabhängigkeit hat längst begonnen!' (We/Switzerland has been selling off its freedom and independence for a long while) (pages 18 and 22 in the respective language versions).

The three other parties in the Federal Council, on the other hand, maintain a discourse which consistently avoids the frequent negative or hostile collocations of the SVP/UDC with respect to foreigners and migrants, and the SPS/PSS even avoids the use of the word 'Ausländer' (foreigners) entirely. Similarly, these distinguish between EU/EEA citizens and other foreigners, giving preference to the former.

On the question of inward migration, the SVP/UDC once more takes what is the extreme position among these parties. Their position can be summed up with their slogan, 'Arbeitskräfte ja, Zuwanderung nein', 'Main d'oeuvre étrangère oui, immigration non' (Workers yes, immigration no) (pages 12 and 40). They consistently avoid the neologism 'Zuwanderer', which in official documents in German normally means 'migrant' (i.e. a nominally temporary resident) as opposed to the permanent 'immigrant', and in its stead employ 'Einwanderer' five times (the older term, meaning 'immigrant' in the English-language sense) with total consistency in negative collocations linked to the topoi of crime or the use of willful deception to enter and remain in the country.

On the other hand, the other parties use 'Zuwanderung', 'Zuwanderer', and even 'Einwanderung' (migration, migrant, immigration). For the CVP/PDC the former occurs in collocations with 'beschränken'/'minimieren'/'Grenzen setzen'/'wird kontrolliert' (limit, minimize, set limits, is being checked) but all of these imply that there *will* be inward migration. The other parties used the terms in collocations indicating restrictions for those coming from outside the EU/EEA countries. The FDP/PRD speaks openly of inward migration even going so far as to use 'Einwanderung' and 'Einwanderer' (immigrant and immigration), but links this overtly and consistently to the development of Swiss interests, as an instrument for the promotion of prosperity (*passim*, pages 9–19 and 20). This theme of the promotion of Swiss prosperity is shared by the CVP/PDC and SVP/UDC. In the latter case, the commodification of such migrants is extreme. The employment of foreign workers is to be linked to the economic cycle, only temporary visas will be granted, and family members will be excluded. This will 'promote economic growth, without increasing migration': (Section 'Ausländerpolitik'/'Politique des étrangers', pp. 12 and 40).

On one important point there is consensus among three of the four parties: the representation of the national space in business terms. The SVP/UDC repeatedly uses 'Wirtschaftsstandort Schweiz' and 'Forschungsstandort', always in positive collocations, and with 'Forschungsstandort' including research being undertaken by business organisations. Even the SPS/PSS employs the term, as does also the FDP/PRD. Only the CVP/PDC avoids it, though repeatedly emphasizing its support of SMBs and 'eine innovative, gerechte und leistungsfähige Marktwirtschaft' (an innovative, just, and productive market economy: section 'Unsere Vision der Schweiz 2007' (Our Vision of Switzerland)).

Integration/security

For all parties 'Integration' represents a solution to a situation or 'problem', though this discourse strand contains very significant variations. For the SVP/UDC and CVP/PDC it is not developed at length: with the former it is restricted to the naturalization process, and with the latter to language acquisition as a social feature, and the facilitated naturalization of persons 'who have in fact have been Swiss for a time' (Section 'Unsere Kernforderungen in der Ausländerpolitik' (Our fundamental demands in the area of foreigners' policy). In fact, although within the same strand, these two positions are clearly opposed, as for the SVP/UDC naturalisation is always under local (municipal or cantonal) control and no appeal is possible after a rejection, while for the long-term residents mentioned by the CVP/PDC it is to be a process 'without bureaucratic hassle and significant obstacles'.

For the FDP/PRD the theme of security is incorporated into what is, among these parties, the most developed manifestation of this strand, totalling 19 occurrences of the term 'Integration'. This explicit association with security policy (and also with foreign policy) comes close to a direct association with the new security discourse. However, the incorporation into the discourse by this and two of the other parties of the theme of criminal activity and drugs reflects the same security concerns.

The SPS/PSS manifesto orients the integration strand around the needs of migrant women or parents and their children and refuses to employ the negative topoi of the other parties. It is also the only one to suggest that in the area of family unification non-EU citizens have at least the same rights as EU citizens. On the other hand, however, it does make a distinction between the two groups and emphasizes the EU/non-EU distinction.

Thus, while there is a harder position on the part of the SVP/UDC towards all non-Swiss, there is a tripartite (FDP, CVP, SPS) position on the preferential ranking of EU/EEA citizens, and a joint quadripartite position on the need for foreign labour for what the minister had earlier called 'la place industrielle et économique suisse'.

To come back for the moment to the initial hypothesis of the over-lapping of two discourses: Just as, previously, the North-American/ European realm of freedom and free enterprise stood in contrast to the eastern area of unfreedom and economic dirigism, so now the polarity is between the European and the business orientation on the one hand, and the extra-European threat to social, political, and civil values, exacerbated by the necessity of having *intra portas* an increasing contingent of foreign labour with a different value structure: or, at least, the discourse presents it as possessing a different value structure and insists on representing it as a 'problem'.

The presence in the current foreigner-management discourse of the mutated post-cold-war security discourse still functions in terms of keeping the state safe against intruders. The representation of the state in business terms in a globalized economy also means that the cold-war representation of international relations as contest is widened. It is a continuation of the struggle for survival – but by other means: commercial, rather than military.

Migration, National Identity, European Identity

This representation of Swiss existence as struggle for preservation of identity and prosperity leaves very little room for ethical considerations related to the deliberate recruiting of highly-skilled specialists from countries of the developing world. If one considers further this question of recruiting specialists within the logic of struggle and competition, then the following situation arises. When the 'foreign' community where the unwanted values originate is explicitly or implicitly represented as harmful or even hostile, then the act of weakening it by taking its best brains in order to support your own welfare – and to strengthen your own competitive position in the world – is certainly a positive act. No-one is saying this or dares say this, but it is an absolutely logical consequence of what IS being said. In addition, within the logic of the state or nation as business enterprise, just as it is in the insiders' interest to have as highly trained and flexible a workforce as possible, so it is also in their interest not to dilute the individual shareholder influence by increasing the number of shareholders (citizen voters) who have a voice in the affairs of the business, hence the resistance to automatic, or even facilitated, access to citizenship, as the failed referenda of 26 September 2004, mentioned at the beginning of this chapter, made unmistakably clear.

In her speech to the party and the public, and also in her German-language radio and television address on 9 September 2000 recommending rejection of the referendum question, and in the printed statements distributed at her press conference on 18 August 2000, the minister discursively constructed a homogenous national identity, that of prosperity resulting from intense, and globalized, business activity. But at the international level there can be no claim that this is the distinguishing mark of Swiss identity. Nor is any such claim made. On the contrary, it is this quality of prosperity, explicitly due to technological advancement and business activity, which identifies Switzerland with the EU member states and makes it politically and logically acceptable to open Swiss borders to EU citizens who, significantly, she never referred to as 'foreigners'. Consequently, what we have here is also the discursive construction of an EU identity and the reduction of national differences within Europe linked to prosperity resulting from intense business activity. With the four parties considered (though to a lesser extent for the SVP/UDC), the same practice of creating a systemic distinction between European (understood as EU-European plus EEA) and non-European is clear.

The integration strand of the political discourse of identity and immigration in Switzerland has been rendered necessary because of the inward migration in response to direct economic demand. Only in this way is it possible for parties and governments to reconcile what they present as the economic imperatives driving them with the need to create among the electorate the conviction that they are able to deal with social issues. Or, to re-state this, but from a slightly different point of view: a discourse of business which on one level deconstructs the role of the nation state (Muntigl, *et al.* 2000; Wodak 2000), is politically acceptable only if counterbalanced by one which asserts the state's ability to deal with social issues, particularly with questions of social cohesion.[9] The function is to persuade the electorate that the party (or government) can manage a situation which, because of the economic dimension, is outside the state's full control and places the country in a situation of dependence on outsiders.

As revealed in these brief analyses of authoritative texts, the situation in Switzerland demonstrates the fundamental paradox of need and suspicion perceptible also in the official political texts of its neighbours. No claim is made, and no inference should be drawn, that Switzerland is a particular case. The necessity of importing labour (particularly, though not exclusively, highly-skilled persons) in response to economic demand and changing demographics, and the realities of providing shelter for refugees conflicts with the self-image and value structure present by implication in large sectors of the population.

It is conceivable that this situation may have problematic results for Switzerland, as, for instance, the interpenetration of the discourses of security, business, and foreigner management as used both by a minister and by parties in the Federal Council gives heightened status and credibility to already existing anti-foreigner topoi; and it represents a hardening of the polarity European/non European. Furthermore, the political practice of verbally constructing or reinforcing this distinction based on the threat topos, incorporating elements of the new security discourse, and founded also in the competition model of the globalization discourse, does not augur well for social peace within any country attempting to deal with significant non-citizen populations, visible minorities, and economic and demographic shifts leading to labour shortages and economic difficulties.

Notes

1. For complementary information on the position of 'job market' and 'skilled labour' in the German and Austrian discourses, see Stevenson (this volume).
2. Each referendum, 'Über die ordentliche Einbürgerung sowie über die erleichterte Einbürgerung junger Ausländerinnen und Ausländer der zweiten Generation' and 'Über den Bürgerrechtserwerb von Ausländerinnen und Ausländern der dritten Generation', was defeated both by a majority of voters in the whole country and by voters in a majority of cantons.
3. When, for instance, statements are made across the political spectrum in Switzerland to the effect that EU/EEA citizens have free access to the labour market, or in Germany that 'since the Treaty of Maastricht EU citizens are no longer foreigners in the traditional sense' (CDU 2001, Section 3.4 'EU-Binnenmigration'), this represents a clear re-drawing of the conceptualizations of 'citizen'.
4. An extensive discourse strand of competition and competitivity is to be found in party manifestos, position papers, and coalition statements in Germany and Austria.
5. Quite explicit in the CDU/CSU manifesto for the 2002 Bundestag elections, and foreshadowed in the position paper in immigration published just one year earlier (CDU 2001 and CDU/CSU 2002).
6. This emphasis on the business dimension is to be found equally in the federal government's publicity brochures urging support for the May 2000 referendum on the treaties with the EU which is referred to by the minister.
7. See the shifting construction of 'foreigner' given in note 3.
8. The CDU position paper just mentioned has a long section devoted to this concept, significantly developing the term's semantic value and function in relation to their 1998 election manifesto.
9. For the German response to this, see Stevenson (this volume).

Primary sources

Christlich-Demokratische Union (2001) 'Zuwanderung steuern und begrenzen, Integration fördern. Beschluss des Bundesausschusses der CDU Deutschlands vom 7. Juni in Berlin'.

Christlich-Demokratische Union/Christlich Soziale Union (2002) 'Leistung und Sicherheit: Zeit für Taten: Regierungsprogramm 2002/2006. Unsere Projekte für Deutschland'.

Freisinnig-Demokratische Partei (2003) 'FDP. Im Einsatz für Freiheit und Verantwortung. Mehr Chancen für die Schweiz. Wahlplattform 2003 der FDP'.

Sozialdemokratische Partei der Schweiz (2003) 'Gleichheit, soziale Sicherheit und Lebensqualität! Wahlplattform der SP Schweiz für die eidgenössischen Wahlen 2003'.

Schweizerische Volkspartei (2003) 'Wahlplattform 2003 bis 2007'.

Union démocratique du centre (2003) 'Plate-forme électoral 2003 à 2001'.

13

Conducting Dissonance: Codeswitching and Differential Access to Context in the Belgian Asylum Process

Katrijn Maryns and Jan Blommaert

Introduction

One of the major inequalities in the field of communication is inequality in access to particular contexts. Context and contextualization, as we have learned from Gumperz and his associates, is the key to understanding and misunderstanding in social interactions. Codeswitching, Gumperz convincingly demonstrated, was a powerful contextualization cue, something which framed and directed people's interpretation of talk (Gumperz 1982a; Gumperz and Roberts 1991; Auer and Di Luzio 1992; Duranti and Goodwin 1992). Contextualization, we now know, is also not a purely 'automatic' or mechanical phenomenon; it is a social act that operates under the constraints of social life – power and inequality are always present. For example, Briggs (1997) has demonstrated how the circulation of discourse across contexts involves, creates and sustains power differences in the construction of a judicial 'case'. Consequently, access to particular contextual spaces allowing particular forms of (authoritative) interpretation, such as for instance legal or judicial-procedural contexts, appears to be an object of inequality, and contexts (as means for interpretation) appear to be unevenly distributed resources in communication (Silverstein and Urban 1996b; Blommaert 2001a). The point here is to understand the connection between contexts and epistemic domains on the one hand, and institutional regulation of access to and circulation through such contexts-and-epistemic-domains on the other. Control over particular contextual spaces involves the authority to formulate particular kinds of knowledge – the epistemic domains mentioned above. It also involves the power to involve or exclude others from formulating – indeed understanding – such kinds of knowledge, even if these kinds of knowledge affect others' lives. This will be the topic of this chapter.

We will discuss examples in which codeswitching as a contextualization cue offers opportunities to regulate access to particular contextual spaces. The data we shall discuss are institutional data from the asylum application procedure in Belgium.[1] Institutions such as those controlling asylum applications in Belgium, while overtly proclaiming an almost clinical neutrality and objectivity *vis-à-vis* all subjects treated by them, are marked by tremendous invisible inequalities and asymmetries, some of which are based on the differential control over access to contextual spaces as stated above. Due to the increasing bureaucratization of public institutions (already observed by scholars such as Gumperz and Cook-Gumperz 1982 and Fairclough 1989), we see an increase of the construction of *text trajectories* as central instruments of institutional practice (Blommaert 2001a). Subjects' individual stories become the input of a sequence of different entextualizations as the story – now turned into a 'case' – moves through the various stages of bureaucratic treatment. These stages of bureaucratic treatment involve sometimes far-reaching reformulations, rewordings and reframings of the original story, often involving momentous transitions in text-structure: from oral to literate, from casuistic and individual to standardized and categorizable, from plain language to jargon, and so on (Sarangi and Slembrouck 1996; Slembrouck 2003). Linguistic ideologies of standard and purity – Collins' (1996) 'textualism' – operate at all levels, and intricacies in structure and effect that may be present in oral storytelling can and do get lost in the construction of bureaucratic textual artefacts (a phenomenon well documented in the essays in Silverstein and Urban 1996a; also Haviland 2003). Stories are recontextualized, refocused and reorganized, and subjects, while still being treated as the 'author' of what has become a whole text trajectory rather than a single text, have hardly any control over the re-entextualization processes.

The problems facing asylum seekers, while being fundamentally similar to those facing every other subject of bureaucratic entextualization, are particularly grave. Asylum seekers often have to tell their stories in nonstandard varieties of languages or in languages that have to be translated by an interpreter. They often have to provide crucial contextual information that may remain unrecorded or is open to disqualification as irrelevant. And they very often face a system based on the presupposition of a literate subject, thus imposing conditions of documentation, precision and detail on people who come from illiterate or semiliterate backgrounds. Though none of this will be extensively discussed in this chapter, it is the backdrop against which the discussion here must be put (see Blommaert 2001b; Maryns and Blommaert 2001, 2002 for extensive discussions). Like in so many other domains of contemporary social life, language is a problem in the asylum procedure, and the denial of its complexity may be a source of rather fundamental, though often invisible, injustices.

The data we shall discuss involve three parties: African asylum seekers, Belgian officials (officers of the asylum application bureau or judges) and outside experts – lawyers assisting the asylum seeker and/or professional interpreters. The interview with the asylum seeker is conducted in a language of his/her choice, but the language of the procedure is in each case Dutch, one of the national languages of Belgium. The patterns that we shall discuss involve shifts in codes between African languages, English and Dutch.

Inclusion and exclusion through codeswitching

We shall discuss three sets of data from interview settings. In each of the cases, the applicant is supposed to provide facts to an official interviewer, using a particular language/code which fits the appropriate discursive practices, and with the target of constructing a record that can be 'fixed' and 'checked' to a certain extent, on the basis of established norms for assessing evidence and truthfulness in legal procedures. The asylum seeker has a degree of control in the sense that s/he is the sole provider of such evidence. S/he also has the right to tell the story in a language of his/her choice, and interpreters will assist him/her whenever appropriate or required. These are the 'rights' officially granted to applicants, and on the face of things these rights provide a degree of control over the event for the applicant.

What is beyond the control of the applicant, however, has to be situated at a much deeper level: the circulation of discourse, i.e. the links between the different discourses produced, the representation and the (de/re)contextualization of the discourse. In other words, 'control' is not simply a matter of accessibility to the required epistemic domains, the required narrative shape, linguistic resources, and so forth, but rather, the links between contextual domains might give birth to new meanings at much more complex and hidden levels. This covert control of the discursive processes can amongst other things be lodged in practices of conversational exclusion through code-switching. Such conversational exclusion entails exclusion from the process of linking up different contexts, which in turn affects the applicant's estimation of and control over his/her case.

Example 1

Here the conversational exclusion emanates from a sudden switch to Dutch. The interpreter (T), like the applicant (AS), is from Sierra Leone. T is fluent in English and Krio and has picked up French and Dutch during his stay in Belgium. As his Dutch is good, interaction between the interviewer (I) and T is in Dutch, rather than English. This in itself already results in conversational exclusion: the applicant (who also knows Krio and English) would have considerable control over the translation process Krio-English, which is not the case now. In the example here, there is confusion about the applicant's exact date of arrival in Belgium and therefore additional questions are asked. Yet, these are not contextualized for the applicant: the main concern here is that the applicant provides the appropriate missing information. The applicant is not informed about the assumed mistake in his file. He has no clue as to the importance attached to the question and answer, he is not informed about the particular status of this bit of information in the whole of his story.

The fragment can be divided into five segments, organized by shifts in participation framework. Each of the shifts is accompanied by a shift in code.[2]

DVZ 6: Brussels, Immigration Office
Interactants: applicant (AS), interviewer (I), interpreter (T)
Applicant's country of origin: Sierra Leone
Language: Krio, English, Dutch
Date: 30/03/01

Segment 1: AS – T (Krio)

　　AS: then they take me done go na house...Mende xx...
　　T: Mende xx
　　AS: yes...one hour...
　　T: ((writes down...))

Translation

　　AS: then they take me to my house...Mende (unclear)...
　　T: Mende (unclear)
　　AS: yes...One hour...
　　T: ((writes down))

Segment 2: T –I (Dutch)

I: hier staat toch den achtentwintigsten xxx
T: achtent ... ach = hier.
I: = zesentwinstigste ja nee nee nee nee nee negenentwintig heeft hij asiel
   aangevraagd en achtentwintig ... in België binnengekomen ... maar
   misschien is da een fout ...
T: 'k zal hem nog ies vragen ... urm welk datum staat daarop
I: zesentwintig

Translation

I: but here it says the twenty eighth xxx
T: twenty ei. oh eigh = here.
I: = twenty sixth yeah no no no no no twenty nine he asked for
   asylum and twenty eight ... arrived in Belgium .. but maybe that is
   a mistake ...
T: I will ask him once more ... urm what date is on it
I: twenty six

Segment 3: T-AS (Krio)

T: so the plane ... The plane na F na Freetown you take at the twenty
   six ...
AS: the helicopter
T: the helicopter sorry
AS: yeah
T: the twenty six xx na. this place
AS: yes
T: urm. the same twenty six now na this na this other place
AS: yes
T: and the same twenty six now you take the plane
AS: yes
T: na the other place you reach at the ... you reach now na Belgium ja xx
AS: the twenty seven

Translation

T: so the plane ... the plane to F to Freetown you took on the twenty
   sixth ...
AS: the helicopter
T: the helicopter sorry
AS: yeah
T: the twenty sixth xx to. this place
AS: yes

T: urm. the same twenty sixth now to this to this other place
AS: yes
T: and on the same twenty sixth no you took the plane
AS: yes
T: now the other place you reached on the...now you reached
    Belgium yah xxx
AS: the twenty seventh

Segment 4: T-I (Dutch)

T: ja...zo that's waarschijnlijk een fout...

Translation

T: yeah...So that is probably a mistake...

Segment 5: AS-T (Krio)

AS: = twenty seven
T: twenty seven...then you reach na x
AS: yes. xxxx day...I meet one black man. I ask
T: uhum uhum

Translation

AS: = twenty seventh
T: twenty seventh...then you reached x
AS: yes...xxxxx day...I meet a black man. I ask
T: uhum uhum

Note that the applicant appears to have a degree of awareness about generic expectations of precision and detail. In the beginning of segment 3, he corrects the interpreter ('the helicopter') and appears to insist on the correctness of details in the event narrative. The purpose of the questions from T, however, only becomes more or less clear as the questioning sequence unfolds and repeated emphasis is put on the dates of departure and arrival. The precise direction of the question, as well as the way in which it fits in the construction of the text-replica of his story (a word-processed report of the story – the next step in the text trajectory), is not flagged to AS; it is discussed in the segments 2 and 4, between I and T. Even if AS has gauged the importance of getting the dates right, the point does not seem to carry much weight in his own narration: he quickly moves on to the storyline he was developing earlier ('yes. xxxx day...I meet one black man. I ask'). Thus, the particular generic and procedural value of this bit of information is not made clear to AS.

Yet, chronological precision is of utmost importance in the asylum application procedure. Applicants are expected to tell a story which is temporally linear and coherent, which contains no contradictions in the sequence and descriptions of events, people, objects and places, and so forth. The reason why such insistence is made on the precise date of arrival is to establish whether AS produces contradictions or whether an error was made previously in recording the story. Knowing the status of such elements of narration in the procedural assessment of stories is a crucial ingredient of generic competence; in this case it is 'blackboxed' – rendered inaccessible to AS – by a shift from Krio to Dutch.

Example 2

In this case, like in the previous one, conversational exclusion is due to a switch from English to Dutch. The fragment can be divided into two segments: first the lawyer (addressed here as 'Meester', the Dutch honorific term for lawyers) and the interviewer discuss the applicant's case, after which the procedural spin-off of this discussion is immediately communicated by the interviewer and the lawyer to the applicant. The lawyer's plea, however, is not translated for the applicant, and AS has no access to the way in which his case is weighed and prospects are judged by I and L.

CGVS 10: Zaventem Airport
Interactants: AS, I, L (lawyer) and T.
Applicant's country of origin: Sierra Leone
Language: Dutch, English (language chosen by the AS)

Segment 1: I-L (Dutch)

I: ok ... Meester

L: urm als ik urm. samen met u ... het relaas. van mijn cliënt zo hoor dan. dan meen ik toch wel dat er urm dat. de Dienst Vreemdelingen- zaken toch wel een beetje snel op op zijn beslissing is overgegaan. urm zeker tot de ontvankelijkheid van die asielaanvraag dat er toch wel grondig onderzoek nodig is ... wat betreft de motieven van de Dienst Vreemdelingenzaken ... en dat hij niet veel zou weten omtrent ... zijn identiteit. zijn nationaliteit waar ie vandaan komt ... ik xx dat tijdens dit gesprek toch wel duidelijk is ge = urm graakt dat hij daar toch wel heel wat van afweet ...; van het land zelf van urm Sierra Leone. welke districten. welke talen er worden gesproken. enz. xxx. urm waarom hij het land heeft verlaten. urm xxx van de burgeroorlog xxxx urm ... goed urm hij kon een. hij kan de preciese datum geven omtrent zijn vertrek hoe lang hij. urm

I: uhum

L: hoe lang hij dus in in dat kamp heeft gezeten waar hij verbleef. in urm Guinea xxxx urm...

I: uhum

L: we kunnen dan nog natuurlijk niet verwijten urm een man die daar ergens urm. xxx maar toch in een urm onderontwikkeld land zit om alles te weten van in het land urm... daarop... [inaudible].
...

Translation

I: ok... Meester (LL.M)

L: if I urm... together with you... hear the account of my client then. then I really believe that urm. that. the Immigration Office has actually come to its decision rather quickly. urm I particular to the admissability of this asylum application that thorough research is actually really necessary... as to the motives of the Immigration Office... and that he would not know much about... his identity. his nationality where he comes from... I xx that during this conversation it yet has become urm clear that he actually knows a lot about it... of the country itself of urm Sierra Leone. what districts. what languages are spoken there etc. xxx urm why he has left the country. urm xxx about the civil war xxxx urm... right urm he could a. he could give the precise date of his departure how long he. urm

I: uhum

L: how long he actually was in that camp where he stayed. in urm Guinea...

I: uhum

L: we can after all obviously not blame urm a man who there somewhere urm. xxx but still lives in an urm underdeveloped country to know everything from within the country urm... therefore... [inaudible]
...

Segment 2: I-L-AS (English)

I: urm listen we'll examine your file... urm. very thoroughly. we'll discuss about it and will take a decision in the coming days... ok... we let you know our decision. by the end of the week or beginning of next week... ok...

L: next week yeah

AS:xx

I: = ok... thanks...

The lawyer's plea contains important statements on the way in which the applicant's story can be related to procedural and legal norms and expectations. It is a reformulation of the story in procedural and legal terms, and in terms of contextual orientation it orients towards the 'centre', i.e. towards those norms and expectations that will be decisive in judging the application. It is thus a new 'text', part of the complex trajectory the story of the applicant moves through. The applicant, however, is not incorporated in this centring exercise: the statement communicated to him in segment 2 is about the 'next steps' in the procedure, not about the way in which his case currently relates to judgments and assessments in the procedure. This, again, can be seen as crucial generic information: it is essential for AS to know how his story relates to what is expected from 'good' stories in the application procedure. Both the lawyer's arguments and the way in which the interviewer responds to them are crucial bits of information, from which he has been excluded by a narrowing of the participation framework through the shift from English into Dutch.

Example 3

In fragment 3, an applicant's case is heard by a judge of the Court of Appeal. Conversational exclusion here emanates from 'filtering' through translation: utterances produced by the judge are drastically rephrased or even simply omitted by the translator. In most cases the rephrasals or omissions concern ironic, doubtful and sometimes arrogant remarks by the judge, which are interpreted by the translator as 'asides not liable to translation'. In this way however, the applicant is no longer capable of estimating and judging the assessment of the judge and hence the evaluation and interpretation of his story. There are three segments in this fragment. The first segment is a statement by AS on the 'absence of phones', translated by T. Segment 2 is a cross-examination started by I. I begins by interrogating AS on the size of the place referred to earlier, and after AS's response she comments extensively, expressing disbelief. Segment 3 starts with AS reiterating what to him is the main point: the absence of phones. This leads to a reinvigorated expression of doubt from I, who now confronts AS's claim about the difficulties of reaching the SDF with the ease with which Belgian authorities could contact that organization.

VBC 5: Brussels, Court of Appeal
Interactants: AS, I (judge), L and T.
Applicant's country of origin: Cameroon

Language: English, Dutch
Date: 04/05/01

Segment 1

AS: there's no telephone in C. xxx
T: er is geen telefoon in C. zegt ie...

Translation:

AS: there's no telephone in C. xxx
T: there is no telephone in C. he says...

Segment 2

I: hoe groot is C.
T: how big is C.
AS: sorry
T: how big. is. C.
AS: just an urm small district...Yeah xx
T: het is een klein district zegt ie
I: maar hoe groot is dit
T: but how big is it
I: hoeveel mensen leven er
T: how many people are living there. roughly
AS: xxxx I can't remember of people living in C...xx there are so many villages in C. I cannot really...urm
T: hij kan dat nie urm
AS: know the population...
I: zo klein is het ook niet. ze hebben een school. een middelbare school...xxx dus het moet al een centrum zijn...middelbare school. een ziekenhuis...dus het is niet een urm...klein urm dorpken in de brousse he...ur zegt u spreekt daar over iets dat...urm. dat al centrum is en dat er daar geen telefoon is...
T: she says urm it cannot be that small they have. urm a secondary school they have a hospital..it cannot be that that small and urm when you say there is no telephone there well...

Translation

I: how big is C.
T: how big is C.
AS: sorry
T: how big. is. C.
S: just an urm small district...Yeah xx

T: it is a small district he says

I: but how big is this

T: but how big is it

I: how many people are living there

T: how many people are living there. roughly

AS: xxxxx I can't remember of people living in C... xx there are so many villages in C. I cannot really... urm

T: he cannot urm

AS: know the population...

I: it is actually not that small. they have a school. a secondary school... xxx so it must already be a centre... secondary school. a hospital... so it is not an urm... tiny little town in the bush hen (?)... you say you talk there about something that... urm. that already is a centre and that there is no telephone there...

T: she says urm it cannot be that small they have. urm a secondary school they have a hospital... it cannot be that that small and urm when you say there is no telephone there well...

Segment 3

AS: yeah there is no telephone in C.

I: nee

T: er is geen

I: = geen telefoon in C. en het is onmogelijk om om de S = SDF te contacteren.. ik bedoel wij hebben het zo eenvoudig om de mensen van het SDF te contacteren te e-mailen te bellen te faxen... en en de SDF leden zelf kunnen dat niet en en bij ons gaat dat in een in een wip en een draai ik bedoel. dat is toch xxx

T: she says ah it's it's not possible to contact the SDF whereas they have it very they can very easily contact the SDF by e-mail. urm by telephone it's and members actual members of the SDF cannot contact urm their party urm that's very strange...

Translation

AS: yeah there is no telephone in C.

I: no

T: there is no

I: = no telephone in C. and it is impossible to to contact the S SDF... I mean we can so easily contact email or fax the people of the SDF... and and the SDF members themselves cannot do that and and we can do it in a skip and a jump I mean. that is rather xxx

> T: she says ah it's it's not possible to contact the SDF whereas they
> have it very they can very easily contact the SDF by e-mail. urm by
> telephone it's and members actual members of the SDF cannot
> contact urm their party urm that's very strange...

The judge's utterances are packed with affect expressions marking
doubt and disbelief (as well as revealing gross ignorance of living conditions in parts of subsaharan Africa), and again we see how factual parts
of the applicant's story are oriented towards 'centring' norms and
expectations of truth, likelihood and veracity. To put it simply: the
judge assesses elements from the story using her own Belgian social
(hence, middle class) common sense as a yardstick for truth, likelihood
and veracity. From this vantage point, it is unlikely that *there is no phone*
in a place where there is a school and a hospital. It may, however, not
be so unlikely that someone like the applicant *does not have access* to
a phone in a place where there is a school and a hospital.

The difference between both issues is due to the direction of contextualization. If one accepts the Belgian middle class cultural norms and
customs as a yardstick, the story becomes unlikely; if an effort is made
to imagine living conditions in Cameroon, and if some attention is
given to the particular forms of expression produced by AS (which are
clearly the product of incomplete competence levels in English: *there is
no phone* may well mean *I couldn't use a phone*), then the story becomes
more plausible. In both cases, the direction of contextualization determines the interpretation of the story, and this is crucial for AS to understand. We notice, however, how T reduces the judge's utterances to bare
reported speech focused on propositional content, not the directions of
contextualization that determine the evaluation of the applicant's
story. The latter are articulated in Dutch, but get lost in English.

Discussion

Shifts from one code into another control and organize shifts in
participation frameworks in each of these cases. In each of these cases,
however, such shifts also involved important shifts in domain and genre,
from unique event narrative to standardized procedural interpretation,
from one focus of contextualization (the local context of the story) to
another (the norms and expectations valid in the asylum procedure).
Particular forms of interpretation went hand in hand with particular
forms of distribution of such knowledge, by means of conversational
closure through codeswitching.

Codeswitching thus marked a transition from one Foucaultian *'pouvoir-savoir'* into another: it marked a transition in domains of knowledge and domains of power. The shift in epistemic frame was conditioned by a shift in participants, and the transition from anecdotal, isolated bits of knowledge to procedurally interpreted and evaluated knowledge was also a transition from individual to institution. This shift was accomplished by means of conversational closure, something that could only be accomplished by the institutional side in this communication process. The asylum applicant needs to be maximally transparent and inclusive in his/her talk; however, the institutional partners could withdraw from time to time from interaction with the applicant, in order to establish the procedural, legal or epistemic validity of the applicant's story. Thus, the way in which this story was injected into other phases of the text trajectory – institutional interpretations and evaluations, re-entextualizations of all sorts – was blackboxed. However, the question is to what extent the institutional partners themselves conceptualize their interactional behaviour in terms of blackboxing practices and power moves. Increasing pressure to force up the procedure prioritizes any time-saving initiative and hence legitimizes interactional moves such as the quick settlement of procedural discussions by switching to one's first language and the omission of what is considered 'redundant translation'. Moreover, these interactional moves have taken on the shape of behaviouralized practices by which any awareness of the potential effects of interactional textuality has disappeared (Silverstein 1997). In other words, the institutional partners no longer realize, let alone question, the way in which they potentially affect the degree of the applicant's control over the case.

This on the one hand demonstrates the increasing complexity of modern bureaucracies in a globalized environment, where intricate plays of territorialized and deterritorialized symbols and forms of expression become the rule rather than the exception. To put it simply: it demonstrates the increasing complexity caused by multilingualism in bureaucratic environments where monoglot ideologies of language and communication are dominant (Silverstein 1996, 1998). On the other hand, it illustrates for the umpteenth time the ways in which language, apparently more so than other symbols and tools, can have the effect of indexing and organizing such fissures and tensions. Contemporary systems of power display a predilection for language regimes – linguistic, generic, pragmatic – as instruments of organizing asymmetries and inequalities. Procedures of contextualization are based on socially and politically sensitive indexicalities, and linguistic-communicative differences are thus not only used to procure 'linguistic-referential' interpretations, but also evaluative aspects of interpretation involving forms of categorization that have effects on people's life chances (Gumperz 1982a).

The power thus exerted is minuscule but effective. It is what Foucault called 'capillary' power, power organized at the extremes of the system, through habituated patterns of behaviour such as language choice, codeswitching and shifts in participation framework, none of which appear as explicit or remarkable manifestations of power. This may be the end of the innocence of multilingualism as a feature of globalization and multiculturalism: the awareness that language is the prime organizer of discrete, often invisible power differences in environments where the absence of power and the prevalence of rights are advertized as house culture. The phenomenon should be well understood by now: whenever claims are made about semiotic-communicative standardization as a tool for safeguarding equality and respect for differences, precisely the opposite may happen.

Notes

1. Fieldwork was conducted at the Belgian asylum authorities in Brussels over a period of 10 months (October 2000–July 2001). The field transcripts have been selected from interviews between asylum seekers and institutional partners at the three institutions making up the Belgian asylum procedure, viz. the Immigration Office (DVZ in the transcript), the Commissioner-General's Office for Refugees and Displaced Persons (CGVS) and the Higher Commission of Appeal (VBC). Maryns (2004) provides an extensive discussion of the whole of the application procedure.
2. Transcription symbols used in these examples are: /for an intonationally marked clause boundary, dots for pauses, = for overlaps and *x* for unclear parts of the utterance. For each segment the code used is given between brackets. For the transcription of Krio and Dutch respectively English and Dutch orthography are used.

14

Multilingual Migrants and Monolingual Teachers: The Discursive Construction of Identity in a Flanders Primary School

Massimiliano Spotti

Introduction

As a result of politically, economically and socially motivated migration, which started in the seventies, Belgium has undergone a considerable demo-linguistic change. Flanders, the Dutch speaking part of Belgium, is no exception to this (see, Ramaut 1998; Verlot and Delrue 2004). While for those immigrants who belong to Western European groups there has been a form of integration within the mainstream culture, a strong case for social (and linguistic) integration still needs to be made for non-western minorities, such as the Turkish and Moroccans (Blommaert and Verschueren 1998). This is also seen in the ambiguous attitude toward minority communities which emerges from the analysis of Flemish educational policy documents. These, in fact, while calling for the preservation and nurturing of group identity and community languages, are in sharp contrast with a minority perspective which demands that minority community members recognize and respect the values and norms of mainstream society, that is, acceptance of cultural boundaries, without being included in them (see, Verlot 2000; De Caluwe *et al.* 2002). Such discrepancy is also perceived in the native – allochtonous divide present in the way the education system refers to pupils drawn from minority groups, their community languages and their teaching within the mainstream school system.[1] Moreover, research makes clear that the presence in the classroom of pupils with a home language other than or alongside Dutch may present a challenging phenomenon to the pedagogic and professional knowledge of teachers with a monolingual background (Bezemer 2003) as well as to the smooth running of classroom conduct during Dutch language lessons (Jaspaert and Ramaut 2000) or to the classroom's language norms (Ramaut 2000). It is also shown (Hunter 1997) that teachers' construction of students' identities in the learning environment is based on reified concepts of ethnicity and proficiency in the language of the majority. These concepts can vary from the students' investment in very different social identities from those actualized through the speaking of the local vernacular or of a community language.

It is in this context that the present article investigates the '(discourse) models' (Gee 1999; Holland and Quinn 1987; Wieder and Pratt 1990) that inform the categorization process through which a recently qualified monolingual Flemish primary school teacher constructs the social identities of immigrant minority pupils in the socio-cultural space[2] of a 5th Grade primary classroom. The theoretical framework that informs the reasoning behind my work will be explained first, followed by my research strategy. I will also give a picture of the city, of the school and of the community languages used by the 5th Grade pupils. I will then move on to present the analysis and interpretation of the teacher's discourse practices, drawing on the construction of pupils' identities.

Social categorization and identity forming

Even though space constraints do not allow for a full discussion, the theoretical lineage I have chosen presents identity as a social product commonly referred to as 'social identity' indicating how a person is categorized within a social environment (Verkuyten 1999). In this respect, category forming – understood as an overarching mostly spontaneous process helping people to make sense of the world around them (Verkuyten 1992) – is at the basis of how social identities are constructed. For a person to form categories, s/he has to have parameters through which people are assigned to a particular group depending on the social context examined. These parameters resulting in 'story lines, families of connected images or (informal) theories stored by people belonging to specific socio-cultural groups' (Gee 1999: 43) are called 'models'. As Aitchison puts it (2002: 5):

> Cultures make sense of the world by building an interlocking set of mental models: some of these are culture specific, others spread across several cultures, others still are universal. 'Good' models achieve cultural resonance and avoid cognitive dissonance: they therefore give the impression of being obvious and timeless.

These models are expressed through verbal and/or written code called 'discourse'. Discourse is therefore authored, issued and authorized by multiple agents that may be either an institutional body producing macro-discourses and/or individuals producing micro-discourses in their social interactions (see, Cherryholmes 1988). For instance, the models that words like 'autochtonous pupil' or 'allochtonous pupil' enact are inserted within a country's macro educational discourse. These, in turn, may be re-formulated and used by educators in informing their pedagogic choices and actions during micro-interactions at classroom level, thus leading them to categorize pupils as belonging to one group or another (see, Koole and Hanson 2002). In order 'to have' a social identity, people have to be constructed as part of a socio-cultural space respecting therefore those 'accepted associations among ways of using language, thinking, acting, valuing and interacting, in the right places and at the right time' (Gee 1999: 43). However, at the moment in which these conditions are not matched, identity negotiation comes into play, social identities become therefore 'a sense of self in relation to others creative of and creative by agents' responses to social forces' (Weis 1990: 1).

Research strategy

The present study adopts a general research framework, based on an ethnographic interpretive approach (Erickson 1986). This follows three pragmatic rules: openness of the researcher, openness of the subject of research and openness of perspectives when analyzing the data emerging from the socio-cultural space used in the research. The general methodology employed is a heuristic one trying to gather from multiple perspectives – that is., teachers, pupils and classroom interactions – how the social identities of pupils drawn from minorities are constructed and whether there are any negotiations or challenges between the understanding held by recently qualified monolingual teachers and those that their immigrant minority pupils may offer. For the purpose of this article, I only consider the data gathered from two of the four interviews carried out with a recently qualified monolingual primary teacher between November and December 2002 during the time spent as non-participant observer in the class. These two interviews were based on the model of the long open-ended interview, given that this approach 'can take us into the mental world of the individual, to glimpse the categories and logic by which he or she sees the world' (McCracken 1988: 9). They were designed to explore, among other things, the class teacher's biography, the approach to multiculturalism and multilingualism in this classroom and the teacher's understanding of pupils' national and ethnic affiliations. The interviews presenting these topics under the guise of prompts based on what I observed in the classroom were carried out in English, even though switching to Dutch was occasionally employed to make the informant feel at ease. Both interviews were audio taped and the recordings were transcribed and made available to the teacher for confirmation of content and accuracy of transcription. They were then analysed through socio-culturally rooted discourse analysis (see, Gee 1999) looking for those 'discourse models' contained in the teacher's discourse that could shed light on how minority pupils' identities are constructed. In the analysis, I let identity construction emerge from my teacher-informant's talk, looking for the construction and articulation of pupils' identities that were presented to me. By sifting through the transcripts, a first tentative analysis was drawn and fed back to the class teacher who elucidated those points that were still unclear. The re-drafted analysis and inter-pretation were again presented to the informant and to other Flemish native research fellows for validation. I then examined ways in which the models I re-constructed could be related to each other trying to achieve and sustain a specific account of the construction of pupils' identities.

The district, the school, the classroom and the pupils

The Rebus Catholic Primary School,[3] in which my case study classroom is located, was founded in 1925. In 1958, it moved to its present loca-tion, a suburban district of a large city in northwest Flanders. In line with the educational measures adopted by the Vlaams Verbond van het Katholiek Basisonderwijs (Flemish Network for Catholic Primary Education), the Rebus Catholic Primary does not cater for either the teaching or the integration in the mainstream classroom of immigrant minority languages.[4] Rather, the school has a Special Entry Programme for those children who have recently migrated to Flanders. This gives the school the possibility to organize an immersion/support programme in the Dutch language for one school year. According to the figures given by the school head teacher, during the school year 2002–2003, 152 pupils were regularly enrolled at the Rebus. The pupils' register shows 23 Moroccans, seven Yugoslavs, five Turkish and a remaining seven pupils with other nationalities: two Pakistanis, one American, one Angolan, one Pole, one Russian, and one Somali respectively. While we are therefore confronted with a linguistically and culturally heterogeneous school clientele, all the class teachers at the Rebus are monolingual speakers of Dutch holding Belgian nationality. The age range of the teaching body varies greatly, as well as its experience with multicultural classrooms combining recently qualified teachers with senior staff members who have been in service for more than 15 years. Around November 2002, the 5th Grade classroom had twelve pupils. Four were Belgian nationals from Flanders who speak (a variety of) Dutch, while one pupil – Sebastian – has come to Belgium only two years ago as a refugee. Sebastian, born in Albania from a Macedonian father and a Kosovan mother, has Macedonian and Italian as self-reported home languages and is entitled to another year of instruction of Nederlands als Tweede Taal (Dutch as a second language) given his late enrolment at the Rebus in the previous school year. Three other pupils – born on Belgian soil – reported having parents born outside Belgium, two in Morocco and one in Poland, with their self-reported home languages being Berber, Arabic and Polish respectively. Three other pupils presented yet another interesting demo-linguistic situation. While all of them reported coming from exogenous marriages – two pupils with Belgian mothers and Turkish fathers and one pupil with a Belgian mother and an Italian father – for the two pupils coming from Turkish-Belgian marriages the Turkish language is the language used in the home. But for the pupil born to Italian–Belgian parents, Anthony, Italian is not used any more given that Anthony's father has left his family. However, it is the language used by his stepfather, French, that is now used besides Dutch in the home environment. The last pupil, Joyce, has a maternal grandfather who is half-Italian, while her paternal grandfather is Spanish. While the Italian language plays no role in the home environment, the Spanish language is reported as her home language, and it is mostly used in interactions with her mother, her father and her paternal grandfather.

Mevrouw Irina

The 5th Grade class teacher, Irina, is 23. She was born to Dutch monolingual Belgian parents, she holds Belgian nationality and alongside Dutch she is quite fluent in French and English. She states that her home language is 'just Dutch' although, jokingly, she makes the remark that ever since teaching at the Rebus, her Dutch has suffered in the presence of the local dialect. Irina's own primary schooling took place in a small Flemish school where she cannot remember having any contacts with pupils coming from other cultures. When looking back at herself as a pupil, she states: '[. . .] I was not stupid (. . .) I was not smart (. . .) I was just (. . .) a good pupil'. Irina's secondary schooling was in moderne talen en wiskunde (modern languages and mathematics), she then moved onto a lerarenopleiding (teacher training college) for primary education. During her studies, Irina wrote a dissertation dealing with the theory and practice of intercultureel onderwijs (intercultural education). Her dissertation centred on lessons that she planned and taught during her teaching practice in a 3rd Grade in the city where this investigation takes place. After completing her teaching studies, Irina was appointed to a Steiner[5] primary school. After one school year, she felt dissatisfied with their educational ethos because 'society is changing and I think that they don't change with it. That is why I left there but it was great to do'. She was then appointed to her current post of 5th Grade teacher at the Rebus Catholic Primary which she has been covering for the last two years. She reports liking this school because 'I like small schools, you know all the children by name (. . .) I think that's important'. She also likes the fact that the pupils call her by first name even though at the beginning, she thought it was impolite because, at the primary school she attended as a child, calling a teacher by their forename was not done.

'They can function like all the others do'

The first discourse model re-constructed from Irina's interviews deals with the ethnic and national affiliation of those pupils drawn from the minorities and with the issue of cultural maintenance and diversity. As we read:

> [I]: They can use the several languages, they can talk about it, what's the difference, in some lessons they can talk about it about cultures or (-), I don't know, they can talk about (. . .)
> [M]: Like they did yesterday talking about the way of cooking?
> [I]: (Uh) yeah, ok for example. Yeah if we are learning about countries, they can tell something about their own country and their language and they can, I don't know, but I (-) it's not a problem and I hope we use it and that's a good thing.

As observed during the period spent in the 5th Grade, Irina's pupils are given the chance to share insights about their own cultural habits and to talk about what Irina calls 'their own country' and 'their language' through incidental intercultural education. My prompting her on the bilingual pupils' national affiliation revealed the following:

> [M]: Do you think that all your children here are Belgian?
> [I]: (. . .) Yes I do.
> [M]: And why?
> [I]: Why (. . .) because they can function just like all the others do in school.

In a follow-up interview I asked Irina to expand on the verb 'to function':

> [M]: But what did you exactly mean with the fact that they can function like all the others do?
> [I]: To function means more than just speaking. I have looked it up in the dictionary, because it is really difficult to re-word it better than what the word in itself does. In there I found 'to fulfil one's function or task'. Given the context of the sentence, it means that the children are able to fulfil the task of an inhabitant of Belgium. Of course we don't get any task by birth but if the children can feel at ease in Belgium, can go to the shop, can follow the lessons, speak, write, read, play together with others, pay respect to the culture then they can 'function' in Belgium.

The utterance 'they can function like all the others do in school' suggested in the first place, that pupils' functionality in school constitutes an indicator of these pupils' being Belgian and it could also be seen as an expression of how, in Irina's view, schooling constitutes the place where those pupils who already function, that is to say those pupils who are Belgian by *jus soli* and *jus sanguini*, are the yardstick of measurement for what functioning is. This is achieved through the fulfilment of tasks among which we find 'paying respect to **the** culture [*my emphasis*]'. Moreover, Irina states:

> [I]: But I know that at home is different because they have the Moroccan culture or the Turkish culture at home, the mother wears a (. . .) something on the head.
> [M]: You mean a *hoofddoek*.
> [I]: Yeah a *hoofdoek* and she can't come out and that is something they, they live with it. So at home it's Moroccan culture.
> [I]: (. . .) but they can function just like all the others (. . .) so these are Belgian kids.

While functionality, within the realms of school and of Belgian society at large, previously emerged as a means of being Belgian, that is, 'but they can function like the others (...) so these are Belgian kids', minority pupils also possess cultural repertoires addressed as belonging to the home environment only. From the adversative clause Irina uses, i.e. 'But I know that at home is different', these repertoires seem not strictly relevant to pupils' functionality as Belgians. While it is true that the private domain offers scope for cultural maintenance (Arends-Tóth 2003), the teacher's perceived adaptation of her minority pupils to the majority's mode of functioning at school and in the public domain is key to categorize them as 'Belgian' while the cultural elements of the home environment are not.

Educationally marginal pupils

Further on, the model re-constructed from Irina's interviews focuses on the social identity of her pupils within the educational establishment. While referring to the Rebus' student population, Irina states that in this school '[...] we take everyone' (I01, 4, 077) followed by:

> [I]: We have a lot of children who have knocked on several doors of schools and they were not welcome [...]

Through her discourse, pupils are addressed as 'everyone' and as those who 'were not welcome' by other schools. This line of argument developed further as follows:

> [M]: In general, what kind of background do they [*5th form pupils*: MS] have overall?
> [I]: (Uh) [*they are*: MS] *een beetje marginaal*,[6] there are just a few kids that are coming out from stable families.
> [I]: And most of them, I think we have ten, ten per cent of the kids even twenty, I don't know, are of the institute for kids [...]

In her discourse, both monolingual and bilingual pupils are categorized not only as those who are refused entry in other schools but also as those having a 'marginal' social background. Irina elaborates on this by stating:

> [I]: There are a lot of kids here who can't follow on a better (...) in a **better school** [*bold for her emphasis*], [...] and they come here because otherwise they have to go to special schools.

The categorization Irina draws, implicitly pictures the social identities of all her pupils as those who are 'not bright' given that these are pupils 'who can't follow [...] in a **better school**' and who otherwise would have to attend special education. Also, the use of the comparative 'better' – referring to better schools than the Rebus Primary – suggests that this school matches the pace at which these pupils can follow; thus implicitly reiterating that these are pupils that work at a low pace. Irina carries on with this reasoning when giving more information about the pace and level of the work her pupils can do:

[I]: [...] there are several children, they are 11, 12 years old and they can not make a sentence.

[I]: I am happy with the things they do because we can understand each other but if you go to another school with that, they will laugh about it.

Her discourse, without drawing any distinction between mainstream pupils and those drawn from immigrant minority communities, suggests that the social identities of all her pupils are constructed as educational underachievers, that is, 'they can not make a sentence', with a marginal social position. While the first utterance contains elements conforming to the insight put forward by Carrington and Short (1989: 122–3) that pupils' social positioning as well as their underachievement are pivotal factors for building teacher's expectations that are key to the understanding of how pupils are assessed, in the second utterance, Irina reports to be 'happy with the things they [*her pupils*] do', even though – as introduced in the adversative clause that follows – these 'things' would be mocked in 'another school' where pupils' work is of higher standards. It seems feasible to advance that Irina's model of educational disadvantage is also instanced through her explicit awareness and acceptance of pupils' low standards of work as compared to the standards set for pupils who 'can follow' in a 'better' school. The model re-constructed here allows yet another key linkage with Anderson-Levitt's (1987) ethnographic study, showing that the effect of school performance is to legitimize and privilege the position of pupils with an already high 'cultural capital'. While it appears that the social identities of those who do not own an already high form of cultural capital – as for Irina's 5th graders – appear constructed within the boundaries of educational disadvantage.

A marginal linguistic repertoire

This model of educational disadvantage finds further supportive evidence when Irina deals with her pupils' language use in the classroom drawing a relationship between linguistic and social variables present in her classroom. As Irina states:

> [I]: We have a dialect in this city, yeah, and it's, I am really fair in it, I don't speak that proper either. Okay?
>
> [M]: You don't speak the dialect or you don't speak [-] (*Irina interrupts*: MS).
>
> [I]: Yeah I do, sometimes I do, and as a teacher maybe it's not allowed to speak the dialect. But sometimes I do because I know that kids will understand me better when I do that.

Irina reports that there is a dialect in the city where the school is located and that she occasionally speaks it in the class, even though, she claims not to speak it properly either if compared to standard Dutch. Irina also explains that her language choice and use of the city dialect between the classroom walls is motivated by the assumption that by doing so, her pupils – without making a distinction between monolinguals and bilinguals – will understand her better than when using Dutch because they are users of the city dialect. In the last quotation, Irina challenges her own didactic reasoning when casting doubt on the fact that 'maybe' this code is 'not allowed' to be spoken by a teacher, as opposed to the Dutch language that is the code in which a teacher should be conducting classroom interactions. Then the socio-linguistic behaviour of her pupils is illustrated as follows:

> [I]: So when I say to them (uh), *bij voorbeeld neem allemaal jullie boek op de volgende pagina*[7]
>
> [M]: Hmm.
>
> [I]: They are going to look at me like: 'Oh my God'.
>
> [M]: Hmm.
>
> [I]: *Ja*, if I say *Neemt uwen boek op die bladzijde* [*].
>
> [M]: Is it the local dialect?
>
> [I]: It 's not correct I know.
>
> [M]: Ok.
>
> [I]: I know but I do it, I don't know why but they understand me better like this (*Irina laughs*: MS) and (…) it's really not correct, I know it but sometimes I do.

[M]: Ok.

[I]: And so they speak the dialect like *wij kosten dat niet doen* [*][8] but it has to be *wij konden dat niet doen* and they even don't know that it is *wij konden*. So they write down *wij kosten* that does not exist (. . .) the dialect, I mean. And that is the problem of this area (. . .).

In the quotations above, her use of 'not correct', which could also be interpreted as the incorrectness of the dialect she speaks, is again motivated by the fact that the use of the local dialect is a didactic tool for allowing a smooth running of her interactions with her pupils. In this context Irina also gives three examples of the language employed in the classroom. First, she reports an utterance in standard Dutch while the other two utterances report the dialect she thinks she uses because by doing so she assumes she is better understood by her pupils. In the first sentence, 'neem allemaal jullie boek op de volgende pagina', the verb 'neem' is the singular imperative form of the infinitive 'nemen' (to take) while 'jullie' (your) is a colloquial form of the possessive pronoun used in referring to the books of her pupils. In the second utterance, 'Neemt uwen boek op die bladzijde [*]', the verb 'nemen' is conjugated into 'neemt' – a formal plural form of the imperative of the verb 'nemen'. While 'uwen' is a morpheme with a zero morph of plurality {ø} that in the dialect takes the bound form morpheme {en} as suffix, resulting in the polymorphemic {uw-en}. Finally in the third example, 'wij kosten dat niet doen', the simple past tense of the verb 'kunnen' (can) is given in what Irina claims to be its dialect form, 'kosten' rather than its standard Dutch form 'konden'. Irina reports that 'kosten' is what all her pupils would write down and this is because by being dialect users her pupils ignore that 'wij kosten' cannot be written because – as Irina argues – dialect in a written form does not exist.

An interpretation of the utterances above can now be suggested. Irina occasionally employs the use of the city dialect as a didactic device, based on the assumption that both her monolingual and bilingual pupils will understand her better. Second, through her discourse bilingual and monolingual pupils' social identities are constructed as those of dialect users although not aware of being so, as instanced in the use of 'kosten'. The result is that Irina's use of the vernacular could be seen as an 'entry ticket' in her pupils' linguistic practices. In fact, the biographic and schooling information gathered from Irina suggests that her socio-linguistic upbringing and schooling was based on other forms of socio-linguistic practice other than the vernacular variety that she chooses to speak to her 5th graders. Irina's own linguistic repertoire therefore is based on a certain form of 'verbal hygiene' that is 'ingrained in every one who has been schooled in using a language' (Cameron 1999: 14). Such form of verbal hygiene does not match those of her bilingual and monolingual pupils who, in her view, are accustomed to using this local vernacular variety of Dutch, thus constituting a binding factor among monolinguals and bilinguals who are pictured as a homogeneous linguistic group that shares 'a body of verbal signs and that is set off from similar aggregates by significant differences in language use' (Gumperz 1971: 114). Moreover, the interview reads:

[M]: And when you teach them Dutch language, how do you deal with the fact that these children have another language [*e.g.* *Arabic*: MS] at home? Does that matter?

[I]: Yes it matters because they [*all her pupils*: MS] don't speak Dutch as well as other kids, when you go to another school you will see the difference.

[M]: Hmm.

[I]: When they have to write something down, it is really hard for them. But actually it's not because they speak another language because the Flemish people (…) the Dutch people also have problems. It's just something (…) we don't know where, where does it come from but we have big problem with Dutch here.

Through the utterance 'they don't speak Dutch as well as other kids [...]', Irina puts together again monolingual and bilingual pupils because both are different in their language use when compared to pupils from 'another school', i.e., a better school than the Rebus. This homogeneity among monolinguals and bilinguals seems to be further supported by the adversative clause 'but actually it's not because they speak another language' explicitly suggesting that the common denominator and common source of problems among monolinguals and bilinguals is the local vernacular. Further on, when asked about the teaching of Dutch to multilingual pupils, we read:

[M]: But how do you teach it [*the Dutch language*: MS] with children with Dutch as a second language? Is there a difference, if any?

[I]: Probably there is a difference because you have to think about a language that is not your mother language and otherwise is just fluent. But that is just a thing. I explained that it is not fluent because of the dialect of this area. So I don't do anything special for kids with a second language (...) as with Dutch as a second language.

[M]: You just work.

[I]: Yeah I just work and it works and if there is a problem I am going to think about it but now there is no problem so (...).

While in the fourth interview Miss Irina expands on this notion stating:

[I]: But I can also help for example with other problems, than only the problems a native Dutch speaker can have. Extra practice on the use of the different articles can be given to the students. Even though this is not a problem a native Dutch speaker will have.

With the utterance 'I don't do anything special for kids with a second language', Irina's bilingual pupils are put again on the same level as their Flemish native counterparts, also confirmed by the adverb 'probably' which casts doubt on whether the bilinguals' mother-tongue could affect their Dutch. Later on though, as reported in the second excerpt, her bilingual pupils are constructed as those facing specific language problems, like article – noun attachment, that a native speaker of Dutch – whether in its standard or vernacular form – would not have. If proficiency is taken to be the gate-keeping notion for being defined as a native speaker of a language, then all her pupils could be seen as native speakers of the local vernacular variety of Dutch (see, Singh 1997) but from the discourse practices analysed above, a paradox seems to emerge. In the first place, the social identities of all her pupils are reified as those who are at a socio-linguistic disadvantage as a consequence of the vernacular they use, therefore excluding them from being native speakers of the standard variety of Dutch that Irina assumes to be spoken in other (better) schools. Further though, Irina's bilingual pupils are not constructed as native speakers of Dutch not only because of the local vernacular, but also because they are speakers of the local vernacular, who, as well as that, have also a mother-tongue that is other than Dutch. In turn, this brings to bear specific language problems that neither speakers of the standard variety of Dutch nor speakers of the local variety of Dutch would have to face. Even though we do not know the extent of these pupils' proficiency in both varieties of Dutch, pupils of Flemish origin appear constructed as speakers of standard Dutch who are penalized by the local vernacular, while bilingual pupils' social identities seem twice legitimized within the boundaries of socio-linguistic disadvantage. First they are users of standard Dutch whose language is penalized by the local dialect, second they are also those who have, as well as the local dialect penalization, the specific problems brought to bear by their (presumed) home languages.

Conclusion

The models re-constructed from the discourse practice of Irina, the 5th Grade teacher, set an initial equity between immigrant minority pupils and their Flemish native counterparts, defining them both as Belgian by adequately functioning at school and in society at large. This equality is also proposed in terms of educational disadvantage, when all the pupils are categorized as those who cannot attend 'better' schools, thus constructing their social identities as 'not bright' learners. Equality occurs again when Irina deals with the socio-linguistic habits of her pupils who are constructed as in a disadvantaged position because of the common problems brought as a result of the local dialect. This third model seems to conform to the process of 'iconization' (Irvine and Gall 2000: 37) where the linguistic features that index a social group appear to be 'iconic' representations, depicting, in this case, the nature of disadvantage of the social group itself. Following this process, linguistic features and codes are often seen as reflecting and expressing socio-culturally specific images of people and of their social identities. Consequently, models about language appear to locate socio-linguistic phenomena 'as part of, and evidence for, what they [*people*: MS] believe to be systematic behavioural, aesthetic, affective and moral contrasts among the social groups indexed' (Blackledge 2002: 200). In fact, despite its initial equity, socio-linguistic disadvantage appears double for those pupils drawn from minority groups given the specific problems brought in by their home languages as well as by the local variety of Dutch.

The present research may have given a glimpse of the complexity of the actual discourse models informing us about how an educator comes to construct the identities of her minority pupils. However, in the approach taken, there is also the danger of generalization. In fact, the categorization emerged from the analysis and interpretation proposed is only a first step in furthering the understanding of these pupils' identity paths within the learning environment and in society at large. Even though we do not know whether these models may lead to an adjustment of pupils' identities as the 'disadvantaged ones' as well as not knowing the extent to which the assumptions informing this teacher's models reflect the actual socio-linguistic reality of these pupils, – for example, the pupils' proficiency in the local variety of Dutch and their ability to apply different language norms to different socio-cultural spaces – we are left with the question of how to move beyond the designation of these pupils as those with an educational and socio-linguistic marginal profile. According to Hall (1988), it is necessary to begin to see pupils drawn from minority communities as members of urban communities emerging as active participants of a process of 'new ethnicities' formation and rather than constructing their social identities as 'passive inheritors of views of nations as culturally homogeneous communities of sentiment' (Gilroy 1987: 59–61) where their cultural and linguistic repertoires remain untapped, they should be accepted into mainstream society.

Acknowledgments

This research has been made possible through a grant from the University of London Scholarship Fund [Ref: AR/CRF/A] and a travel bursary from the Westminster Society, Westminster Institute of Education at Oxford Brookes.

Notes

1. Examples of this jargon are: 'allochtone leerlingen' (allochtonous pupils), 'migrantenleerlingen' (migrant pupils), 'doelgroepleerlingen' (target group pupils) for pupils belonging to minority groups. 'Migrantentalen' (migrant languages) and 'eigen taal en cultuur' (own language and culture) for community languages cultures and 'onderwijs in eigen taal en cultuur' (education in own language and culture) for the teaching of the above in mainstream education (see, Extra and Gorter 2001 for a complete discussion).
2. See, Auer and Dirim 2003: 224.
3. School, teacher and pupils' names are fictitious for privacy protection.
4. Onderwijs in Eigen Taal en Cultuur (OETC) can be organized by the school in the mainstream classroom if there is a minimum of 20 immigrant minority pupils in the school and if two thirds of the parents agree to their children being taught about the language and culture of the parental 'homeland'.
5. Rudolph Steiner: Austrian philosopher was the founder of the anthroposophical movement.
6. The direct translation of the term *marginaal* in English is 'insignificant' (Oxford Advanced Learners Dictionary (4th Edn.) 1989: 761). Given the strong negative connotation of this term and the context of the utterance I translated it as 'marginal'.
7. '(. . .) for example: all of you turn your book to the next page.' [*]
8. 'We could not do that.'1

15
Changing Media Spaces: The Transformative Power of Heteroglossic Practices

Brigitta Busch

Introduction

For many years a central role has been attributed to the media[1] in the rise of standard and national languages (Innis 1997). Recent developments, however, may well be contributing to the de-centring of national and standard languages. The monolingual habitus of media which address a national audience, their normalizing and standardizing role, is not an inherent feature of particular mass media technologies, but is rather due to the way media technologies are socially appropriated. In the period of the emerging nation-states a process of hierarchization of languages was set in motion through censorship and licensing procedures, which fostered state or national languages. At the same time the media began to fulfil a controlling function through the 'correct' use of a unitary language on the one hand and through metalinguistic discourses on the other. National broadcasting was able to create 'a sense of unity – and of corresponding boundaries around the nation', 'turn previously exclusive social events into mass experiences' and 'link the national public into the private lives of citizens' (Morley 2000: 107).

The western European media order as it was established in the aftermath of World War II remained relatively unchallenged until the 1970s, when processes of regionalization and localization, of privatization, of European integration and later of globalization began to de-centre the national public spheres. In the process of economic globalization and the transformation of the world political order, supranational and sub-national institutions are gaining in importance in the developing power vacuum due to the retreat of the traditional nation-state (Castells 2003).

Nevertheless, the state remains a relevant political entity, it has constantly to define and redefine its role (Foucault 1986). On a supranational level core functions are being abandoned to international organizations (in terms of language policy and cultural policy especially the EU and UNESCO) and to international expert bodies, such as the WTO, which defy largely democratic control. On a sub-state level regional and local bodies are gaining in importance. Increasingly, intermediaries and private bodies are becoming more important actors. This development also applies to language policies in education, a domain which has traditionally been under direct state influence.

In the past two decades, there has been a radical marketization of public services, which means that hospitals, schools and universities increasingly have to operate like private businesses. These processes also involve a marketization of language, whereby the language of the market conquers the public service domain. Marketization entails a shift in social relations and social identities, which results in ambivalent and contradictory authority relations. The 'consumers' gain in power, the power to shop around and choose (Fairclough 2000: 163–4). In parallel with the changing media order, a process of de-centring of standard languages has become visible on several levels: supranational media seek to embrace whole language areas as one single audience and market, and follow different strategies of addressing this nationally and linguistically heterogeneous audience. In regional and local media varieties, minority languages or urban codes – before only present in niches – now assume a more comprehensive communicative function. Media enterprises have largely become actors in their own right as far as language policies are concerned.

Several factors determine language policy orientations in the media: the way audiences are being imagined and relationships with the audiences are being structured; how different modes of communication and communication technologies are being appropriated; how the production process is organized; and which resources can be used. I shall discuss and illustrate these factors in the following sections.

Focus on urban local media

Due to migration and labour mobility life worlds in European metropolitan centres are multilingual. The monolingual biography of the individual speaker – which was never more than a projection, a sort of ideal construct (see the chapters by Gal and Brumfit, this volume) – cannot therefore be upheld as the norm. For example, in Vienna almost a quarter of the population (Waldrauch and Sohler 2004: 153) uses a language other than German or in addition to German in daily life. Through the internet and satellite technology, media are available almost everywhere in a huge range of different languages, although local media still play an important role in daily media habits.

Discussing examples from local radio stations in urban areas which produce programmes for migrants, I will show how these media question the monolingual habitus and transgress the imperative of linguistic purity. Radio MultiKulti, the multilingual local broadcasting station in Berlin, is one of the most documented and researched examples (see, for example, Vertovec 2000; Echchaibi 2002; Kosnick 2002; Busch 2004). Founded in 1994 as part of the Landesmedienanstalt Berlin–Brandenburg (Berlin–Brandenburg Media Authority), it is bound to the principles of the public service media sector. Radio MultiKulti claims to assure the continuity of so-called foreign language programmes broadcast for the *Gastarbeiter*[2] migration in Berlin since 1974.

Examining state migration policies and public service broadcasting policies in a historical perspective reveals direct correlations: when labour policies were aiming at a rapid turnover of workers and assumed that the workers would return after a temporary short stay, programmes in the languages of the larger migrant groups saw their mission as building bridges to the countries of origin. Later, when the idea of integration and assimilation began to dominate migration policies, the focus of the radio programmes changed. German language programmes with an intercultural orientation had the effect not only of decreasing the number of 'foreign' language programmes, but also of strengthening ties with the new environment and raising understanding and good will among the majority population (Kosnick 2000). Similar developments have taken place in other European countries. Franchon and Vargaftig (1995), for example, show in a Europe-wide study of public service television and immigration in the mid-1990s that there was already a clear tendency to abandon or outsource programmes in 'minority' languages to niches within the programme schedule or to the private sector.

Today Radio MultiKulti broadcasts in more than twenty languages. Most of the programmes in languages other than German are located in a programme slot between 5 p.m. and 10 p.m. During day time – that is, during the peak listening hours – the main language of transmission is German. There is a clear correlation between the size of particular migrant groups in Berlin and the amount of time allocated to programmes in 'their' languages.

In many European cities non-commercial private radio stations began to develop after the fall of the state broadcasting monopolies in the 1970s and 1980s. Right from the beginning, despite their different history and organizational structure, a multilingual orientation became one of their common characteristic features (Kleinsteuber 1991: 321–2). In many local community stations, like Radio LoRa in Zurich, Radio Fro in Linz or Radio Orange in Vienna, programmes in languages other than the 'national' language account for approximately 15 per cent to 20 per cent of the time on air (Busch 2004: 123). The range of languages which can be heard differs from Radio MultiKulti in so far as languages which do not figure prominently in the cities' census statistics can also be found. Furthermore, there is a high proportion of bi- and multilingual programmes which aim at addressing diverse audiences as one public. The strong presence of 'small' language groups suggests that the radio programmes on the community stations fulfil a compensatory function for those that are excluded from access to (national) media. It is not a coincidence that many of the minority programmes on community stations have titles like 'the voice of the voiceless'.

Imagining the audience – the fiction of a homogeneous national target group

On Radio MultiKulti programmes in the now separate languages spoken in the area of former Yugoslavia (Bosnian, Croatian and Serbian) have their own slots. The website of the 'Emisija na Bosankom jeziku' (Programme in Bosnian Language) addresses the listeners directly:

Dobar dan i maksuz selam!
U akšame rane Emisija na bosanskom jeziku se svakog radnog dana obraća Vama, građanima Bosne i Hercegovine – Bošnjacima, Hrvatima i Serbima – koji su u ovom gradu 'kod kuće' na duže ili kraće vrijeme. (...) Dajemo Vam priliku da se čuje i Vaš glas, na Vašem jeziku i da zahori Vaša pjesma i donese malo sevdaha, meraka i rahatluka u večeri rane.

(Good day and a cordial greeting!
Every day in the early evening hours the programme in the Bosnian language addresses you, the citizens of Bosnia and Herzegovina – Bosnjaks, Croats and Serbs – who have been 'at home' in this city for a longer or shorter time. (...) We offer the possibility that your voice can be heard in your language and that your song brings a little bit of love, joy and contentment in the early evening.)

The programme is conceived for a multiethnic audience which is imagined as a single national community. Listeners are addressed in their capacity as citizens of the state (whose passport they often do not possess) and as migrants who have chosen Berlin as a new home. The programme reports relevant news from the *Heimat* (homeland) as well as from 'the community' in Berlin. It defines itself as a bridge to the country of origin and as a promoter of the integration process. The focus on national belonging also finds expression in the micro-linguistic choices. Expressions like *maksuz selam* (cordial greetings) or *malo sevdaha, meraka i rahatluka* (a bit of love, joy and contentment) were considered as dialectal, as Turcisms, when Bosnian, Croatian and Serbian were still regarded as one single Serbocroatian/Croatoserbian language. During the process of the disintegration of the Yugoslav state and the drawing of new borders, linguistic demarcation served as a means of emphasizing differences (see, for example, Busch and Kelly-Holmes 2004a; and Voss, this volume) and when the three separated national languages were proclaimed, expressions such as those mentioned above were incorporated into the new Bosnian written standard as markers of distinctness. The text on the web site suggests that a 'correct' and 'pure' Bosnian language is being used here. Similarly, the programme in Croatian on Radio MultiKulti announces that it reports about 'what is new in Croatia' and 'what Croats in Berlin and Germany should know', just as the Serbian programme focuses on Serbia and Montenegro.

During day time, on Saturdays and in the late evening hours Radio MultiKulti broadcasts a programme which might be characterized as 'world music'. It addresses a particular Berlin scene that defines itself through a multicultural life style. The following text is an extract from the website which introduces the presenters of the German language programmes:

> Der Wahl-Berliner und überzeugte Neapolitaner Giò di Sera alias Don Rispetto ist ein Szene-Held und Allround-Künstler mit vielen Talenten. (. . .) Dabei bedient sich Don Rispetto einer besonderen Sprache, einer 'Misch-lingua', dem 'Berlingo'. . . a cool mix of Deutsch, Italiano and English u.a. per tutti i fratelli della musica!

> (The adoptive Berliner and through and through Neapolitan Giò di Sera alias Don Rispetto is a hero of the scene and an all-round artist with multiple talents. (. . .) Don Rispetto uses a special language, a 'mix-lingua', 'Berlingo'. . . a cool mix of Deutsch, Italiano and English amongst others per tutti i fratelli della musica!)

The 'mix-lingua' is meant to contribute to the multicultural feeling. Unlike in the non-German language programmes, the audience is not imagined as a national/ethnic community but in terms of a life style expressed in a particular kind of music. Whereas the requirement of 'linguistic correctness' – which reigned in public service broadcasting until the 1980s/1990s – still seems to operate for the programmes broadcast in languages other than German in the early evening hours, it seems to have lost its force in certain German language programmes. The elements from other languages or codes in this case are less expressions of the heteroglossia present in the city than elements of style that refer to a certain life style.

Most of the urban community radio stations in Austria, Germany and Switzerland also feature programmes which address listeners from the space of former Yugoslavia. Some of the independent stations – like Radio Fro in the Austrian town Linz – even schedule a whole range of such programmes. Some of them are run by 'traditional' migrant organizations and address ethnic or national communities; more frequent are programmes which cater for a particular taste or address a particular scene or generation. At the Viennese station Radio Orange the programmes 'Yu-radio' and 'Radio Nachtwerk' are run by owners of discos. Both programmes aim not only at maximizing their radio audiences but also at attracting as many visitors as possible to the disco venues with a programme addressing people from the whole Balkan area. Consequently the journalists avoid as far as possible expressions which can be identified immediately as markers of difference for one of the three 'new' standards, Bosnian, Croatian and Serbian. Some commercial media produced in the space of former Yugoslavia (such as the diaspora version of Pink TV or the magazine Svet Plus) employ a similar strategy of addressing the whole former Serbocroatian linguistic space as a single potential audience (Busch 2004: 211 ff).

The following text comes from the introductory sequence of a programme broadcast on a community radio station in Austria. It avoids national/ethnic labelling not for commercial but for political reasons:

To je emisija na vašem i našem jeziku, ili barem jeziku za koji nikome nije potreban prevod, jeziku, koji svi razumemo. Muzika je (xxx) izkjučivo od naših izvođača i autora, geografski gledano od sredine tunela Karavanke pa do granične rampe sa Grčkom.

(This is the programme in your and in our language, a language for which nobody needs a translation, which we all understand. The music is exclusively by our artists and authors, geographically speaking from the middle of the Karavank tunnel right to the border barrier with Greece.)

The broadcasting language is defined as 'a language for which nobody needs a translation, which we all understand' avoiding at the same time both the 'new' national labels and the 'old' unitary name. Irony is used as a stylistic resource to distance the speaker from ascribed national identities. The programme positions itself as an alternative programme, as a counter-discourse to the dominant national discourses. This is visible not only in the contents of the programme and in the linguistic choices but also in the ways the programme is designed and organized. For example, the emphasis is on dialogic forms, and live discussions and phone-in programmes encourage listeners to participate via telephone, email and text messages. Therefore a broad range of codes, registers, and styles is present in the programme.

It is in fact the producer-audience relationship and the ways in which audiences and their expectations concerning texts are imagined that determine how the text is shaped. The notion of the target audience, which encompasses a spatial (local, regional, national, global) and/or a social (social status, income, age, gender) dimension, is based on rigid and reified audience categories. The notion of media coverage and definitions of target audiences are instruments of market research and correspond to criteria established by the advertising industry. Ang (1991) demonstrates that this approach is based on a discursive construct of audience that is unable to capture the actual relationship between media and audiences. Following McQuail (1987), she distinguishes between two main orientations: audience-as-public and audience-as-market.

The first is generally associated with the public service media sector, in which the addressee is seen as a citizen (of a state), the relationship with the audience is paternal and the aim is to transmit values, habits and tastes. It is linked to the so-called transmission model of communication, in which the transmission of a message and the ordered transfer of meaning is the intended consequence of the communication process. Monolingual orientation and linguistic 'purity' dominate in this paternalistic model.

The second audience configuration is associated with the private commercial media sector. Audiences are addressed as consumers in a double sense: as consumers of the media product and as potential consumers of the products advertised in the programmes. In the attention model of communication, communication is considered successful as soon as attention is actually aroused in audiences. The transfer of meaning plays a secondary role. The scoop, the extraordinary, and the scandal gain in importance as means of arousing attention. On the level of linguistic choices, standard forms lose their central position: for example, elements from other codes are built in to attract attention.

In the alternative media sector, by contrast, the conception of the audience is determined by the idea of an active public that participates in social action and media production. The aim is to overcome the division between producers and audiences, to move closer to a situation in which 'the Other' is able to represent itself, in which the heterogeneity of 'authentic informants' is not reduced (Atton 2002: 9). Alternative or 'third sector' media are consequently closer to the ideal of representing the multi-voicedness of society in all three dimensions which Bakhtin (Todorov 1984: 56) described: heterology (raznorečie), that is the diversity of discourses, heteroglossia (raznojazyčnie), the diversity of language(s), and heterophony (raznoglossie), the diversity of individual voices. However, the three sectors cannot be separated neatly. It has, for example, been observed that the public service sector is becoming more market-oriented, at least in some segments of its programmes, and that formats and genres developed in a certain sector are taken up – sometimes in a transformed way – by others. The different basic orientations in conceiving the producer-audience relationships result in preferences for particular media formats (for example, authoritative information-centred programmes, market-oriented infotainment programmes, dialogic forms such as phone-in programmes) and in different linguistic practices. They also determine the way in which discourses are shaped, reproduced and transformed.

Multimodality – decentring the role of standard languages

Media communication is inherently multimodal communication: language in written and spoken form is only one of several modes available for expressing a meaning potential. For instance, in print media layout and image are available in addition to the written word, in radio language is present in its spoken form, alongside music and different sound sources, and in television all of these modes can be drawn upon in a context in which the moving image holds a central position. Similarly, in computer-mediated communication a wide range of modes is available (Kress 2002: 6).

How these modes interact is not only a question of technical availability but rather a question of social appropriation and convention, as Kress and van Leeuwen (2001) point out in their multimodal social semiotic theory. The interplay between the different modes has undergone substantial changes in media history. Writing was considered in many cultural environments as the central mode for the transfer of canonical knowledge and authoritative discourse. The predominance of the written text influenced radio production so that practically all radio texts in the early days of the medium were first produced in written form and then read in front of the microphone. Even on television news broadcasts were read for some time without transmitting the image of the speaker as it was considered that the moving image might distract the audience's attention. Linguistic practices and text genres from established media exerted, and continue to exert, a considerable influence on 'new' media and vice versa.

The programmes on urban multilingual radio stations discussed earlier use different communication channels and therefore also different media (each with their own technical and stylistic possibilities) in their contact with their audiences. The web pages designed by the editors of different radio programmes stick closely to the conventions established in print media. A 'correct' and elaborate standard language is the norm as is the case for the websites of the Bosnian programme cited above or of Don Rispetto's music programme on Radio Multikulti. Commercially oriented or alternative radios do not differ substantially in their linguistic practices for this kind of web site.

Some of the radio programmes accommodate interactive spaces on their web sites. In guest books or chat rooms the rules and practices traditionally attached to the written mode seem less powerful (see also Bleichenbacher, this volume). The following example from Radio Nachtwerk (nw), one of the Bosnian/Croatian/Serbian programmes on Radio Orange in Vienna, shows a mix of elements current in oral communication, in text messages and in 'netspeak'. Both messages in the guest book refer to a concert with the popular singer Seka:

Example 1
ich fands ganz super das seka in nw war cmok an das nw team nw 4ever
(It was great for me that Seka was in nw kiss for the nw team nw 4ever)

Example 2
Ej nemogu da erwartenim da vidim seku!!! es wird sicher geil!!!! wahnsinn...
(Oh, I cannot wait to see Seka!!! it will be cool!!!! amazing...)

In both messages there are features of speech current among German and Bosnian/Croatian/Serbian speaking youth in Vienna such as amalgamating different codes: in example 1 'cmok', listed in Bosnian, Serbian or Croatian dictionaries as 'loud kiss', interrupts a predominantly German netspeak flow. In the second example, codeswitching occurs not only after the first sentence but also with the German 'erwarten' which is inserted into the first sentence with a Slavic verb-suffix attached to it. In both messages graphic elements also play a role. Messages from the internet guest book or from emails sent to Radio Nachtwerk are sometimes read during the broadcast, so that (written) web practices make their way into the spoken mode. Music can also serve as a door-opener for 'impure' practices in the sense that song texts in other languages or codes can interrupt the monolingual orientation of programmes.

Recontextualization and linguistic transformation – the availability of resources

Media production is regulated by institutional routines, media reception by everyday practices and arrangements; both depend on available resources. The production of media texts can be seen as a series of transformations, a chain of communicative events which links sources in the public domain to the private domain of media reception (Fairclough 1995: 48–9). Media production encompasses the collection and selection of 'raw material'. At each stage in media production, earlier versions of the text are transformed and recontextualized in ways that correspond to the priorities and goals of the current stage. Due to the economic imperative of reducing the fixed costs in media enterprises, the amount of genuine journalistic work decreases in favour of 'ready-made products' such as news agency material, pre-produced programme elements and formats.

Journalistic work thus becomes more a matter of selection than of investigation. This process is encouraged by an oligopolistic owner structure and practices of cross-referencing between different media (Siegert 2003). However, it would be too simplistic to say that these developments lead necessarily to a homogenization of cultural production. Different media develop their particular policies of material collection and selection in which the search for the unusual and the surprising also has a certain value, so that elements from all kinds of (sub-cultural) codes have their market value. For the journalist current developments in media production also mean an increasing specialization on narrower fields of reporting, on particular genres, topics and so forth, while the traditional division of labour between the technical and journalistic parts of production is disappearing. With the increasing responsibility for the final media product the journalist becomes the designer and producer of a multimodal text.

Returning to local radio stations, it is noteworthy that the public service Radio MultiKulti in Berlin is also organized in a more traditional way. It is part of a hierarchically structured media institution, in which the organization of work is based on a division of labour. According to the company's employment guidelines, journalists for programmes in languages other than German must have an accent-free command of their 'mother tongue' and most of the journalists employed as editors of these programmes have completed the major part of their education in their 'mother land'. Similarly, for the programmes broadcast in German journalists should have mastered German perfectly, but a certain 'foreign flavour' in the voice is considered an advantage. For short interviews, opinion polls and so on within the German language programmes, the editors explicitly want voices that display an immediately noticeable 'foreign' accent. In this context the accent is not a reflection of the social heteroglossia but functions as a marker of ethnicity or as Kosnick (2002: 125) in her ethnographic study of Radio MultiKulti puts it: 'Visual appearances, central to the process of categorization along ethnic and racial stereotypes, cannot function as indicators of ethnic belonging in a purely oral context, and so language plays a central role in signaling ethnic otherness.' Although 'untamed and impure' practices like code-mixing, codeswitching and speaking with a Berlin accent are slowly penetrating the German language and 'foreign' language programmes, the situation is somewhat paradoxical as language policies on this local station, while emphasizing a multicultural and multilingual orientation, exclude a range of heteroglossic local linguistic practices. To keep costs low, Radio MultiKulti re-broadcasts programmes or parts of programmes from other radio stations. Among their partners are public service radio stations in different German Länder and the BBC World Service news programmes in different languages. Radio MultiKulti's multilingual language policy, with its complicated set of rules, gives the impression that 'other' voices, immigrant voices, are represented on air; only a closer analysis reveals that this policy is still very much based on a nation-state principle and on the assumption of distinct and bounded ethnic and cultural identities.

In local community radio stations the programme schedule is usually the result of a process of negotiation between different groups of producers. Groups or individuals that can guarantee regular programme production can apply for time on air. They receive basic technical and journalistic training and are then entitled to use the radio infrastructure, but do not receive any remuneration from the station for their product. Often – especially for programmes in languages other than the dominant one – very diverse initiatives with diverging interests are present on the same station. Producers include traditional migrants' associations, second generation initiatives, commercial 'ethnobusiness' enterprises, groups with an emancipatory orientation, and cultural initiatives. The resulting multiperspectivity and multivoicedness draws attention to the fact that migrant groups within one city cannot be seen as ethnically, linguistically or nationally homogeneous groups of 'others'.

In community radios each group of journalists is responsible for the respective programme and its realization. Traditional press agency material only very rarely figures as source material; producers rely to a large extent on personal contacts and on local material. Connections with other media function in a translocal or transurban framework rather than in an international or transnational one. An example of an already relatively structured translocal network is Cross Radio (www.crossradio.org), which started in 2001 when a group of radio activists from Radio B92 (Belgrade), Radio Student (Zagreb) and Radio Student (Ljubljana) began to exchange programmes on a regular weekly basis. Each radio station produces a 20-minute long feature about current activities in the local cultural scene with a special emphasis on new, young, independent cultural activities. Today the Cross Radio project brings together in this way twelve radio stations from Serbia, Bosnia and Herzegovina, Slovenia, Kosovo, Macedonia and Switzerland (produced by members of the Bosnian community in Zurich). Cross Radio has adopted a specific language policy: programmes are rebroadcast by the partners in the original languages (except the programme from Pristina/Kosovo, which is in English), so the listeners are exposed to language in use in Serbia, Croatia, Macedonia, Slovenia and among the diaspora.

Conclusions

Increasingly creative responses to the challenge of heteroglossic societies can be found in the third sector. But community radio stations also have an impact on developments in other media sectors as they usually allow space for experimentation and creativity. Independent stations were the first to produce interactive formats such as phone-in programmes, duplex programmes which are produced on two stations simultaneously, or bi- and multilingual programmes which search for approaches other than simple translation.

Such linguistically diverse programmes can succeed in bringing together diverse audiences into one single public. The following example from Radio Helsinki in Graz (Austria) shows that this design feature also has an impact on the level of discourse. On the occasion of a football match between Turkey and Austria two editorial teams decided to produce a common bilingual programme. The idea was that listeners would watch the live TV transmission of the match, and switch off the sound provided by TV while listening to the alternative commentary on the radio. The co-presence of the mode 'moving image' enabled the presenters to move away from conventional broadcasting routines and experiment with innovative commentary patterns.

Sometimes the commentators commented on the match consecutively in Turkish and German, sometimes – especially when one of the teams was approaching the goal – in both languages simultaneously. From time to time the Turkish- and German-speaking journalist translated and both sets of commentators engaged in a discussion. In the studio the Turkish-speaking journalist soon took the lead, determining the dynamic of the programme. For the German-speaking audience the Turkish-speaking journalist's ability to switch between the two codes becomes obvious. It gives this part of the audience the opportunity to experience everyday multilingualism from another perspective than that of a deficit, in which the bilingual speaker is often identified as the one who speaks with an accent, the one who does not conform to the standard norm.

Both the Turkish-speaking and the German-speaking journalists have inside knowledge relevant to their tradition of sport reporting (that is, in Turkey and in Austria respectively). Their inside knowledge adds a surplus value for the other part of the audience as they can interpret, for example, the meaning of a particular team formation from this insider position. The most striking feature is that the deictic frame of reference is very different from that normally found in sports programmes. Listener-inclusive 'we-constructions' addressing the listeners as Turkish or Austrian nationals are very rare, as are metonymy and personification using the names of the two countries when the two teams are meant. Much more frequent are inclusive we-constructions meaning the two commentary teams in the studio, or listener-inclusive we-constructions – referring to the people following the match through the programme – that bring the two (the German-speaking and the Turkish-speaking) audiences together.

This bilingual commentary on the football match therefore represents a new genre, another social practice in sport reporting. At the core is the fact that it addresses two audiences separately in acknowledging their difference, but at the same time it merges the two audiences into one in which parallelisms, differences and convergences can be experienced, in which the space between begins to emerge.

As I have tried to show in this chapter, the predominantly monolingual habitus of the mainstream media appears to be linked to the ideal of a single national public sphere. This ideal, which aimed at homogenizing diverse populations, tended to marginalize and exclude segments of society which did not correspond to the dominant role model and to dominant discourses. The current fragmentation of the national public sphere that is accompanying the process of globalization is resulting in a reconfiguration of media spaces in which supranational as well as local media are gaining in importance at the expense of nationally organized media. Furthermore, while the rise of national and standard languages was connected with the nation-state project, the de-centring of the nation-state as the organizing principle in society seems to favour the de-centring of national and standard languages. The presence of a multitude of languages and codes in the media enhances the visibility of diversity within society, but does not in itself cater for social cohesion and dialogue. Therefore it is necessary to allow for interfaces, public spaces in which the heteroglossia of society is represented and in which negotiation can take place.

Notes

1. The data used in this chapter were collected in the context of the research project 'Changing city spaces', which was carried out within the 5th Framework Programme of the European Union (2002–05).
2. The term *Gastarbeiter* (guest worker) was coined to designate the (predominantly male) workers that came to Western European countries in the period of rapid economic growth in the 1960s and 1970s. It was meant to replace the term *Fremdarbeiter* (foreign worker).

Websites

Radio multikulti Berlin: http://www.multikulti.de
Radio orange, Wien: http://www.orange.or.at
Nachtwerk, Wien: http://nachtwerk.at

16

Dobry den Košice – üdvözlöm Kassát – Hello Kosice: Language Choice in a Slovak Internet Guestbook

Lukas Bleichenbacher

Introduction

Policies and paradoxes

Kosice, the metropolis of Eastern Slovakia, is the country's second largest city and, due to its beautifully restored historic town centre, one of its major tourist destinations. To the linguistically interested visitor however, Kosice presents a number of intriguing paradoxes. The city's rich history of societal multilingualism, which can be gleaned even from a superficial glance at the inscriptions in its historical monuments, is contrasted in current public discourse by a 'Slovak only' ideology vigorously defended even by those who entertain close and unproblematic relations with people of non-Slovak ethnolinguistic background. Hungarian especially is a language frequently to be heard in Kosice, and Hungary itself is only a twenty minute's drive away, but there is no teaching of Hungarian as a foreign language to Kosice's ethnic Slovak majority. Instead, parents prefer to send their children to playgroups where English or German are used, these being the two major foreign languages in Slovakia's educational system (Eurydice 2001: 7). Furthermore, it is an uncontested practice that in all Slovak schools with teaching in one of the minority languages, Slovak is intensively taught as an obligatory second language. And when in August 2003, some thirty foreigners attended a Slovak language course in Kosice, this event was covered not only on the city's local TV channel, but also on a nation-wide radio programme – and even made it to the prime time TV news.

According to Spolsky (2004: 5), any description of language policies has to account for three major components: language practices, beliefs about language, and specific efforts to influence the linguistic behaviour of the speech community in question. Spolsky believes that in most cases, the actual outcome of overt language policies does not correspond to its authors' intentions (2004: 223); a similar point is made by Thomas (2000) with reference to Slovakia.

In this chapter, I will argue that the nationalist and monolingual ideologies underlying language policies on both sides of the Slovak-Hungarian border have indeed proved to be successful at least on a local and regional level, albeit at the expense of members of linguisitic minorities (see Rouillard and Stevenson, both in this volume, on similar observations in an Estonian and German/Austrian context, respectively). In present-day Slovakia however, the intensification of foreign contacts, involving foreign trade, tourism, academic exchanges and, most significantly, the continuing attachment of Slovak emigrants and their descendants to Slovakia, is likely to result in a rather different picture in the near future.

My observations are based on an analysis of language choice (i.e. Spolsky's practices) and metalinguistic statements (beliefs) in a multilingual online text, namely the guestbook of Kosice's official internet website, www.kosice.sk (Mesto Košice: 2003). In this guestbook, contributors from Slovakia as well as from all over the world post messages to comment on the website or the city, greet their friends or relatives, or discuss their Slovak ancestry. At first glance, English is the dominant language in the Kosice guestbook, but by no means the only one, especially in the entries written by European contributors. Therefore, an account of the interrelations between the contributors' countries of origin, the purpose and content of their entries, and the languages they use, will allow me to draw some conclusions on the relation between multilingual policies and practices in a present-day Central European context.

Languages in Kosice – past and present

Since the city of Kosice was first mentioned in 1230 as 'Villa Kassa', it has been referred to by the names of Latin *Cassovia*, Hungarian *Kassa*, German *Kaschau* and, most recently, Slovak *Košice*. *Košice* is currently the only official name of the city, but the other ones are still in use; even *Cassovia* was chosen only recently as the name of a new shopping centre. Like most of present-day Slovakia, the city had belonged to the

Kingdom of Hungary since the Middle Ages, and urban multilingualism in Hungarian, German, Yiddish, and Slovak had characterized the city's everyday life up to the 19th century. However, in the decades following the Austro-Hungarian *Ausgleich* of 1867, an exceedingly strict Hungarian-only policy was enforced, outlawing the use of the Slovak language in nearly all spheres of public life (Němec *et al.* 1994: 11; Mannová and Holec 2000: 196ff.) and aggravating the relationship between the two ethnolinguistic groups for generations to come. When Hungary lost its claims to most of its territories after the First World War, Kassa became Kosice and what had been the Hungarian *felvidék* (highland) became a part of the first Czechoslovak Republic. Throughout the twentieth century, it was the ethnic Hungarians' turn to suffer under equally rigid Slovak-only policies, especially in the wake of the Second World War (during which parts of Southern Slovakia, including Kosice, had again been occupied by Hungary). Hungarian, the once dominant language, was gradually replaced by Slovak. Whereas in 1910, around 75 per cent of the Kosice inhabitants declared themselves as ethnic Hungarians (Jiroušek 2003: 139), only 3.79 per cent did so in 2001. In the entire republic, the percentage of ethnic Hungarians is almost 10 per cent, as can be seen from Table 16.1 (source: Statistical Office of the Slovak Republic 2004; Mesto Košice 2004b).

The early years of post-socialist transformation in no way improved the lot of Slovakia's linguistic minorities – on the contrary, they were denied even basic language rights in a language law issued by the Slovak parliament in 1995. Slovak is still the only language mentioned by name in the national Constitution, but with the implementation of a more tolerant language legislation in 1998, interethnic tensions between Slovaks and Hungarians (and, on a larger scale, the two republics) have recently grown somewhat fainter, without, however, disappearing altogether.[1]

Today, Kosice is the industrial and commercial centre of Eastern Slovakia, the main economic earners being heavy industry, education

Table 16.1 Slovak vs Kosice residents by ethnic structure, 2001 census

	Slovakia	%	Kosice	%
Slovak	4,614,854	85.79	210,340	89.10
Hungarian	520,528	9.68	8,940	3.79
Romani	89,920	1.67	5,055	2.14
Czech	44,620	0.83	2,803	1.19
Other	109,533	2.04	8,955	3.79
Total	5,379,455	100	236,093	100

and transportation (Mesto Košice: 2004c). Kosice has its own international airport and direct train links to major destinations in all
neighbouring countries to the Republic. A motorway from the capital
Bratislava (which will eventually lead to the Ukraine), and another one
from Miskolc in North-Eastern Hungary, are currently under construction; they are expected to promote foreign investment and fuel economic
growth in the region still the poorest in the country, which will also
have its effects on the linguistic situation. The increase of the need for
major Western European languages like English, German, French and
Spanish as well as intensified cross-border tourism to and from Hungary
and Poland are likely to contribute to a further intensification of the
city's multilingual character. Crucially, while the status of Russian,
formerly Slovakia's first and obligatory foreign language, rapidly sunk
after 1989, a renewed emphasis on the learning of Eastern Slavonic
languages would seem reasonable, given Kosice's aspiration to perform
the function of a bridgehead towards its Eastern neighbour, the Ukraine
(Kreyenbühl: 2004).

The Kosice website

Language choice on Slovak city websites

The www.kosice.sk website appears in a Slovak and a slightly reduced
English version, which suggests a preference for the international lingua
franca at the expense of the minority and neighbouring languages. This
very fact is repeatedly referred to in the guestbook itself: While some
contributors compliment the designers on the inclusion of English, others
suggest making the website available in Hungarian, German or French
as well. As shown by an overview of the language versions available on
the official websites of twelve major Slovak cities, a combination of Slovak
and English is not an unusual choice. The same option is offered by the
capital Bratislava and by two other major Western Slovak cities (Trnava
and Zilina (see Table 16.2)):

Monolingual Slovak websites are featured in four cities, all of which,
despite being attractive university towns, share the disadvantage of relatively poor traffic links. The use of German in the case of Trencin, Martin
and Komarno, three cities relatively close to Austria, is clearly aimed at
visitors from German-speaking countries. The status of German as one
of Slovakia's minority languages, however, does not lead to its inclusion
on the website of Poprad, a city which, under the name of *Deutschendorf*,
used to be centre of Saxon settlement. Hungarian and Polish are present

Table 16.2   Language versions of official websites in Slovak cities

Slovak cities	Language versions of official websites
Banska Bystrica, Nitra, Presov, Zvolen	Slovak
Bratislava, **Kosice**, Trnava, Zilina	Slovak, English
Trencin, Martin	Slovak, English, German
Poprad	Slovak, English, Polish
Komarno	Slovak, English, German, Hungarian

on only one website each, the two cities in questions being in close vicinity of the respective borders: Komarno is right across the Danube from its Hungarian twin city Komarom, whereas Poprad is dominated by the Tatra mountain range, which forms a natural border between Slovakia and Poland.

Textlinguistic features of the Kosice guestbook

Visitors of the *www.kosice.sk* website access the entry page of the guestbook through a direct link from the introductory page. There, a short introductory text in English and Slovak invites comments on the website or on Kosice itself by posting entries. Alternatively, the visitor can read through the other entries, which are filed in hyperlinked archives, one for every year from 1998 through 2003. Since every contributor is asked to enter their name, e-mail address, and place of origin, and nearly all actually do so (rather than using a pseudonym), most entries can be categorized not only according to the language(s) used, but also geographically. For this study, the complete guestbook archive was analyzed, a total of 414 entries posted between 1998 and 2003, with an average length of 48.5 words per entry. Although three quarters of all entries contain some linguistic realization of address, there is no visible interaction between the contributors. Thus, the entries are not addressed to other guestbook participants, but rather to the website programmers, to people in and from Kosice, or to a more general web audience. The most frequent topics of the guestbook entries are (1) explaining the contributor's link to Kosice (61 per cent of all entries), (2) commenting on the website (58 per cent), (3) commenting on the city of Kosice (40 per cent), (4) announcing one's visit to Kosice (26 per cent), (5) specific questions or requests (22 per cent), and (6) greeting Kosice or Slovak people (10 per cent). Furthermore, 37 or 8.9 per cent of all entries bear some form of metalinguistic content, the major issues being aspects of the contributors' linguistic autobiographies, or comments on language use in Kosice or on the website itself.

Origin of the guestbook entries

In 406 of 414 entries, guestbook contributors from 39 countries in all 5 continents name the place from where they are writing. Figure 16.1 shows an overview, sorted by geographical regions:

More than a quarter of the guestbook entries are from Slovakia, its three Central European neighbours, or from Germany, Austria and Switzerland. These countries have been preferred destinations for recent Slovak emigrants and are important foreign investors in Slovakia, which is also true for Great Britain, the Netherlands and France. North America is where most extraterritorial Slovaks live, however, which is well illustrated by the fact that nearly 50 per cent of all entries reach the Kosice guestbook from the USA and from Canada. The remainder come from various countries in Central and South America, the Near East and elsewhere. Obviously, these figures do not only reflect interest in Kosice, but also varying degrees of internet access. This partly explains the noteworthy absence of any contribution from the Ukraine, while there is one entry each of Russian and Byelorussian origin; both are written in English.

Languages used in guestbook entries

Whereas 357 or 86 per cent of the entries are written in one language only, some form of switching into another language occurs in as many as 57 entries (14 per cent). In these 'bilingual' messages, one language is always clearly dominant, that is, used for more than half of the entry's text – except in two cases where the same text appears in two language versions (French–English and English–Hungarian). Figure 16.2 shows the number of languages used as the only or the dominant language, sorted by their frequency.

The two main languages, English and Slovak, are chosen for 385 or 93 per cent of all entries. 16 contributors write in one of four neighbouring languages of Slovakia, while other languages (Spanish, French and Serbo-Croatian) are chosen in only 5 further cases. Judging from the content, origin and degree of interlanguage visible in the entries, it could be safely assumed that in at least 61 cases, the contributors use a foreign language for their entry. Of these foreign language entries, 47 are in English, 13 in Slovak, and one entry from Poland is written in foreign language Czech (example 2 below). In the following section, an analysis of language choice patterns sorted by the origin of the guestbook

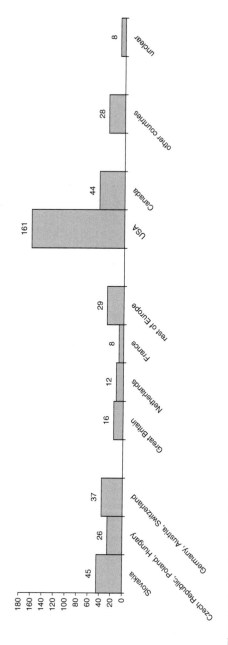

Figure 16.1 Origin of guestbook entries

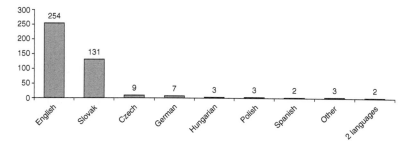

Figure 16.2 Dominant language of entries

entries will shed light on the question of who uses which language to what purpose when an international online community talks about Kosice.

Patterns of language choice in the Kosice guestbook

Guestbook contributors from Slovakia, at least 20 of which live in the city itself, most often write to comment on the website, pay compliments to its designers or suggest additions, for instance local bus timetables. Value judgments about the city itself, practically always of a positive nature (this is true for the entire corpus), also appear frequently in entries from Slovakia, as in example (1) below.[2] Slovak only is used for this entry as in almost all entries from Slovakia, although a different language choice would seem sensible in this very example, where foreign visitors are indirectly addressed:

(1) Naše mesto je vel'mi pekné preto radím cudzincom aby ho navštívili.

(Our city is very nice, therefore I advise foreigners to visit it.)

Table 16.3 Entries from Slovakia, the Czech Republic, Poland and Hungary

Origin of entry	Dominant language of entry				
	Slovak	English	Czech	Polish	Hungarian
Slovakia	43	2	–	–	–
Czech Rep.	2	–	5	–	–
Poland	4	4	1	3	–
Hungary	3	1	–	–	1
Total	52	7	6	3	1

It does not come as a surprise that Czech is used by all contributors from the Czech Republic, except by one Slovak emigrant, given the genetic closeness of these two West Slavonic languages, and a long tradition of bilingual intercommunication where both Czechs and Slovaks typically used their L1 and were understood by their interlocutors.[3] Since Slovaks are still frequently exposed to both written and spoken Czech, no alteration to this pattern can be expected in the near future. A more complex picture is visible in the entries from Poland, where the same high level of linguistic intercomprehension cannot be expected, and language choice has to be carefully negotiated. Polish contributors write in Polish, English, Slovak as a foreign language and even in the lingua franca Czech. The author of example (2) below makes his choice of Czech explicit by apologizing for not knowing Slovak, and expressing his uncertainty as to whether writing in Polish might suit his potential pen pals in Kosice:

(2)   Dobry den! Prominte, mluvim jen cesky a polsky (cesky jen trochu). Jsem Polak. Moze zrozumie mnie kto z kosic po polsku? Bardzo chtel by korespondowac z jakim kosicanem.:)

(Hello! Excuse me, I speak only Czech and Polish (Czech only a bit). I'm Polish. Maybe somebody from Kosice understands me in Polish? I'd like very much to correspond with somebody from Kosice.:)

The use of English (rather than, for instance, Russian or German) as a lingua franca for cross-border communication in Central Europe appears as a viable option. Example (3), where a Polish contributor switches from English into Polish for a final greeting, illustrates that these entry writers manage to make themselves understood despite their imperfect command of English:

(3)   [...] Unfotunetly I don't make my own page, but I think about it. **Pozdrowienia z Polski:)**

([...] **Greetings from Poland:**))

Only five entries in the guestbook are from Hungary, which is a strikingly low number considering Kosice's undeniable appeal for Hungarian tourists (owing to, for instance, the birthplace of the writer Sándor Márai and the resting place of Ferenc Rakoczi, an 18th century freedom fighter immortalized on the Hungarian 500 Forint banknote). Whilst three contributors write in Slovak and one in English, Hungarian is used only in one case, by a descendant of emigrants from Kassa/Kosice complaining about the absence of Hungarian and German on the website:

(4) [...] Kitünő, részletes igényes az oldal, csak a magyar nyelvű verziót hiányolom, meg a német nyelvűt. Remélem lessz a jövőben ilyen.

([...] The website is excellent, detailed and demanding, I only miss the Hungarian and also the German language version. I hope they will be there in the future.)

Although German is never used as a lingua franca in the guestbook, contributors from German-speaking countries confidently use this language even when addressing a specific question to the website staff, as in example (5) below. English is used still more frequently, however; and some contributors spice their entries with a switch into Slovak for place names, to greet and express sympathy towards their audience, or even, as in (6), to evoke a romantic atmosphere:

(5) Herzliche Grüsse aus Zürich. Wir haben viel Gutes über eure Stadt gehört. Unsere Mutter wuchs in Kosice auf (**Ulica Rasinova**). Können Sie uns sagen, wie die Strasse heute heisst? [...]

(Warm greetings from Zurich. We have heard much good about your town. Our mother grew up in Kosice (**Rasinova street**). Can you tell us what this street is called today? [...])

Table 16.4   Entries from Germany, Austria and Switzerland

Origin of entry	Dominant language of entry			
	Slovak	*English*	*German*	*Hungarian*
Germany	6	11	4	2
Switzerland	2	5	2	–
Austria	2	2	1	–
Total	10	18	7	2

(6) hi kosice!greetings from a 21 year-old austrian student!!!!!!!!a nice town with such a cute habitant!**dvatsat bozkov:**)))))))))

([...] **twenty kisses:**)))))))))

Slovak and Hungarian are also used for entire entries, namely by first generation emigrants to these German-speaking countries. For members of the Slovak expatriate community, the Kosice website is a welcome means to stay in touch with their country of origin, greet other Slovaks abroad or express their feelings of homesickness. For such in-group communication, Slovak is the obvious choice:

(7) Ahoj Kosice! Pekna Stranka! Uz sa tesim na vianoce, ked konecne znova uvidim MOJE MESTO.

(Hi Kosice! Nice site! I'm already looking forward to Christmas, when I finally see MY CITY again.)

Similar patterns of language choice can be observed in the rest of Europe, where English is the default choice for non-Slovak contributors both from Great Britain and the continent. Example (8) from the Netherlands and (9) from Denmark illustrate how English is used with very different levels of proficiency:

(8) i just want to tell that i like kosice. it is a warm town and compared to bratislava there is real streetlife. [...]

(9) it is very nice with your page, so us turister can find information about kulture, zoo, sport yes everthing we need before we trewel too Slovakiet it's very nice. [...]

Table 16.5   Entries from the rest of Europe

Origin of entry	Dominant language of entry						
	Slovak	English	French	Italian	Spanish	Serbo-Croatian	2 languages
GB	6	9	1	–	–	–	1
Netherlands	–	14	–	–	–	–	–
France	–	7	1	–	–	–	1
rest	9	16	–	1	1	1	–
Total	15	46	2	1	1	1	2

Only five contributors choose to write in languages other than English and Slovak, which results in a strikingly low representation of Europe's three major Romance languages. Slovak is again the preferred option for first generation emigrants, but it is also chosen for complete entries by two foreign language users. One of them is a former student at a Kosice university living in Sweden, whereas the Italian author of (10) sends season's greeting from Italy to Kosice, where he spent time as a steel worker long ago:

(10) vesele vianoce a stcasni novy rok vsetkim kosicanom a okolie vam praje giuseppe p.s. som tam bol vroku 1966 a 1972 na montase vsz ciao [. . .]

(merry christmas and a happy new year to all the inhabitants of kosice and surroundings from giuseppe. p.s. i was there in the years 1966 and 1972 working on assembly at the vsz. bye [. . .])

The results for the Northern American entries substantiate the findings of Hammerová and Ripka's (1994) survey of the Slovak Americans' linguistic behaviour. Large-scale Slovak (especially Eastern) emigration to this part of the world began towards the end of 19th century, but linguistic assimilation took place fairly rapidly – it was generally members of the second generation who abandoned their parents' languages in favour of English. However, 'Slovak self-identification has persisted into the third and fourth generations' (1994: 67). Unsurprisingly, many Northern American contributors to the Kosice guestbook are from a Slovak background but they rarely write entries entirely in Slovak unless, as they most often state explicitly, they are first generation emigrants. Interestingly, the percentage of Slovak-language entries from Canada is much higher as opposed to the US, which might be linked to the different attitudes towards multilingualism in the two

Table 16.6 Entries from North America

Origin of entry	Dominant language of entry		
	Slovak	English	Czech
USA	23	136	2
Canada	17	27	
Total	40	163	2

countries. For members of later generations, family roots remain an important issue, which they highlight in their entries by regretting their language loss, as in example (11), or by adding some Slovak phrases, as in (12) by a descendant of Slovak emigrants living in Washington State:

(11) [...] Until I was 6 years old, I spoke only the Slovak of my grandparents who came to the US in the early 1900's. I slowly lost much of the language after they passed away, & my English orientation took over. Couple years ago, at a State (NJ) Slovak Festival, I overheard a visiting Slovak soccer team talking. I understood only a word here and there. My language is weak, but my love for Slovakia is forever. [...]

(12) **Ahoj, 'Slovak som a Slovak budem.'** Kosice is a beautiful city. My wife and I visited my **stary otec's** birthplace in Kysta.We had the trip of a lifetime! [...]
(**Hi, 'Slovak I am and Slovak I will be.'** [...] my **grandfather's** birthplace [...])

The inverse phenomenon, switches into English in mainly Slovak entries, are often triggered by meta-medial comments related to information technology, as in example (13) with its striking misrepresentation of present-day Slovak infrastructure. The author of (14), a former university EFL teacher at Kosice's Air Force Academy, also uses English in his comment about the website, but resists the temptation to continue in English and switches back into Slovak twice:

(13) [...] Vas **website** je skutocne krasny. Moja manzelka to nasla lebo ja som si ani nemyslel ze na Slovenku maju pocitace **(computers let alone websites).** [...]

([...] Your **website** is really beautiful. My wife found it, for I wouldn't have even thought that there are computers in Slovakia **(computers let alone websites).** [...])

(14) Ahoj! **This is a great website!** Volam sa [...] Dejakujem tebe na ta navstevna kniha! **I wish my Slovak was better!** Dovidenia! [...].
(Hi! **This is a great website!** My name is [...] Thank you for this guestbook! **I wish my Slovak was better!** Goodbye! [...]

Table 16.7 Entries from various other countries

Origin of entry	Dominant language of entry		
	Slovak	English	Spanish
Central and South America	1	6	1
Near East and Asia	5	7	–
Africa, Australia and New Zealand	6	3	–
Unknown origin	3	5	–
Total	15	21	1

The findings for Europe and Northern America are confirmed in the case of the remaining parts of the world, from where emigrants and other people with Slovak links write to the Kosice website. Spanish is the only other language used once by a Chilean, otherwise non-Slovak contributors choose English. Slovak is used even in cases such as example (15), where an emigrant has been living in South Africa for over 30 years:

(15) Ja sa este stale pokladam za Kosicana i ked zijem v Juhoafrickej Republike od 1968-ho roku. [...]

(I still declare myself a Kosican although I have lived in the Republic of South Africa since 1968. [...])

In five cases however, Slovak is clearly used as a foreign language by contributors who lived in Kosice as foreign workers or students. The Syrian author of example (16) below displays a learner variety of Slovak which is as grammatically fossilized as it is rich in vocabulary. His use of Slovak ties in with his expression of profound sympathy towards his former host country, and his Slovak-only entry is the second longest in the entire guestbook:

(16) [...] mily priatelia! mily kosicanom! vsetkym vam zelam z celeho srdca zdaravie, vela uspechov vo vase stranke, ozaj vy slovensky narod ste velmy pohostiny. [...]

([...] dear friends! dear kosicani! From the bottom of my heart I wish you all good health, good luck with your website, really you the Slovak people are very hospitable [...])

This exemplifies two major findings of this analysis: On the one hand, the globalization of the Slovak language, and on the other hand, the guestbook contributors' self-confident use of albeit imperfect foreign language writing skills: the objective to get their message across often overrules their anxieties about making 'mistakes' in writing.

Conclusions

This study has shown that despite the large number of languages potentially available to the Kosice guestbook contributors, two languages dominate while many others are largely absent. The predominance of English is mainly due to the importance of the US, Canada and Great Britain as targets of Slovak emigration. This is unlikely to change at least in the near future with respect to Great Britain, where citizens of the new EU member states may join the labour market much more easily than on the continent. Whilst most entries in English are thus written by contributors from English-speaking countries, the language also performs the functions of both a global and a European lingua franca. No other language, apart from the above-mentioned single instance of Czech, is used to this purpose in the Kosice guestbook. English does not, however, compromise the use of the Slovak language in intra-Slovak interaction; nor does the medium of communication, the internet, cause the Slovak contributors to choose English rather than their L1, which underlines Crystal's point that the web is becoming increasingly multilingual (2001: 216ff). Slovak is also used in some cross-border interaction by Poles and other foreigners with strong professional or academic links to Slovakia. This suggests that the gradual transformation of Slovakia into a target of different forms of immigration does not pose any risk to the status of the Slovak language itself. Foreigners who are well integrated in Slovak society gladly learn the language, express pride in their acquired proficiency and spread the word back home, rather than trying to impose the use of, say, English on their Slovak interlocutors.

The strikingly low number of entries in other languages reflects the limited choice of languages – English and Slovak – by the website designers, a fact repeatedly referred to by the guestbook contributors. Indeed, if other languages like Hungarian, German, Polish or French were added to the website, more contributors might feel confident in using them in their entries. In a similar vein, cases where contributors write in two languages to address a larger audience are very rare. Instead, language switching in the guestbook entries mainly aims at expressing the contributors' multilingual identities, and also their sympathy with specific target groups. Both language switching and metalinguistic accounts of language identity are a distinctive feature of the Kosice guestbook – crucially however, this is not the case in entries from Slovakia itself. The fact that multilingualism is neither performed, nor even referred to by autochtonous Slovaks illustrates the extent to which Slovak-only ideologies have proved to be successful.

The success of Slovakia's reintegration into Europe – not only as an administrative project, but as a multiplication of real-life contact situations across both political and linguistic borders, depends on the finding of alternatives to these monolingual mindsets. If the Slovaks of all ethnolinguistic groups recognize the cultural, touristic and economic benefits of multilingualism rather than considering it as a disadvantage or even a sign of segregation, the country, and especially the structurally weaker Eastern Slovak area around Kosice, will greatly profit. In this sense, and with respect not only to Hungarian, but to other languages as well, it can be hoped that *Quasimodo*'s Christmas wish may become true: When in December 2002, the Slovak newspaper *SME* printed a list of Christmas wishes they had previously asked their readers to contribute, material presents were what most people had in mind. The person writing under the pseudonym of *Quasimodo*, though, had more of a linguistic request, which summarizes the recommendations of this paper in an elegant way:

Quasimodo: Milý Ježiško, nauč, prosím Ťa, Maďarov po slovensky a Slovákov po maďarsky. Aspoň počúvať' a trošku viac chápat'.

(Quasimodo: Dear Baby Jesus, please teach the Hungarians some Slovak, and the Slovaks some Hungarian. At least to listen and to understand a bit more.)

(from: s.n., Čo by si želali pod stromček čitatelia *SME* [What *SME* readers wish for Christmas], *SME*, 23 December 2002: 6).

Notes

1. Whereas societal multilingualism in and around Slovakia was not a major issue for pre-1989 sociolinguistics (see Hammer: 1995), the extent of the language strife is well reflected in the somewhat partial nature of many scholarly contributions published since the 1990s. On the one hand, Slovak linguists insisted that the minority languages were catered for well enough and stressed the need to defend the Slovak language against Hungarian. See, for instance, Dorula 1997; Kačala 1994, 1997; Števček 1995. Duszak (this volume)

describes similar conservative undercurrents in Polish linguistics. These positions were met with strong opposition from the viewpoint of the linguistic minorities, such as Simon and Kontra 2000 or Daftary and Gál 2000. Some notable exceptions, based on more scientific than ideological approaches, are the works of Ondrejovič 1996a; Langman and Lánstyák 2000; Lánstyák 2000.

2. All non-English quotations are followed by my translations. Switching into another language is indicated with bold face.

3. Aspects of Czech–Slovak bilingualism since the split of Czechoslovakia in 1993 are discussed in Berger 2000; Buzássyová 1995a, b; Nábělková 1999.

Websites

Mesto Košice (2003) 'Guestbook = Navstevna Kniha www.kosice.sk' http://www.kosice.sk/guestbk/

Mesto Košice (2004a) 'Mesto Košice' www.kosice.sk

Mesto Košice (2004b) 'Demografické údaje = Demographic data' http://www.kosice.sk/info/basic/demograf.htm

Mesto Košice (2004c) 'Hospodársko-ekonomické informácie = Economic information' http://www.kosice.sk/info/basic/hosp_eko.htm

References

Aarbakke, V. (2003) *Ethnic Rivalry and the Quest for Macedonia (1870–1913)* (New York: East European Monographs, 629).

Ahrens, R. (ed.) (2003) *Europäische Sprachpolitik* (Heidelberg: Winter).

Aitchison, J. (2002) 'Birdy birds and bubbles: identifying and evaluating mental models', in Cormeraie *et al.* (2002), 1–12.

Alexander, N. (1985a) 'Nation and ethnicity in South Africa', in Alexander (1985) *Sow the Wind: Contemporary Speeches* (Johannesburg: Skotaville), 41–56.

Alexander, N. (1985b) 'Race, ethnicity and nationalism in social science in Southern Africa', in Alexander (1985), 126–53.

Alexander, N. (1989) *Language Policy and National Unity in South Africa/Azania* (Cape Town: Buchu).

Alexander, N. (2002) *An Ordinary Country: Issues in the Transition from Apartheid to Democracy in South Africa* (Pietermaritzburg: University of Natal Press).

Althusser, L. (1971) 'Ideology and ideological state apparatuses', in Althusser (1971), 85–126.

Althusser, L (ed.) (1971) *Lenin and Philosophy* (New York/London: Monthly Review Press).

Anderson, B. (1983, 2nd edn, 1991) *Imagined Communities: Reflections on the Origin and Spread of Nationalism* (London: Verso).

Anderson-Levitt, K. (1987) 'Cultural knowledge for teaching first grade: an example from France', in Spindler and Spindler (1987), 171–92.

Andriuškevičius, A. (1995) 'Semi-nonconformist Lithuanian painting', in Rosenfeld and Dodge (1995), 218–26.

Androutsopoulos, J. and Georgakopoulou, A. (eds) *Discourse Constructions of Youth Identities* (Amsterdam: Benjamins).

Ang, I. (1991) *Desperately Seeking the Audience* (London: Routledge).

Anusiewicz J. and Siciński, B. (eds) (1994) *Język polityki a współczesna kultura polityczna* (Wroclaw: Towarzystwo Przyjaciół Polonistyki Wrocławskiej).

Appadurai, A. (1996) *Modernity at Large: Cultural Dimensions of Globalization* (Minneapolis: University of Minnesota Press).

Arends-Tóth, J. (2003) *Psychological Acculturation of Turkish Migrants in the Netherlands: Issues in Theory and Assessment* (Amsterdam: Dutch University Press).

Arendt, H. (1951) *The Origins of Totalitarianism* (New York).

Atton, C. (2002) *Alternative Media* (London: Sage).

Auer, P. and Di Luzio, A. (eds) (1992) *The Contextualization of Language* (Amsterdam: John Benjamins).

Auer, P. and Dirim, İ. (2003) 'Socio-cultural orientation, urban youth styles and the spontaneous acquisition of Turkish by non-Turkish adolescents in Germany', in Androutsopoulos and Georgakopoulou, (2003), 223–46.

Austin, J. L. (1962) *How to Do Things with Words* (Cambridge, Mass.: Harvard University Press).

Baker, S. (ed.) (2002) *Language Policy: Lessons from Global Models* (Monterey, CA: Monterey Institute of International Studies).

Bakhtin, M. M. (1981) *The Dialogic Imagination: Four Essays* (Austin: University of Texas).

Balibar, E. (2001) *Nous, citoyens d'Europe: les frontières, l'état, le peuple* (Paris: Editions la Découverte).

Barbour, S. and Carmichael, C. (eds) (2000) *Language and Nationalism in Europe* (Oxford: Oxford University Press).

Barth, F. (1969) *Ethnic Groups and Boundaries: The Social Organization of Cultural Difference* (Long Grove: Waveland Press).

Bassel, N. (2002) *Сопричастность: сборник статей и докладов* (Tallinn: Estonian American Business College).

Baudrillard, J. (1988) *America* (London: Verso).

Bauman, R. and Briggs, C. (2003) *Voices of Modernity: Language Ideologies and the Production of Inequality* (Cambridge: Cambridge University Press).

Belloc, H. (1925) *The Cruise of the Nona* (London: Constable).

Berger, T. (2000). 'Die Rolle des Tschechischen in der heutigen Slowakei', in Panzer (2000), 179–196.

Bezemer, J. (2003) *Dealing with Multilingualism in Education – A Case Study of a Dutch Primary School Classroom.* (Amsterdam: Aksant).

Biko, S. (2004) *I Write What I like: A Selection of His Writings* (Johannesburg: Picador Africa).

Billig, M. (1995) *Banal Nationalism* (London: Sage).

Bjelić, D. I. and Savić, O. (eds) (2002) *Balkan as Metaphor: Between Globalization and Fragmentation* (Cambridge, Mass., London: The MIT Press).

Blackledge, A. (2002) ' "What sort of people can look at a chicken and think dofednod?" – Language, ideology and nationalism in public discourse', *Multilingua*, 21, 197–226.

Blackledge, A. (2004) 'Constructions of identity in political discourse in multilingual Britain', in Pavlenko and Blackledge (2004), 68–92.

Blackledge, A. and Pavlenko, A. (2002) 'Introduction', *Multilingua* 21 (2/3), 121–40.

Blackledge, A. and Pavlenko, A. (eds) (2004) *Negotiation of Identities in Multilingual Contexts* (Clevedon: Multilingual Matters).

Blommaert, J. (ed.) (1999a) *Language Ideological Debates* (Berlin/New York: Mouton de Gruyter).

Blommaert, J. (1999b) 'The debate is open' in Blommaert (1999a), 1–38.

Blommaert, J. (2001a) 'Context is/as critique', *Critique of Anthropology* 21 (1), 13–32.

Blommaert, J. (2001b) 'Investigating narrative inequality: African asylum seekers' stories in Belgium', *Discourse & Society* 12 (4), 413–49.

Blommaert, J. (2003) 'Commentary: a sociolinguistics of globalisation', *Journal of Sociolinguistics*, 7 (4), 607–24.

Blommaert, J. and Verschueren, J. (eds) (1991) *The Pragmatics of Intercultural and International Communication* (Amsterdam: John Benjamins).

Blommaert, J. and Verschueren, J. (1998a) 'The role of language in European nationalist ideologies', in Schieffelin *et al.* (1998), 189–210.

Blommaert, J. and Verschueren, J. (1998b) *Debating Diversity: Analysing the Discourse of Tolerance* (London: Routledge).

Blunkett, D. (2005) *A New England: An English Identity Within Britain*, speech to the Institute for Public Policy Research, 14 March 2005 (London: ippr).

Boeckmann, K-B., Eder, U., Furch, E. and Plutzer, V. (2003) ' "Sprich Deutsch und du gehörst zu uns!" Deutsch als Zweitsprache bei der Integration von

MigrantInnen und in der LehrerInnenaus- und -fortbildung', in Busch and de Cillia (2003), 43–62.

Bond, P. (2004) *Talk Left, Walk Right: South Africa's Frustrated Global Reforms* (Scottsville: University of KwaZulu-Natal Press).

Bourdieu, P. (1981) *Language and Symbolic Power* (Cambridge: Harvard University).

Boykov, V. and Bassel, N. (eds) (2000) *Русские в Эстонии на пороге XXI века: прошлое, настаящое, будущее* (Tallinn: Russian Research Centre in Estonia).

Bradford, H. (1984) 'Mass movements and the petty bourgeoisie: the social origins of ICU leadership, 1924–1929', *Journal of African History* 25.

Bralczyk, J. (2003) *O języku polskiej polityki lat osiemdziesiątych i dziewięćdziesiątych* (Warszawa: Trio).

Bralczyk, J. and Mosiołek-Kłosińska, K. (eds) (2000) *Język w mediach masowych* (Warszawa: Oświata).

Bralczyk, J. and Mosiołek-Kłosińska, K. (eds) (2001) *Zmiany w publicznych zwyczajach językowych* (Warszawa: RJP).

Brand, G. (2004a) 'Taalpolitiek as studieterrein' (Language politics as a field of study), *Akripolis*: 'Pols 2004' www.akripolis.org

Brand, G. (2004b) 'Demokrasie na 10 jaar – winste en verliese' (Democracy after 10 years – gains and losses), *Woord en Daad / Word and Action* Winter edition.

Brecht, R. and Rivers, W. (2002) 'The language crisis in the United States: language, national security and the federal role', in Baker (2002), 76–90.

Brenneis, D. and Macaulay, R. (eds) (1996) *The Matrix of Language: Contemporary Linguistic Anthropology* (Boulder: Westview Press).

Briggs, C. (1997) 'Notes on a "confession": On the construction of gender, sexuality and violence in an infanticide case', *Pragmatics* 7 (4), 519–46.

Brown, K. (2003) *Macedonia's Child-Grandfathers: The Transnational Politics of Memory, Exile and Return 1949–1998* (Washington: Donald W. Treadgold Papers series, 38).

Browne, T. (1658/1906) *Hydriotaphia: Urn Burial* (London: Dent).

Brubaker, R. (1996) *Nationalism Reframed: Nationhood and the National Question in the New Europe* (Cambridge: Cambridge University Press).

Brumfit, C. J. (2001) *Individual Freedom in Language Teaching* (Oxford: Oxford University Press).

Brunner, G. and Lemberg, H. (eds) (1994) *Volksgruppen in Ostmittel- und Südosteuropa* (Baden-Baden: Nomos Verlag).

Brutt-Griffler, J. (2002a) *World English: A Study of Its Development* (Clevedon: Multilingual Matters).

Brutt-Griffler, J. (2002b) 'Class, ethnicity and language rights: an analysis of British colonial policy in Lesotho and Sri Lanka and some implications for language policy', *Journal of Language, Identity, and Education* 1 (3), 207–34 (and the Forum discussing this paper, *Journal of Language, Identity, and Education* 3 (2), 2004: 127–60).

Busch, B. (2004) *Sprachen im Disput. Medien und Öffentlichkeit in multilingualen Gesellschaften* (Klagenfurt/Celovec: Drava).

Busch, B. and de Cillia, R. (eds) (2003) *Sprachenpolitik in Österreich. Eine Bestandsaufnahme* (Frankfurt: Peter Lang).

Busch, B. and Kelly-Holmes, H. (2004a) 'Language boundaries as social, political and discursive constructs', in Busch and Kelly-Holmes (2004b), 1–13.

Busch, B. and Kelly-Holmes, H. (eds) (2004b) *Language, Discourse and Borders. Current Issues in Language and Society* (Clevedon: Multilingual Matters).

Butler *et al.* (eds) (1987) *Democratic Liberalism in South Africa: Its History and Prospect* (University Press of New England).

Butler, J. (1993) *Bodies that Matter: On the Discursive Limits of 'Sex'* (New York/ London: Routledge).

Butler, J. (1997) *Excitable Speech: A Politics of the Performative* (New York/London: Routledge).

Butler, J. (1999 [1990]) *Gender Trouble: Feminism and the Subversion of Identity* (New York/London: Routledge).

Buttler, D., Kurkowska, H. and Satkiewicz, H. (1971) *Kultura języka polskiego* (Warszawa: PWN).

Buzássyová, K. (1995a) 'Aspekty kontaktov slovenčiny a češtiny', in Ondrejovič and Šimková (1995), 163–182.

Buzássyová, K. (1995b) 'Vzt'ah slovenčiny a češtiny a jazyková kultúra', in Dorul'a (1995), 87–95.

Calvet, L-J. (1987) *La Guerre des Langues et les Politiques Linguistiques* (Paris: PUF).

Calvet, L-J. (1994) 'Les politiques de diffusion des langues en Afrique Francophone', *International Journal of the Sociology of Language*, 107, 67–76.

Cameron, D. (1999) *Verbal Hygiene* (London: Routledge).

Cameron, D. and Kulick, D. (2003), *Language and Sexuality* (Cambridge/New York: Cambridge University Press).

Canagarajah, S. (2004) 'Multilingual writers and the struggle for voice in academic discourse', in Pavlenko and Blackledge (2004), 266–89.

Carrington, B. and Short, G. (1989) *Race, Ethnicity and the Primary School*. (London: NFER–Nelson).

Carter, R. (2004) *Language and Creativity* (London: Routledge).

Castells, M. (2003) *Das Informationszeitalter III. Jahrtausendwende* (Opladen: Leske+budrich).

Ceaser, J. W. (1997) *Reconstructing America: The Symbol of America in Modern Thought* (New Haven: Yale University Press).

Chambers, J. K., Schilling-Estes, N. and Trudgill, P. (eds) *Handbook of Language Variation and Change* (Oxford: Basil Blackwell).

Cherryholmes, C. (1988) *Power and Criticism: Post-structural Investigations in Education*. (New York: Teachers College Press).

Chinn, J. and Kaiser, R. (1996) *Russians as the New Minority: Ethnicity and Nationalism in the Soviet Successor States* (Boulder, Colorado: Westview Press).

Chloupek, J. and Nekvapil, J. (eds) (1987) *Reader in Czech Sociolinguistics* (Amsterdam: John Benjamins).

Clark, H. (1996) *Using Language* (Cambridge: Cambridge University Press).

Clogg, R. (ed.) (2002) *Minorities in Greece. Aspects of a Plural Society* (London: Hurst & Company).

Clyne, M. (ed.) (1997) *Undoing and Redoing Corpus Planning* (The Hague, Berlin: Mouton de Gruyter).

Coleman, J. (1996) *Studying Languages: Survey of British and European Students – the Proficiency, Background, Attitudes and Motivations of Students in Foreign Languages in the United Kingdom and Europe* (London: CILT).

Collins, J. (1996) 'Socialization to text: Structure and contradiction in schooled literacy', in Silverstein and Urban (1996), 203–28.

Cope, B. and Kalantzis, M. (eds) (2000) *Multiliteracies. Literacy Learning and the Design of Social Future* (London: Routledge).

Cormeraie, S., Killick, D. and Parry, M. (eds) *Revolutions in Consciousness: Local Identities, Global Concerns in 'Language and Intercultural Communication'* (Leeds Metropolitan University: International Association for Languages and Intercultural Communication).

Cortese, G. and Duszak, A. (eds) (2005) *Identity, Community, Discourse: English in Intercultural Settings* (Bern: Peter Lang).

Coupland , N. (2003) 'Introduction: sociolinguistics and globalisation', *Journal of Sociolinguistics*, 7 (4), 465–73.

Coupland, N., Sarangi, S. and Candlin, C. (eds) (2001) *Sociolinguistics and Social Theory* (Harlow: Longman).

Crawford, J. (1992) *Hold Your Tongue. Bilingualism and the Politics of 'English Only'* (Reading MA: Addison-Wesley).

Crowley, T. (1991) *Proper English?* (London: Routledge).

Crystal, D. (1997) *English as a Global Language* (Cambridge: Cambridge University Press).

Crystal, D. (2001) *Language and the Internet* (Cambridge: Cambridge University Press).

Daftary, F. and Gál, K. (2000) 'The new Slovak Language Law: Internal or External Politics?' http://www.ecmi.de/doc/download/working_paper_8.pdf

Dahlstedt, K.-H. (1976) 'Societal ideology and language cultivation: The case of Swedish', *International Journal of the Sociology of Language* 10, 17–50.

Daneš, F. (1987) 'Values and attitudes in language standardization', in Chloupek and Nekvapil (1987), 206–45.

Danforth, L. (1995) *The Macedonian Conflict. Ethnic Nationalism in a Transnational World* (Princeton: University Press).

Danthine, J.-P. (2001) 'A propos de la mondialisation', http://www.hec.unil.ch/jdanthine/Press/24heures/mondiali.pdf

Daun, Å. (1996) *Swedish Mentality* (University Park: Pennsylvania State University Press).

De Beaugrande, R. (1996) *New Foundations for a Science of Text and Discourse* (Norwood: Ablex).

De Caluwe, J. *et al.* (2002) *Taal Variatie & Taalbeleid: Bijdragen aan het Taalbeleid in Nederland en Vlaanderen.* (Antwerp–Apeldoorn: Garant–Nederlandse Taalunie).

De Swaan, A. (2001) *Words of the World: The Global Language System* (Cambridge, UK: Polity Press).

Delrue, K. *et al.* (1996) *Optimaliseringsmodellen van Onderwijs in Eigen Taal en Cultuur* (Gent/Leuven: Steunpunt ICO, Vakgroep Pedagogiek/Steunpunt NT2).

Derrida, J. (1991 [1972]) 'Signature event context', in Kamuf (1991), 80–111.

Dimitrov, B. (2000) *Desette lăži na makedonizma* (Sofia: Aniko).

Dodge, N. and Hilton, A. (eds) (1977) *New Art from the Soviet Union: The Known and Unknown* (Washington: Acropolis).

Dorul'a, J. (ed.) (1995) *Spisovná slovenčina a jazyková kultúra* (Bratislava: VEDA).

Dorul'a J. (1997) 'Jazyk a identita, jazyk a zákon', in Ondrejovič (1997), 108–112.

Drew, A. (2002) *Discordant Comrades: Identities and Loyalties on the South African Left* (Pretoria: UNISA Press).

Dubow, S. (1987) 'Race, civilization and culture: the elaboration of segregationist discourse in the inter-war years', in Marks and Trapido (1987).

Duranti, A. and Goodwin, C. (eds) (1992) *Rethinking Context: Language as an interactive phenomenon* (Cambridge: Cambridge University Press).

Duszak, A. (2004a) 'Exploring a new ecology for Critical Discourse Analysis: some remarks on critical linguistics in Poland'. Paper read at International Conference on Critical Discourse Analysis, Valencia, 5–8 May 2004.

Duszak, A. (2004b) 'Globalisation as interdiscursivity: on the spread of global intertexts', in Duszak and Okulska (2004), 117–32.

Duszak, A. (2005) 'Between styles and values: an academic community in transition', in Cortese and Duszak (2005), 91–94.

Duszak, A. and Okulska, U. (eds) (2004) *Speaking from the Margin. Global English from a European Perspective* (Frankfurt/M: Peter Lang).

Echchaibi, N. (2002) '(Be)longing media: minority radio between cultural retention and renewal', *javnost/the public* 9 (1), 37–51.

Edwards, J. (2001) 'No good past Dover', *English Today* 17, 3–12.

Edwards, J. (2003) 'Contextualizing language rights', *Journal of Human Rights* 2, 551–71.

Ehn, B., Fyrkman, J. and Löfgren, E. (eds) *Försvenskningen av Sverige. Det nationellas förvandlingar* (Stockholm: Natur och Kultur).

Eisenlohr, P. (2004) 'Language revitalization and new technologies: Cultures of electronic mediation and the refiguring of communities', *Annual Review of Anthropology* 33, 21–45.

Ellegård A. (1989) 'Engelskan i svenskan', *Språk i Norden 1989*, 67–76.

Erickson, F. (1986) 'Qualitative methods in research on teaching', in Wittrock (1986), 119–61.

Eurydice (2001) 'Foreign language teaching in schools in Europe. Situation in: Slovakia' http://www.mszs.si/eurydice/pub/eurydice/fltndsk.pdf

Everly, R. (1997) 'Ethnic assimilation or ethnic diversity? Integration and Estonia's citizenship law', in Kirch (1997), 106–21.

Extra, G. and Gorter, D. (eds) (2001) *The Other Languages of Europe* (Clevedon: Multilingual Matters).

Extra, G. and Yağmur, K. (eds) (2004) *Urban Multilingualism in Europe – Immigrant Minority Languages at Home and School.* (Clevedon: Multilingual Matters).

Fairclough, N. (1989) *Language and Power* (London: Longman).

Fairclough, N. (1995) *Media Discourse* (London: Edward Arnold).

Fairclough, N. (2000) 'Multiliteracies and language. Order of discourse and intertextuality', in Cope and Kalantzis (2000) 162–81.

Fairclough, N. (1992) *Discourse and Social Change* (Cambridge: Polity Press).

Feinstein, S. C. (1977) 'The avant-garde in Soviet Estonia', in Dodge and Hilton (1977), 31–4.

Fietz, Martina (1999) ' "Wir müssen den Zuzug von Ausländern klar begrenzen" ' (*Die Welt* 28 December 1998) http://www.welt.de/daten/1998/ 12/28/1228de83861.htx

Fishman, J. (1968) 'Nationality-nationalism and nation-nationism', in Fishman *et al.* (1968), 39–52.

Fishman, J. (1989) *Language and Ethnicity in Minority Sociolinguistic Perspective* (Clevedon: Multilingual Matters).

Fishman, J. (1991) *Reversing Language Shift: Theoretical and Empirical Foundations of Assistance to Threatened Languages* (Clevedon: Multilingual Matters).

Fishman, J., Ferguson, C. and Das Gupta, J. (eds) (1968) *Language Problems of Developing Nations* (New York: John Wiley and Sons).

Foucault, M. (1986) 'La gouvernementalité: texte d'une leçon', in *Actes. Les Cahiers d'action juridiques*, No. 54.

Foucault, M. (1998 [1978]) *The Will to Knowledge; The History of Sexuality: Vol 1* (London: Penguin).

Franchon, C. and Vargaftig, M. (eds) (1995) *European Television: Immigration and Ethnic Minorities* (London: Libbey).

Friedman, V. (2001) 'Romani multilingualism in its Balkan context', *Sprachtypologie und Universalienforschung* 54, 146–59.

Fyfe, A. and Figueroa, P. (eds) (1993) *Education for Cultural Diversity* (London: Routledge).

Gajda, S. (2000) 'Media – stylowy tygiel współczesnej polszczyzny', in Bralczyk and Mosiołek-Kłosińska (2000), 19–27.

Gal, S. (1978) 'Peasant men can't get wives: language change and sex roles in a bilingual community', *Language in Society* 7, 1–16.

Gal, S. (1979) *Language Shift: Social Determinants of Linguistic Change in Bilingual Austria* (New York: Academic Press).

Gal, S. (1991) 'Bartók's funeral: Europe in Hungarian political rhetoric', *American Ethnologist* 18 (3), 440–58.

Gal, S. (1993) 'Diversity and contestation in linguistic ideologies: German-speakers in Hungary', *Language in Society* 22 (3), 337–59.

Gal, S. and Woolard, K. (eds) (2001a) *Languages and Publics: The Making of Authority* (Manchester: St.Jerome).

Gal, S. and Woolard, K. (2001b) 'Constructing languages and publics: authority and representation', in Gal and Woolard (2001a), 1–12.

Gardt, A and Hüppauf, B. (eds) (2004) *Globalization and the Future of German* (Berlin/New York: Mouton de Gruyter).

Gee, J. (1999) *An Introduction to Discourse Analysis – Theory and Method* (London: Routledge).

Gelazis, N. M. (2003) 'The effects of EU conditionality on citizenship policies and the protection of national minorities in the Baltic states', in Pettai and Zielonka (2003), 46–74.

Gellner, E. (1983) *Nations and Nationalism* (New York: Cornell University Press).

Giddens, A. (1991) *Modernity and Self-Identity: Self and Society in the Late Modern Age* (Cambridge: Polity).

Giddens, A. (1995a) *Consequences of Modernity* (Stanford: Stanford University Press).

Giddens, A. (1995b) *Beyond Left and Right: The Future of Radical Politics* (Stanford: Stanford University Press).

Gilbert, P. (2000) *Peoples, Cultures and Nations in Political Philosophy* (Edinburgh: Edinburgh University Press).

Giles, H. (ed.) (1977) *Language, Ethnicity and Intergroup Relations* (London, New York, San Francisco: Academic Press).

Giliomee, H. (2003) *The Afrikaners: Biography of a People* (Cape Town: Tafelberg).

Gilroy, P. (1987) *There Ain't No Black in the Union Jack*. (London: Routledge).

Glenny, M. (1999) *The Balkans 1804–1999* (London: Granta).

Głowiński, M. (1990) *Nowomowa po polsku* (Warszawa: PEN).

Gogolin, I. and Kroon, S. (eds) *'Man schreibt, wie man spricht': Ergebnisse einer international-vergleichenden Fallstudie über Unterricht in vielsprachigen Klassen* (Münster: Waxmann).

Goldsworthy, V. (2002) 'Invention and in(ter)vention: the rhetoric of Balkanization', in Bjelić and Savić (2002), 23–38.

Goosen, D. (2000) ' "Wat staan ons te dinke?" Enkele notas rondom die republikeinse gedagte' ('What are we to think?' Some notes around the republican idea), *Fragmente* 6, 61–74.

Görlach, M. (2002) *English in Europe* (Oxford: Oxford University Press).

Gould, R. (2000) 'Integration, Solidarität and the Discourses of National Identity in the 1998 Bundestag election manifestos', *German Life and Letters* 53 (4), 529–51.

Gowers, T. (2002) *Mathematics: A Very Short Introduction* (Oxford: Oxford University Press).

Graddol, D. (1997) *The Future of English* (London: British Council).

Granger, C. A. (2004) *Silence in Second Language Learning* (Clevedon: Multilingual Matters).

Grin, F. (2003) *Language Policy Evaluation and the European Charter for Regional or Minority Languages* (New York: Palgrave).

Grin, F. (in press) 'Economic considerations in language policy research', in Ricento (in press, a), 77–94.

Grünbaum, C. (1986) 'Hur vill vi ha det i det allmänna språkbruket?', *Språkvård* 1-1986, 24–7.

Grybosiowa, A. (2000) 'O dystansie, szacunku i tolerancji w mediach', in Bralczyk and Mosiołek-Kłosinska (2000), 60–6.

Gumperz, J. (1971) *Language in Social Groups* (Stanford: Stanford University Press).

Gumperz, J. (1982a) *Discourse Strategies* (Cambridge: Cambridge University Press).

Gumperz, J. (ed.) (1982b) *Language and Social Identity* (Cambridge: Cambridge University Press).

Gumperz, J. and Cook-Gumperz, J. (1982) 'Introduction: language and the communication of social identity', in Gumperz (1982b), 1–21.

Gumperz, J. and Roberts, C. (1991) 'Understanding in intercultural encounters', in Blommaert and Verschueren (1991), 51–90.

Gupta, A. and Ferguson, J. (eds) (1997a) *Culture, Power, Place: Explorations in Critical Anthropology* (Durham: Duke University Press).

Gupta, A. and Ferguson, J. (1997b) 'Beyond 'culture': space, identity and the politics of difference', in Gupta and Ferguson (1997a), 33–51.

Hall, S. (1988) 'New ethnicities', in Rattansi and Donald (1992), 252–9.

Hallik, K. (2002) 'Nationalising policies and integration challenges', in Lauristin and Heidmets (2002), 65–88.

Hamel, R. E. (2003) *The Development of Language Empires*, Universidad Autónoma Metropolitana, México, D. F. (unpublished working paper).

Hammer, L. B. (1995) 'Sociolinguistic research in the former Czechoslovakia', in Harlig and Pléh (1995), 109–23.

Hammerová, L. B. and Ripka, I. (1994) *Speech of American Slovaks – Jazykové prejavy amerických Slovákov* (Bratislava: VEDA).

Harlig, J. and Pléh, Cs. (eds.) (1995) *When East Met West: Sociolinguistics in the Former Socialist Bloc* (Berlin, New York: Mouton de Gruyter).

Haviland, J. (2003) 'Ideologies of language: Reflections on language and US law', *American Anthropologist* 105, 764–74.

Helme, S. and Saar, J. (eds.) (2001) *Nosy Nineties: Problems, Themes and Meanings in Estonian Art in the 1990s* (Tallinn: Center for Contemporary Arts).

Herlitz, G. (1995) *Swedes: What We Are Like and Why We Are As We Are* (Uppsala: Konsultförlaget).

Hester, S. and Housley, W. (eds.) *Language, Interaction and National Identity: Studies In the Social Organisation of National Identity in Talk-in-interaction* (Burlington: Ashgate).

Heugh, K. (2000) 'The case against bilingual and multilingual education in South Africa: Laying bare the myths', *Perspectives in Education* 20 (1).

Hinnenkamp, V. (2003) 'Mixed language varieties of migrant adolescents and the discourse of hybridity', *Journal of Multilingual and Multicultural Development* 24 (1 & 2), 12–41.

Hobsbawm, E. J. (1990) *Nations and Nationalism Since 1780: Programme, Myth, Reality* (Cambridge: Cambridge University Press).

Hoernlé, R. (1939) *South African Native Policy and the Liberal Spirit* (Johannesburg: University of Witwatersrand Press).

Hofstadter, R. (1989) quoted in Michael Kazin, 'The right's unsung prophet', *The Nation* 248 (Feb. 20), 242.

Hogan-Brun, G. and Wolff, S. (eds) (2003) *Minority Languages in Europe* (Basingstoke: Palgrave).

Holland, D. and Quinn, N. (eds.) (1987) *Cultural Models in Language and Thought* (Cambridge: Cambridge University Press).

Howe, J. (2004) *Language and Political Meaning in Revolutionary America* (Amherst: University of Massachusetts Press). http://www.transcomm.ox.ac.uk, 6, 1–31.

Hunter, J. (1997) 'Multiple perceptions: social identity in a multilingual elementary classroom'. *TESOL Quarterly* 31 (3), 603–11.

Huntington, S. P. (2004a) 'The Hispanic challenge', *Foreign Policy*, Mar./Ap., [Online], available from: http://www.foreignpolicy.com/story/cms.php?story_id =2495 [13 September 2004].

Huntington, S. P. (2004b) *Who Are We?: The Challenges to America's National Identity* (New York: Simon & Schuster).

Hüppauf, B. (2004) 'Globalization: threats and opportunities', in Gardt and Hüppauf (2004), 3–25.

Hyltenstam, K. (ed.) (1996a) *Tvåspråkighet med förhinder? Invandrar- och minoritetsundervisning i Sverige* (Lund: Studentlitteratur).

Hyltenstam, K. (1996b) 'Svenskan, ett minoritetsspråk i Europa – och i världen?', in Ivars *et al.* (1996), 9–33.

Hyltenstam, K. (1999a) 'Inledning: Ideologi, politik och minoritetsspråk', in Hyltenstam (1999c), 11–40.

Hyltenstam, K. (1999b) 'Svenskan i minoritetsspråksperspektiv', in Hyltenstam (1999c), 205–40.

Hyltenstam, K. (1999c) *Sveriges sju inhemska språk* (Lund: Studentlitteratur).

Ignatieff, M. (1993) *Blood and Belonging: Journeys into the New Nationalism* (London: Chatto & Windus).

Innis, H. A. (1997) *Kreuzwege der Kommunikation. Ausgewählte Texte*, ed. Karlheinz Back (Vienna, New York: Springer).

Instituto Cervantes (2000) *El español en el mundo; Anuario 2000* Centro Virtual Cervantes http://cvc.cervantes.es/obref/anuario/

Integration Foundation (2002) *Integration Yearbook 2001: One State, One Society* (Tallinn: Integration Foundation).

Irvine, J. and Gal, S. (2000) 'Language ideology and linguistic differentiation', in Kroskrity (2000), 35–84.

Ismajli, R. (1988) 'Mbi statusin e shqipes standarde ne RSF te Jugosllavise', *Gjuha Shqipe* 7 (2), 1–22.

Ivars, A.-M., Londen, A.-M., Nyholm, L., Saari, M. and Tandefelt, M. (eds.) (1996) *Svenskans beskrivning 21. Förhandlingar vid tjugoförsta sammankomsten för svenskans beskrivning, Helsingfors den 11–12 maj 1995* (Lund: Stundentlitteratur).

Jaffe, A. (1999) *Ideologies in Action: Language Politics on Corsica* (Berlin: Mouton de Gruyter).

James, C. (1980) *Contrastive Analysis* (London: Longman).

Jaspaert, K. and Ramaut, G. (2000) ' "Don't use English Words in Dutch". Portrait of a Multilingual Classroom in Flanders', in Gogolin and Kroon (2000), 27–40.

Jelavich, B. (1983) *History of the Balkans*, Vol.1 (Cambridge: Cambridge University Press).

Jiroušek, A. (2003) *Košice na začiatku tretieho tisícročia* (Košice: Jes).

Johnston, B. H. M., Mitchell, R. F., Ford, P. K., Myles, F. J. and Brumfit, C. J. (2004) 'The contribution of residence abroad to student critical development'. Paper presented to conference of British Educational Research Association (BERA), Manchester, September 2004.

Joseph, J. (2004) 'Linguistic identity and the limits of global English', in Duszak and Okulska (2004), 17–34.

Journal of Sociolinguistics (2003) Theme issue: 'Sociolinguistics and Globalisation', 7 (4).

Joyce, J. (1916/1983) *Portrait of the Artist as a Young Man* (London: Collins).

Jurančič, J. (1986) *Srbskohrvatsko-slovenski slovar* (Ljubljana: Državna založba).

Kačala, J. (1994) *Slovenčina – vec politická?* (Martin: Matica Slovenská).

Kačala, J. (1997) *Kultúrne rozmery jazyka. Úvahy jazykovedca* (Bratislava: Korene).

Kachru, B. B. (1990) *The Alchemy of English* (Urbana: University of Illinois Press).

Kamińska-Szmaj, I. (1994) *Judzi, zohydza, ze czci odziera. Język propagandy politycznej w prasie 1919–1923* (Wrocław: Towarzystwo Przyjaciół Polonistyki Wrocławskiej).

Kamuf, P. (ed.) (1991) *A Derrida Reader: Behind the Blinds* (New York: Columbia University Press).

Karakasidou, A. (2002) 'Cultural illegitimacy in Greece: the Slavo-Macedonian "non-minority" ', in Clogg (2002), 122–64.

Kibbee, D. A. (2002) 'L'autorité de l'état et l'autorité linguistique', *Histoire Epistémologie Langage* 24, 5–27.

Kirch, A. (ed.) (1997) *The Integration of Non-Estonians into Estonian Society: History, Problems and Trends* (Tallinn: Estonian Academy Publishers).

Kirch, M. and Kirch, A. (1997) 'Identity changes and the emergence of a new integration paradigm', in Kirch (1997), 142–58.

Kleinsteuber, H. (ed.) (1991) *Radio – Das unterschätzte Medium. Erfahrungen mit nicht-kommerziellen Lokalstationen in 15 Staaten* (Berlin: Vistas).

Kochan, M. (1994), Przyklejanie etykietek', czyli o negatywnym określaniu przeciwnika', in Anusiewicz and Siciński (1994), 85–90.

Kofos, E. (1992) 'The making of Yugoslavia's People's Republic of Macedonia', in: *Macedonia Past and Present: Reprints from Balkan Studies* (Thessaloniki: Institute for Balkan Studies), 147–68.

Kontra, M. (ed.) (2000) *Language Contact in East–Central Europe* (Berlin: Mouton de Gruyter).

Koole, T. and Hanson, M. (2002) 'The category "Moroccan" in a multi-ethnic class', in Hester and Housley (2002), 211–32.

Kosnick, K. (2000) 'Building bridges. Media for migrants and the public service mission in Germany', in *European Journal of Cultural Studies*, 3(3), 321–44.

Kosnick, K. (2002) *Reaching Beyond the Local: A study of Turkish Migrant Broadcasting in Berlin, Germany* Dissertation at the New School University USA.

Koven, M. (2004) 'Transnational perspective on sociolinguistic capital among Luso-Descendants in France and Portugal', *American Ethnologist* 31 (2), 270–90.

Krauss, M. (1992) 'The world's languages in crisis', *Language* 68, 4–10.

Kress, G. (2002) 'The multimodal landscape of communication', in *MedienJournal* 4, 4–19.

Kress, G. and van Leeuwen, T. (2001) *Multimodal Discourse. The Modes and Media of Contemporary Communication* (London: Arnold).

Kreyenbühl, T. (2004) 'Reportagen aus dem Herzen des "Neuen" Europa', *Neue Zürcher Zeitung*, 20/21 March 2004, 29.

Kroskrity, P. (ed.) (2000a) *Regimes of Language: Ideologies, Polities, and Identities* (Sante Fe: School of American Research Press).

Kroskrity, P. (2000b) 'Regimenting languages: language ideological perspectives', in Kroskrity (2000a), 1–34.

Kruslov, G. and Kroon, S. (eds) (1998) *The Challenge of Multilingualism to Standard Language Teaching: Cases from Flanders, England, The Netherlands, Germany and Russia* (Moscow: INPO).

Kruusvall, J. (2002) 'Social perception and individual resources of the integration process', in Lauristin and Heidmets (2002), 117–64.

Kymlicka, W. and Patten, A. (2003) *Language Rights and Political Theory* (Oxford: Oxford University Press).

Labov, W. (1972) 'The study of language in its social context', in Pride and Holmes (1972), 180–202.

Laitin, D. (1998) *Identity in Formation: the Russian-speaking Populations in the Near Abroad* (New York: Cornell University Press).

Laius A., et al. (eds) (2000) *Estonia's Integration Landscape: from Apathy to Harmony* (Tallinn: Avatud Eesti Fond and Jaan Tõnissoni Instituut).

Lakoff, G. and Johnson, M. (1999) *Philosophy in the Flesh: The Embodied Mind and Its Challenge to Western World* (New York: Basic Books).

Langman, J. and Lánstyák, I. (2000) 'Language negotiations in Slovakia: views from the Hungarian minority', in Kontra (2000), 55–72.

Lanstyák, I. (1995) 'A magyar nyelv központjai', *Magyar Tudomány* 10, 1170–85.

Lanstyák, I. (2000) 'Bilingual versus bilingual education: the case of Slovakia', in Phillipson (2000), 55–72.

Lauristin, M. and Heidmets, M. (eds) (2002) *The Challenge of the Russian Minority: Emerging Multicultural Democracy in Estonia* (Tartu: Tartu University Press).

Leith, D. (1983) *A Social History of English* (London: Routledge).

Lieven, A. (1993) *Baltic Revolution: Estonia, Latvia, Lithuania and the Path to Independence* (New Haven: Yale University Press).

Linsinger, Eva (2002) 'Du müssen integrieren' (*Der Standard* 9 February 2002) http://derstandard.at/standard.asp?page=archshow&artfn=\Archiv\20020209\161.htm

Lippi-Green, R. (1997) *English with an Accent: Language, Ideology and Discrimination in the United States* (London / New York: Routledge).

Ljung, M. (1986) 'Undersökningen Engelskan i Sverige', *Språkvård* 1-1986, 5–10.

Löfgren, O. (1993) 'Nationella arenor', in Ehn *et al.* (1993).

Lubaś, J. (1996) 'Polszczyzna wobec najnowszych przemian społecznych', in Miodek (1996), 153–61.

Lubaś, W. (2000) 'Słownictwo potoczne w mediach', in Bralczyk and Mosiołek-Kłosińska (2000), 83–95.

Magistrát Hlavného Mesta SR Bratislavy (2004) 'Bratislava' www.bratislava.sk

Makoni, S. and Meinhof, U. (2004) Unpublished paper presented to AILA Colloquium on Applied Linguistics in the Real World, Portland, Oregon, May 2004.

Malkki, L. (1997) 'National geographic: the rooting of peoples and the territorialization of national identity among scholars and refugees', in Gupta and Ferguson (1997a), 52–74.

Maltsev, Y. (2000) 'Вехи путей православия в Эстонии', in Boykov and Bassel (2000), 112–17.

Mangena, M. (2001) 'South Africans must learn to speak in many tongues', *Sunday Times*, 22 July http://www.suntimes.co.za/2001/07/22/insight/in12.htm

Mannová, E. (ed.) (2000) *A Concise History of Slovakia* (Bratislava: Historický Ústav SAV).

Mannová, E. and Holec, R. (2000) 'On the road to modernization 1848–1919', in Mannová (2000), 185–240.

Manz, S. (2004) 'Constructing a normative national identity: the *Leitkultur* debate in Germany 2000–2001', in *Journal of Multilingual and Multicultural Development* 25 (5 & 6), 481–96.

Markowski, A. (2000) 'Jawne i ukryte zapożyczenia leksykalne w mediach', in Bralczyk and Mosiołek-Kłosińska (2000), 96–111.

Marks, S. (1975) 'The ambiguities of dependence: John L. Dube of Natal', *Journal of Southern African Studies* 1 (2).

Marks, S. and Trapido, S. (eds) (1987) *The Politics of Race, Class and Nationalism in Twentieth Century South Africa* (London/New York: Longman).

Mar-Molinero, C. (2000) *The Politics of Language in the Spanish-Speaking World* (London / New York: Routledge).

Mar-Molinero, C. (2004) 'Spanish as a world language: language and identity in a global era', *Spanish in Context* 1, 1, 3–20.

Maryns, K. (2004) *The Asylum Speaker: Language in the Belgian Asylum Application Procedure.* PhD dissertation, Ghent University.

Maryns, K. and Blommaert, J. (2001) 'Stylistic and thematic shifting as a narrative resource: assessing asylum seekers' repertoires', *Multilingua* 20 (1), 61–84.

Maryns, K. and Blommaert, J. (2002) 'Pretextuality and pretextual gaps: on de/ refining linguistic inequality', in *Pragmatics* 12 (1), 11–30.

Maurais, J. and Morris, M. A. (eds) (2003) *Languages in a Globalising World* (Cambridge: Cambridge University Press).

May, S. (2001) *Language and Minority Rights: Ethnicity, nationalism and the politics of language* (Harlow: Longman).

May, S. (2003) 'Misconceiving minority language rights: implications for liberal political theory', in Kymlicka and Patten (2003), 123–52.

McCracken, G. (1988) *The Long Interview* (London: Sage).

McQuail, D. (1987) *Mass Communication Theory: An Introduction* (London: Sage).

Mesto Banská Bystrica (2004) 'Banská Bystrica' www.banskabystrica.sk

Mesto Košice (2003) 'Guestbook = Navstevna Kniha www.kosice.sk' http:// www.kosice.sk/guestbk/

Mesto Košice (2004a) 'Mesto Košice' www.kosice.sk

Mesto Košice (2004b) 'Demografické údaje = Demographic data' http://www.kosice. sk/info/basic/demograf.htm

Mesto Košice (2004c) 'Hospodársko-ekonomické informácie = Economic information' http://www.kosice.sk/info/basic/hosp_eko.htm

Mesto Martin (2004) 'martin.sk' www.martin.sk

Mesto Nitra (2004) 'Mesto Nitra' www.nitra.sk

Mesto Poprad (2004) 'Mesto Poprad' www.poprad.sk

Mesto Prešov (2004) 'Prešovský informačný server' www.pis.sk

Mesto Trenčín (2004) 'Oficiálne stránky mesta Trenčín' www.trencin.sk

Mesto Trnava (2004) 'Mesto Trnava' www.trnava.sk

Mesto Žilina (2004) 'Žilina online' www.zilina.sk

Mesto Zvolen (2004) 'Mesto Zvolen' www.zvolen.sk

Mestský Rad Komárno (2004) 'Komárno' www.komarno.sk

Metzler-Arnold, R. (2000) 'La politique à l'égard des étrangers n'a que faire de quotas'. http://www.ejpd.admin.ch/doks/red/content/red_view-f.php?redID=47 &redTopic=Auslaender

Migration Online Austria (2002) http://www.illegalisiert.at/MUND/integrationsvertrag.htm

Mill, J. (1996) *On liberty*, in Morgan (1996).

Milroy, L. (2001) 'The social categories of race and class: language ideology and sociolinguistics', in Coupland *et al.* (2001), 235–60.

Minnich, R. (1988): 'Speaking Slovene – being Slovene. Verbal codes and collective self-images: some correlations between Kanalska Dolina and Ziljska Dolina', *Slovene Studies* 10 (2), 125–47.

Miodek, J. (ed.) (1996) *O zagrożeniach i bogactwie polszczyzny* (Wrocław: Towarzystwo Przyjaciół Polonistyki Wrocławskiej).

Mitchell, R. and Brumfit, C. J. (1993) 'Language and cultural diversity', in Fyfe and Figueroa (1993), 177–86.

Morley, D. (2000) *Home Territories. Media, Mobility and Identity* (London: Routledge).

Muntigl P., Weiss G. and Wodak R. (2000) *European Union Discourses on Un/ Employment: An Interdisciplinary Approach to Employment, Policy-Making, and Organizational Change* (Amsterdam and Philadelphia: John Benjamins).

Münz, R. and Ulrich, R. (2001) 'Alterung und Wanderung: Alternative Projektionen der Bevölkerung der Schweiz', www.avenir-suisse.ch/uploads/media/ alterung_wanderung_03.pdf

Nábělková, M. (1999) 'Slovenčina a čeština dnes. Kontakt či konflikt', in Ondrejovič (1999), 75–93.

Nelde, P. (1996) *Euromosaic: The Production and Reproduction of the Minority Language Groups of the EU* (Luxembourg: European Communities).

Němec, Z. *et al.* (1994) *Košice 1780–1920* (Sečovce: Pergamen).

New York Times (2002) 'Census finds 'American' identity rising in U.S.', 9 June, 27.

O'Reilly, C. (ed.) (2001) *Language, Ethnicity and the State*, 2 vols. (Basingstoke: Palgrave).

Oakes, L. (2001) *Language and National Identity: Comparing France and Sweden* (Amsterdam/Philadelphia: John Benjamins).

Oakes, L. (2002) 'Multilingualism in Europe: An effective French identity strategy?', *Journal of Multilingual and Multicultural Development* 23 (5), 371–87.

Office fédéral de la statistique (1996) 'Le défi démographique: perspectives pour la Suisse'.

Ondrejovič, S. (1996a) 'Z výskumu jazykovej situácie na južnom Slovensku', in Ondrejovič (1996b), 141–47.

Ondrejovič, S. (ed.) (1996b) *Sociolingvistika a areálová lingvistika* (Bratislava: VEDA).

Ondrejovič, S. (ed.) (1997) *Slovenčina na konci 20. storočiaę jej normy a perspektívy* (Bratislava: VEDA).

Ondrejovič, S. (ed.) (1999) *Slovenčina v kontaktoch a konfliktoch s inými jazykmi* (Bratislava: VEDA).

Ondrejovič, S. and Šimková, M. (eds.) (1995) *Sociolingvistické aspekty výskumu súčasnej slovenčiny* (Bratislava: VEDA).

Painter, D. (2002a) 'English economies: Everyday accounts of language in South Africa', *Proceedings of the 8th Annual Qualitative/Critical Methods Conference: 'Something for Nothing: Subjectivity and the new economy'* www.critical-methods.org/proceed.mv

Painter, D. (2002b) 'What's that got to do with language? Perspectives on language and race in South Africa', *The Researcher* 1.

Painter, D. (2003) 'Kies vir jou 'n taal: Engels, liberale ideologie en rassisme' (Pick your language: English, liberal ideology and racism) http://www.litnet.co.za/taaldebat/painter1.asp

Painter D. and Baldwin, R. (2004) ' "They all speak your language anyway...": Language and racism in a South African school', *South African Journal of Psychology* 34.

Palmer, S. and King, R. (1971) *Yugoslav Communism and the Macedonian Question* (Hamden/Connecticut: Archon Books).

Pan Africanist Congress Publications Collection, 1958–1995 (University of Fort Hare, National Heritage Cultural Studies Centre) http://www.si.umich.edu/fort-hare/pac_pub.htm

Panagl O. and Stürmer, H. (eds.) (2002) *Politische Konzepte und verbale Strategien: Brisante Wörter – Begriffsfelder – Sprachbilder* (Frankfurt, Vienna: Lang).

Panzer, B. (ed.) (2000) *Die sprachliche Situation in der Slavia zehn Jahre nach der Wende* (Frankfurt am Main: Peter Lang).

Patrick, P. (2001) 'The speech community', in Chambers *et al.* (2001), 573–97.

Pavelson, M. and Luuk, M. (2002) 'Non-Estonians on the labour market: a change in the economic model and differences in social capital', in Lauristin and Heidmets (2002), 89–116.

Pavlenko, A. and Blackledge, A. (eds) (2004) *Negotiation of Identity in Multilingual Contexts* (Clevedon: Multilingual Matters).

Pennycook, A. (1994) *The Cultural Politics of English as an International Language* (London / New York: Longman).

Pennycook, A. (1998) *English and the Discourses of Colonialism* (London / New York: Routledge).

Pennycook, A. (2004) 'Performativity and language studies', *Critical Inquiry in Language Studies*, 1 (1) 1–19.

Pettai, I. (2000) 'Integration paradigm of Estonians and non-Estonians', in Laius *et al.* (2000), 70–107.

Pettai V. and Zielonka J. (eds) (2003) *The Road to the European Union, Volume 2: Estonia, Latvia and Lithuania* (Manchester: Manchester University Press).

Phillipson, R. (1992) *Linguistic Imperialism* (Oxford: Oxford University Press).

Phillipson, R. (ed.) (2000) *Rights to Language: Equity, Power, and Education* (Mahwah: Lawrence Erlbaum Associates).

Phillipson, R. (2003) *English-Only Europe?: Challenging Language Policy* (London: Routledge).

Phillipson, R. and Skutnabb-Kangas, T. (1995) 'Linguistic Rights and Linguistic Wrongs', *Applied Linguistics* 16 (4), 483–504.

Piller, I. (2001) 'Naturalization language testing and its basis in ideologies of national identity and citizenship', in *International Journal of Bilingualism* 5 (3), 259–77.

Pisarek, W. (ed.) (1999) *Polszczyzna 2000* (Kraków: RJP).

Pisarek, W. (2000) 'Język w mediach, media w języku', in Bralczyk and Mosiołek-Kłosińska (2000), 9–18.

Pisarek, W. and Zgółkowa, H. (eds) (1995) *Kultura języka dziś.* (Poznań: Kurpisz).

Pitt, L. (1976) *We Americans: Vol. I: Colonial Times to 1877* (Glenville, IL: Scott-Foresman).

Popper, K. R. (1994) *The Myth of the Framework* (London: Routledge).

Prantl, Heribert (2002) ' "Ich möchte keine zweisprachigen Ortsschilder haben": Interview mit Bundesinnenminister Otto Schily' (Süddeutsche Zeitung 26 June 2002) http://www.sueddeutsche.de/deutschland.artikel/945/8937/print.html

Pride, J. B. and Holmes, J. (eds) (1972) *Sociolinguistics: Selected Readings* (Harmondsworth: Penguin).

Proos, I. (2000) 'Significance of Estonian language in integration of non-Estonians', in Laius *et al.* (2000), 108–36.

Quirk, R. (1990) 'Language varieties and standard English', *English Today* 21, 3–10.

Ramaut, G. (1998) 'The state of minority languages in Flemish multilingual schools', in Kruslov and Kroon (1998), 266–70.

Ramaut, G. (2000) 'Language norms in multilingual Flemish nursery schools', in Gogolin and Kroon (2002), 41–61.

Ramphele, M. (1995) *Mamphela Ramphele – a Life* (Cape Town: David Philip).

Rampton, B. (1990) 'Displacing the "native-speaker": Expertise, affiliation and inheritance', *ELT Journal* 44, 97–101.

Rampton, B. (1995) *Crossing* (Harlow: Longman).

Rampton, B. (1999) '*Deutsch* in inner London and the animation of an instructed foreign language', *Journal of Sociolinguistics* 3 (4), 480–504.

Rattansi, and Donald, A. (eds) (1992) *'Race', Culture and Difference.* (London: Sage/Open University).

Ricento, T. (2003) 'The discursive construction of Americanism', *Discourse & Society*, 14 (5), 611–37.

Ricento, T. (ed.) (in press, a) *An Introduction to Language Policy: Theory and Method* (London: Blackwell).

Ricento, T. (in press, b) 'Language rights and language resources in the United States: limitations and false hopes in the promotion of linguistic diversity', *Journal of Sociolinguistics*.

Rosenfeld, A. and Dodge N. (eds) (1995) *Nonconformist Art: The Soviet Experience 1956–1986* (New York: Thames and Hudson).

Rossouw, J. (2003) 'Afrikaners en 'n Suid-Afrikaanse politieke middeweg' (Afrikaners and a South African political middle-road) http://www.groep63. org.za/dok2003/g63_rossouw.html

Ruiz, R. (1984) 'Orientations in language planning', *NABE Journal* 8, 15–34.

s.n. (2002) 'Čo by si želali pod stromček čitatelia *SME*', *SME*, 12–23-2002, 6.

Sarangi, S. and Slembrouck, S. (1996) *Language, Bureaucracy and Social Control* (London: Longman).

Satkiewicz, H. (2000) 'Językowe przejawy agresji w mediach', in Bralczyk and Mosiołek-Kłosińska (2000), 28–33.

Schäffner, C. (2002) 'Auf der Suche nach dem Feind: Anmerkungen zum NATO-Diskurs', in Panagl and Stürmer (2002), 169–84.

Schieffelin, B., Woolard, K. and Kroskrity, P. (eds) (1998) *Language Ideologies: Practice and Theory* (Oxford: Oxford University Press).

Schily, O. (2004) 'Pressemitteilung zum Abschluss der Verhandlungen zum Zuwanderungsgesetz' http://www.bmi.bund.de/dokumente/Pressemitteilung/ ix_95108.htm

Scholtz, G. (1954) *Het die Afrikaanse volk 'n toekoms?* (Does the Afrikaans nation have a future?) (Johannesburg: Voortrekkerpers).

Seepe, S. (2000a) 'The role of language in science teaching', in Seepe and Dowling (2000).

Seepe, S. (2000b) 'A pedagogical justification for mother tongue instruction', in Seepe and Dowling (2000).

Seepe S. and Dowling, D. (eds) (2000), *The Language of Science* (Johannesburg: Vivlia).

Shore, C. (2000) *Building Europe: The Cultural Politics of European Integration* (London, New York: Routledge).

Siegert, G. (2003) 'Im Zentrum des Taifuns: Die Ökonomisierung als treibende Kraft des medialen Wandels?', in *MedienJournal* 1, 20–31.

Siguan, M. (1992) *España plurilingüe* (Barcelona: Ariel).

SIL (Summer Institute of Linguists) (2002, 14th edn) *Ethnologue* www.ethnologue.com

Silverstein, M. (1992) 'The uses and utility of ideology: some reflections', *Pragmatics* 2 (3), 311–23.

Silverstein, M. (1996) 'Monoglot "standard" in America: Standardization and metaphors of linguistic hegemony', in Brenneis and Macaulay (1996), 284–306.

Silverstein, M. (1997) 'Commentary: Achieving adequacy and commitment in pragmatics', *Pragmatics* 7 (4), 625–33.

Silverstein, M. (1998) 'Contemporary transformations of local linguistic communities', *Annual Review of Anthropology* 27, 401–26.

Silverstein, M. and Urban, G. (eds) (1996a) *Natural Histories of Discourse* (Chicago: University of Chicago Press).

Silverstein, M. and Urban, G. (1996b) 'The natural history of discourse', in Silverstein and Urban (1996a), 1–17.

Simon, S. and Kontra, M. (2000) 'Slovak linguists and Slovak language laws: An analysis of Slovak language policy', in Kontra (2000), 73–94.

Simons, H. J. and Simons, R. E. (1969) *Colour and Class in South Africa 1850–1950* (Harmondsworth: Penguin).

Singh, R. (ed.) (1997) *The Native Speaker: Multilingual Perspectives*. (London: Sage).

Slembrouck, S. (2003) 'Class and parenting in accounts of child protection: A discursive ethnography under construction', *Pragmatics* 13 (1), 101–34.

Slovo, J. (2004) 'Has socialism failed?' http://www.sacp.org.za/docs/history/failed.html

Smit, U. (2002) 'Multilingual Vienna past and present: between internationalisation, integration and assimilation', paper given at Sociolinguistics Symposium 14, Gent, 4–6 April, 2002.

Spindler, G. and Spindler., L. (eds) (1987) *Interpretative Ethnography of Education at Home and Abroad*. (Hillsdale: Lawrence Erlbaum).

Spolsky, B. (2004) *Language Policy* (Cambridge: Cambridge University Press).

Statistical Office of the Slovak Republic (2004) 'Population and housing census 2001: Permanently resident population by nationality and by regions and districts' http://www.statistics.sk/webdata/english/census2001/tab/tab3a.htm

Števček, P. (ed.) (1995) *Slovaks and Magyars: Slovak–Magyar Relations in Central Europe* (Bratislava: Správa Kultúrnych Zariadení MK SR).

Stewart, M. (1989) ' "True speech": Song and the moral order of a Hungarian Vlach Gypsy community', *Man* 24 (1), 79–102.

Stroud, C. (2004) 'Rinkeby Swedish and semilingualism in language ideological debates: A Bourdieuean perspective', *Journal of Sociolinguistics* 8 (2), 163–230.

Sturgis, J. (1982) 'Anglicisation of the Cape of Good Hope in the early nineteenth century', *Journal of Imperial and Commonwealth History* 11.

Svede, M.A. (1995) 'Nonconformist art in Latvia: smaller measures to equal effect', in Rosenfeld and Dodge (1995), 189–200.

Tamarón, Marqués de (ed.) (1995) *El peso de la lengua española en el mundo* (Valladolid: INCIPE).

Taylor, C. and Gutman, A. (1994) *Multiculturalism* (Princeton, NJ: Princeton University Press).

Teleman, U. (1992) 'Det svenska riksspråkets utsikter i ett integrerat Europa', *Språkvård* 4–1992, 7–16.

Teleman, U. (2003) *Tradis och funkiš. Svensk språkvård och språkpolitik efter 1800* (Stockholm: Nordstedts Ordbok).

Teleman, U. and Westman, M. (1997) 'Behöver vi en nationell språkpolitik?', *Språkvård* 2–1997, 5–22.

Terreblanche, S. (2002) *A History of Inequality in South Africa, 1652–2002* (Pietermaritzburg: University of Natal Press).

Teubert, W. (2002) 'Die Bedeutung von *Globalisierung*', in Panagl and Stürmer (2002), 149–67.

Thomas, D. (2000) 'Slovakia: Language and national unity', *Parliamentary Affairs* 53 (1), 135–41.

Todorov, T. (1984) *Mikhail Bakhtin. The dialogic principle* (Manchester: Manchester University Press).

Treier, H. (2001) 'In search of an identity', in Helme and Saar (2001), 216–26.

Troebst, S. (1994) 'Makedonische Antworten auf die "Makedonische Frage": Nationalismus, Republiksgründung und nation-building in Vardar-Makedonien 1944–1992', in Brunner and Lemberg, 203–21.

Trudgill, P. (1983a) *On Dialect* (Oxford: Blackwell).

Trudgill, P. (1983b) 'Language contact, language shift and identity. Why Arvanites are not Albanians', in Trudgill (1983a), 127–40.

Trudgill, P. and Tzavaras, G.A. (1977) 'Why Albanian-Greeks are not Albanians: language shift in Attica and Biotia', in Giles (1977), 171–84.

Urla, J. (2001) 'Outlaw language: Creating alternative public spheres in Basque free radio', in Gal and Woolard (2001a), 141–63.

van Brakel, J. (1998) *Interculturele communicatie en multiculturalisme* (Intercultural communication and multiculturalism) (Leuven: Universitaire Pers).

van Dijk, T. (1993) 'Principles of critical discourse analysis', *Discourse & Society* 4, 249–83.

van Dijk, T. (1998) *Ideology: A Multidisciplinary Approach* (London: Sage).

Vann, E. (2000) *Language, Ehtnicity and Nationality in the German–Polish Borderland* (unpublished PhD thesis, University of Chicago) (Ann Arbor: University Microfilms).

Vassberg, L. M. (1993) *Alsatian Acts of Identity: Language Use and Language Attitudes in Alsace* (Clevedon: Multilingual Matters).

verbal (2002) *Stellungnahme im Rahmen des Begutachtungsverfahrens zum Bundesgesetz, mit dem das Fremdengesetz 1997 und das Asylgesetz 1997 und das Ausländerbeschäftigungsgesetz geändert werden* (Vienna: Österreichischer Verband für angewandte Linguistik).

Verkuyten, M. (1992) *Zelfbeleving van jeugdige allochtonen: een socio-psychologische benadering.* (Amsterdam: Swets & Zeitlinger).

Verkuyten, M. (1999) *Etnische Identiteit: theoretische en empirische benaderingen.* (Amsterdam: Het Spinhuis).

Verlot, M. and Delrue, K. (2004) 'Multilingualism in Brussels', in Extra, G. and Yağmur, K. (2004), 221–50.

Verlot, M. (2000) 'Allochtone Anderstaligheid in de Vlaamse en Fraanse Gemeenschap van België – een Vergelijkend Onderzoek naar de Culturele Premissen van Onderwijsbeleid', *Tijdschrift voor Onderwijs Recht en Onderwijs Beleid.* 2000–2001/1. Sept.–Oct. 2000.

Verschueren, J. (1999) *Understanding Pragmatics* (London: Arnold).

Vertovec, S. (2000) 'Fostering Cosmopolitanisms: A Conceptual Survey and a Media Experiment in Berlin', *Transnational Communities Working Paper Series.*

Vihalemm, T. (1999) *Formation of Collective Identity Among Russophone Population of Estonia* Dissertationes de mediis et communicationibus Universitatis Tartuensis (Tartu: Tartu University Press).

Vihalemm, T. (2002) 'Usage of language as a source of societal trust', in Lauristin and Heidmets (2002), 199–218.

Voss, C. (forthcoming) *Das makedonische Standard/Dialekt-Kontinuum. Sprachplanung und Sprachverhalten in der Republik Makedonien (Vardar-Makedonien) und im nordgriechischen Minderheitensprachraum (Ägäis-Makedonien).* (Habilitation, University of Freiburg).

Walczak, B. (1994) 'Co to jest język polityki?', in Anusiewicz and Siciński (1994), 15–20.

Walczak, B. (1995) 'Norma językowa wobec elementów obcego pochodzenia', in Pisarek and Zgółkowa (1995), 120–33.

Waldrauch, H. and Sohler, K. (2004) *Migrantenorganisationen in der Großstadt. Entstehung, Strukturen und Aktivitäten am Beispiel Wien* (Vienna: Europäisches Zentrum).

Weber, E. (1976) *Peasants into Frenchmen: The Modernization of Rural France, 1800–1914* (Stanford: University Press).

Webster, J. (1612) *The White Devil*, Act V, Scene 1 (cited from *Webster & Tourneur*, 1959. London: Ernest Benn).

Weis, L. (1990) *Working Class Without Work: High School Students in a De-industrializing Economy* (New York: Routledge).

Whiteley, P. (2003) 'Do "language rights" serve indigenous interests? Some Hopi and other queries', *American Anthropologist* 105 (4), 712–21.

Wieder, D. and Pratt, L. (1990) 'On being a recognizable Indian among Indians', in Carbaugh (1990), 45–64.

Wierzbicka, A. (1991) *Cross-Cultural Pragmatics: The Semantics of Human Interaction* (Berlin: Mouton de Gruyter).

Wittrock, M. (ed.) (1986) *Handbook of Research on Teaching* (New York: Macmillan).

Wodak, R. (2000) *Does Sociolinguistics Need Social Theory? New Perspectives in Critical Discourse Analysis* http://www.cddc.vt.edu/host/lnc/lncarchive.html.

Wodak, R., de Cillia, R., Reisigl, M. and Liebhart, K. (1999) *The Discursive Construction of National Identity*, trans. by A. Hirsch and R. Mitten (Edinburgh: Edinburgh University Press).

Woolard, K. (1998) 'Introduction: Language ideology as a field of inquiry', in Schieffelin, Woolard and Kroskrity (1998), 3–47.

Woolard, K. (2002) 'Bernardo de Aldrete and the Morisco problem: A study in early modern Spanish language ideology', *Comparative Studies in Society and History* 44 (3), 446–80.

Woolard, K. A. and Schieffelin, B. (1994) 'Language ideology', *Annual Review of Anthropology* 23, 55–82.

Wright, S. (2000) *Community and Communication: The Role of Language in Nation Building and European Integration* (Clevedon: Multilingual Matters).

Wright, S. (2004) *Language Policy and Language Planning: From Nationalism to Globalization* (Basingstoke: Palgrave Macmillan).

Yarian, C. (2004) *Language and Integration in Estonia: The Negotiation of Authority* (unpublished MA thesis: University of Chicago).

Źiółkowski, M. (1994) 'Pragmatyzacja świadomości społeczeństwa polskiego', *Kultura i społeczeństwo* 38 (4), 11–28.

Zuwanderung gestalten – Integration fördern (2001) Bericht der Unabhängigen Kommission Zuwanderung (Berlin: Bundesministerium des Innern).

Index